ADOPTED BY GOD

Adopted by God

Bringing the children of Poland into God's Kingdom

Jasia Gazda with Sara Bruce

HODDER AND STOUGHTON
LONDON SYDNEY AUCKLAND

Copyright © 1995 by Jasia Gazda and Sara Bruce

First published in Great Britain in 1995 by Hodder and Stoughton
a division of Hodder Headline PLC

The rights of Jasia Gazda and Sara Bruce to be identified as the
authors of this work has been asserted by them in accordance with
the Copyright, Designs and Patents Act 1988.

10 9 8 7 6 5 4 3

British Library Cataloguing in Publication Data

A catalogue record for this book is available from the British Library

ISBN 0 340 61229 0

Typeset by Hewer Text Composition Services, Edinburgh
Printed and bound in Great Britain by
Cox & Wyman Ltd, Reading, Berks

Hodder and Stoughton Ltd,
A division of Hodder Headline PLC
338 Euston Road
London NW1 3BH

For Tatusiek and Mamuska
who nurtured me in their garden
that I might take the Rainbow Garden to others

Some would gather money
Along the path of life;
Some would gather roses,
And rest from worldly strife,
But I would gather children
From among the thorns of sin;
I would seek a golden curl
And a freckled, toothless grin.

For money cannot enter
In that land of endless day;
And roses that are gathered
Soon will wilt along the way.
But, oh, the laughing children,
As I cross the Sunset Sea,
And the gates swing wide to Heaven . . .
I can take them in with me!

Author unknown

CONTENTS

PREFACE

This book will take you to a garden, though one that is not, perhaps, as you might expect. In it you will meet a Master Gardener without whom the place would be a wilderness. You will see flowers – some fragile, some strong, all of them blossoming and causing the garden to multiply. You will meet gardeners, too, and one in particular, a stubborn, wilful, self-assured character who could get nowhere until she came under the Master Gardener's care.

Most of those figuring in this garden could be written about freely. A few, however, might have been embarrassed by the role they have played. In those cases, we have changed names and one or two other details to prevent them being recognised. Otherwise the garden's story has been told precisely as it happened, with the weeds that threatened it, the storms that blasted it, the tools that nurtured it, the cool rain that watered it and the "Son"shine that caused it to grow.

It has always been my dream to tell the story of this garden and, after long years of prayer, I thanked God when He sent me a ghostwriter in Sara Bruce. Although we came from opposite ends of the earth, the Lord gave us unity in spirit concerning this vision and Sara easily captured the story on paper.

Sara became more than a colleague. During my bouts of illness, she willingly served as "charwoman" and nursemaid as well. She stood beside me during the life-threatening moments of my sickness, and became my sister in Christ, reading God's Word to me when I could not do so for myself.

She kept my eyes on the vision when the illness threatened to overwhelm me.

She and her family sacrificed a great deal to bring the book into being. The others managed without her during the long months of travel required for the research and writing. Her husband, Michael, constantly gave me encouragement and support, exhorting me to complete the task. Their two boys, David and Joshua, did the same – since early childhood they have been prayer partners in the children's work.

This family encouraged me in another way, too. Michael and Sara have trained their two children so fully in the Lord that, when I observed their walk with Him, I found my own vision for children's work strengthened. Their example proves that it works!

As well as the Bruce family, there have, of course, been others who have helped with the garden and contributed to the book itself. First and foremost, my chocolate-eyed Mamuska has interceded daily for this book as she has for every other facet of my life, surrounding me with her love and inspiring me with her faith. She is my greatest prayer partner. Mamuska has been given excellent care by Ewa Lazar, my adopted sister. Ewa's unfailing help has been a life-saver, not only to Mamuska, but to me as well. She has often made it possible for me to go on when sickness would otherwise have stopped me.

The debt of gratitude I owe them both can never be expressed, nor can the debt to my two Uncles in the vision: Jozef Prower and Sam Doherty. These two men set me on my path towards the garden and, although Uncle Jozef is now in Heaven, Uncle Sam still guides me forward as we see the growth the Master Gardener is bringing about.

God has given me other family in the garden as well. The workers at Child Evangelism Mission are my beloved first-born in the work. Henry and Alina Wieja, too, have been as a brother and sister in the vision for Poland. I am grateful to them all.

More broadly, scattered across Poland, are the many young

people who have given their lives to Jesus Christ and, having thus been "adopted by God", have become a wider family to me. I thank Him for each one's strategic contribution to the work.

In this rather extraordinary garden, some of the gardeners involved are located well beyond the borders of Poland. Chief among them is Evelyn Walker, an Australian I have never met, yet one who has typed endless transcripts and given help at both practical and spiritual levels to see the vision for children go forward. Evelyn also gave us the title for the book.

My grateful thanks go also to those who, in other ways, helped bring the book into being. Ken and Jane Henderson provided accommodation and ongoing support to see this project through. The Glowacki family provided for Sara's travel to Poland and have given constant encouragement. Jo Wilson opened her home to allow us a place for work. Dick and Helen Cadd produced videos of the work. Noelene Poole and her family made provision for much needed medical care. Judy Butler has found an assortment of ways to help – medical supplies, long distance research calls, even a national costume for promotion! An anonymous donor gave a laptop computer for Sara's writing.

Moreover, there have been those who, for many years, have fenced in the garden with their prayer, fellowship and support: Pauline Challender, Chris Fox, Trevor Manning, the Shrewsbury church, the Hegnauer family, the Noordink family, the Schmid family, Barbara MacLeod, Grannie Joan, Grannie Helen and the Admiral, together with the wonderful Aussie prayer force they have mustered.

Finally, I am deeply grateful for the counsel and help given by Hodder and Stoughton, in particular Carolyn Armitage and Bryony Benier.

All of these people, together with many there is no room to name, have helped our garden to blossom and flourish. The garden's growth is not yet complete, however. Something great is yet to happen in this garden, not only in my country, but throughout the world. After you have read this book, take a good look around you. If you don't see a similar garden nearby, plant one!

Jasia Gazda
1994

FOREWORD

Jasia Gazda demonstrates the power of the Gospel of Jesus Christ in her personal life. Hearing the Gospel as a child, God's truth and light made a lasting impact on her. God used other sources to water that seed, which turned into a full-blown, Christ-honouring life.

Her moving story is a theological statement on evangelising children, stronger than most. This is a needed emphasis in the Church today where the power of the Gospel in a child's life is often not taken seriously. "Wait until they're more mature, later," say the child development experts. Jasia's story demonstrates the value that God puts on a child's soul and His keeping power.

We believe children can and do get converted. Some 80 per cent of all full-time Christian workers were converted at fifteen years of age and younger. Jasia's story confirms it, enhances it and gives glory to God.

Be blessed by reading her wonderful story.

Dr Luis Palau
Luis Palau Evangelistic Association
Portland, Oregon
1994

GUIDE TO POLISH PRONUNCIATION

To help those unfamiliar with the Polish language, Polish words have been presented throughout the book in an anglicised form, without the use of Polish letters and accents. Here is a basic guide to the pronunciation of the main words and names used. The "a" is pronounced as in "car" and the "ou" as in "would". The syllable to be stressed is underlined.

Coreczka	SUR ETCH KA
Dziegielow	JEN GIE LOV
Gierek	GEA RECK
Gomulka	GOM UW KA
Jadwiga	YAD VEE GA
Jagiello	YAG YELL WO
Jaruzelski	YAR OU ZEL SKI
Jasia	YA SHA
Kochana	KOH A NA
Kolacz	KO WATCH
Kosciusko	KOST CHOU SKO
Mamuska	MAM OUSH KA
Mazowiecki	MAZ OV YET SKI
Mickiewicz	MIS KIEV ITCH
Morcinek	MOR CHIN ECK
Piernik	PI AIR NICK
Suchocka	SU HOT SKA
Tatusiek	TA TOUSH ECK
Walesa	VA WEN SA

Wojtyla	VOY <u>TI</u> WA
Wujek	<u>VOU</u> YECK
Wyszynski	VI <u>SHIN</u> SKEE
Za swe	<u>ZA</u> SFA

1

BUTTER ON MY HEAD

The soldier's well-trained eyes pierced mine.

"What's in your bags?" he demanded.

"Just my personal belongings," I replied, trying to look nonchalantly out of our train window as we came to the border between Czechoslovakia and Poland.

He scrutinised the four bulging suitcases on the shelf above me. "A lot of luggage for personal belongings," he said, icily. "Open this one!"

I caught my breath. I would go to prison if he searched that bag. It was laden with forbidden, mimeographed material. Polish law stated that only literature produced on government presses was permitted in the country.

The other passengers were watching. They knew the suitcase had been too heavy for me to lift alone, though none had asked why. Among Poles, however, solidarity is a way of life and I saw sympathy in their upturned faces.

The officer tensed at my hesitation. He clicked his heels and two soldiers with him straightened.

"I said, 'Open it!'"

I had known it was dangerous when I packed this literature, but to me it had seemed worth the risk.

Its message could, I believed, raise again the stooped shoulders of my disillusioned people. It could return the light of hope to their weary eyes. It could give them an inner freedom beyond the reach of any gun.

Offering an unspoken prayer, I climbed on to the seat and reached for the handle of my bag.

"Which of you is sitting in seat 36b?" An immigration officer suddenly filled the doorway of our compartment.

"I am," I answered in surprise, hand still on my suitcase.

"You are wanted for questioning! Come with me!"

I almost cried out with relief. Polish law also dictated that no bag could be searched in the absence of its owner. The frustrated customs officer could only stare in defeat as I stepped past him into the passageway.

I followed the green-uniformed officer as our train rolled through no man's land. Outside, the track was lined with enormous rolls of menacing barbed wire. Above them, soldiers in watchtowers surveyed the scene through binoculars. There would be no mercy for any offender caught here, I thought, as fear tugged at me once more. Beyond the ugliness of the border lay the sight I loved most in all the world: the leafy green mountains of my Polish home. Would I be permitted to enjoy them in freedom? Or would I be detained in one of Poland's soulless prisons? In that moment, I feared the worst.

The commander pulled back a drab, railway-issue curtain and bowed deferentially to a man sitting behind it. I wondered why. The seated man was not in uniform. He wore only an expensive leather jacket and stylish, imported pants. With a smug look, he gestured for me to sit too.

"So we've finally come back to Poland, Pani," he said and paused for effect.

"Yes, Pan." I tried to sound respectful. "Pan" is the polite way to address a Polish man, and "Pani" the proper term for a woman. Somehow, though, my interrogator made the word drip with sarcasm.

"And, Pani, we've had a very long time in the West, haven't we?" He consulted his notes. "Given permission to be away one year . . . stayed more than two. We like the luxuries of Western capitalism, do we, Pani?"

Was that jealousy I heard behind his condescension? The cigarette he smoked was French and his coffee tin was German.

"Well, of course I enjoyed the West, but . . ."

"So why bother to return to Poland? You no doubt lived in luxury over there!"

He was definitely jealous.

"Because I love my country," I answered.

He looked at me for a long moment, distrust narrowing his eyes.

"I don't believe you. You have come back for some other reason."

"What?" I asked.

He raised his hand to silence me. "Pani, I will ask the questions, not you!" The man lit a new cigarette and I, always allergic to smoke, began to cough. That pleased him and he puffed the more. Clearly, this was to be a war of nerves.

"You extended your stay in England. Why?"

"I was learning English. I wanted to speak it properly."

"Yes, and now you can't speak Polish properly! Or is that accent just for effect?"

"No!" Did I really speak with an accent? I had noticed my fellow passengers hiding smiles at some of my phrases.

"Yes!" He leaned across the table, his angry eyes level with mine. "You want to be thought of as foreign, Pani. You are wearing foreign clothes. You speak with a foreign accent. And," he blew the smoke into my face, "we have reason to believe you have come home with foreign ideas as well. Huh?"

I shivered. "But I'm proud to be Polish!"

"But I'm proud to be Polish!" he minced, lifting one shoulder and imitating my accent. I could hear it myself now.

The conductor poked his head through the curtains to see if we were finished.

"Finished? We haven't even begun!" my interrogator shouted. "Since this pani has to get off at the border station, you'll just have to hold the train until we're done."

"But what about all the passengers going on to Warsaw?" asked the nervous conductor.

"They'll arrive late!" the interrogator said, his eyes never leaving mine. "We have been waiting more than twelve months for this woman to return to Poland. Your passengers can wait a little too."

Incessant questioning followed. He approached his subject from every angle, writhing with the truth like a snake with its prey.

What had I learned from Poles living in exile? Had I given interviews to the BBC? Why had I travelled to other countries in Europe? Why had I attended church? Was I a Christian? Why? Had I intended to marry while in the West? Why didn't I? Was I returning with a large sum of money? Why not? I had been involved in secret activities before I had left Poland, hadn't I? Had I something to hide?

The snake was on full alert, waiting for any wrong move.

"Something about you doesn't add up, Pani," the man said, at last. "You have no money in your pocket. You have turned your back on a career in the West. You have left behind the man you were to marry. What is the real reason you came back to grey Poland?"

"It's not grey in my eyes, Pan."

He lit another cigarette. "So how will you live without coffee and ham, fine clothes and travel abroad?"

"There are more important things in life."

"Is that so?" Involuntarily, he straightened his imported coat and stared into his cup of German coffee. Only people with Party approval had access to such luxuries. Were they, I wondered, the reason he did this kind of work?

"No country on earth is as special as Poland," I continued. "We have beautiful mountains, lakes and forests, wonderful poets and musicians, exquisite arts and crafts. No, Pan, to me Poland isn't grey. I love my people and I love their faith and courage. I never want to be anything but Polish."

He dangled his cigarette from his lower lip and began slow, heavy clapping. "A poet and a philosopher! We're quite the sentimentalist, aren't we?" he said, spitting out the words. Then he crashed his hand on the table. "My patience is exhausted. You will tell me the truth!"

How could I tell him I meant every word? How could I express the love I felt for my people and my conviction that they needed a reason to believe after a lifetime of lies and broken promises? How could I explain that too many generations in Poland had suffered, for too long, with too little hope? How could I say that I planned to dedicate my life to one end: helping the next generation find a different path?

If I gave any clue it could prompt a search of the bags in my compartment.

The questioning went from one hour into two, he threatening and I searching for ways to answer. The battle was punctuated only by the continued lighting of his cigarettes and anxious interruptions from the conductor. He kept the train waiting two hours before he finally released me.

"You may go, Pani, but now that you are back in Poland you had better tread carefully!" he said.

"Thank you, Pan. I will."

"Be sure you do!" He gave a conspiratorial smile. "Or we'll know!"

Was he saying I would be watched? I could not tell.

"Get out of here!" he barked by way of conclusion, and I knew I was dismissed.

There was no time left for customs to check my suitcases. The overwrought conductor pulled them down and all but threw them and me on to the station before blowing his whistle for departure.

I sat on my bags, too exhausted to move, and watched the train disappear from view.

This encounter had been much harder than I had expected. Was I right about the vision that had brought me home to Poland? Was it worth this kind of opposition?

It had to be. Since my earliest years, life had proved to me that there was only one way to live. I had made too many mistakes to allow the next Polish generation to grow up in the confusion that had marked my childhood and nearly cost me my life. I had to go on.

World War Two had left Poland weeping. The fighting had wrought havoc in our nation and in its wake weary families were burying their dead and searching for their living. Mamuska, my brown-eyed, round-faced mother, was among them.

She and Tatusiek had married in 1941, dressed in the mandatory black of those bleak years at a solemn ceremony attended by few. They had enjoyed just one week of married life before she placed a Bible in his pocket and a kiss on his cheek and watched him return to the front.

Hitler and Stalin had cut Poland in half at the start of the war and, since Germany now considered our Polish region part of the Third Reich, the Nazis had conscripted Tatusiek.

"But I'll shoot all my bullets into the air," he told Mamuska. "I'll hurt no Pole." She waited for news. A letter told her he had soon escaped from the German army and joined the Polish resistance. Another letter told her that the Nazis had caught up with him and, by way of punishment, sent him to the dreaded Russian front in Stalingrad. Mamuska heard nothing more from Tatusiek.

After the war, he did not come home. Everybody around her said he must have died, but Mamuska did not believe it. "I've prayed for him and Pan Jezus has not told me he is dead!" she declared, and that was that.

Mamuska and Pan Jezus; they were quite a pair. Her faith was the glue that held her life together even in the face of impossible odds. She rented two tiny rooms and painted them in Tatusiek's favourite colours. She collected cast-off furniture and painted it to match. She even found a piece of fabric to sew into curtains.

Several years passed and people tapped their heads in a meaningful way. It was whispered that grief had sent the poor young woman crazy. In September 1948, however, she was harvesting potatoes for her parents-in-law when an emaciated soldier rounded the corner of the road. He walked with a limp and his uniform hung in shreds from his haggard shoulders, but she was sure it was Tatusiek. Shaking the dirt from her old harvesting skirt, she ran through the fields to meet him.

"God told me you would come," she said, holding him close and laughing too hard to worry about the lice that crawled from his wretched clothing on to hers.

"And it is Pan Jezus we must thank!" he told her, hoarsely. "It is thanks to the Good Book that I am alive!"

"It gave me strength to cope too," she whispered.

The wind blew his tattered uniform against his body and she saw how thin he was. "It was not only my strength," he told her. "It literally saved my life. An enemy bullet was headed for my heart but," he reached into his breast pocket, "that was where I kept the Bible. The book took the bullet instead of me."

She stared at the little Bible, her eyes moist. Its pages were burned through, but Tatusiek had come home from the war alive.

They began life together, learning to cope with the new yoke of oppression which had harnessed our people: Communism. Few of Poland's then twenty-four million people had wanted it, but after the war the nation was too weakened to resist the Soviet imposition of the Communist state.

Tatusiek and Mamuska always met hardship the same way. "Pain refines" was their creed and, like gold in the fire, they allowed suffering to turn them into people of faith, courage and humour.

In 1950 I had come into the world and they had tried, from my earliest memories, to teach me the same.

For centuries, indeed, survival under oppression had been a way of life for Poles. Each generation had taught the next how to cope; outwardly complying with the ruling power, but inwardly holding fast to one's true belief. A kind of national schizophrenia marked our people, and my own childhood was no exception.

"Jasia, remember what I have taught you. Don't show the customs officer where we put the cheese, and keep everything else hidden too."

Because our home was located in the south of Poland, near Czechoslovakia, much of my training in clandestine things was given at the border.

"Yes, Mamuska. I'll be careful."

At five years of age, I was her apprentice in smuggling goods from Poland to our relatives in Czechoslovakia.

"There's no other way to manage!" she had fumed while packing each item into its secret place. "That wretched Stalin has stolen everything from our country. We can't get coal. We can't get meat. We have to queue for milk and bread. Prices go up all the time. If we couldn't get to Czechoslovakia now and then, I don't know how we'd cope." Neighbouring Czechoslovakia had different goods available than Poland and, as a rule, slightly better ones. Mamuska had a barter arrangement with her sister across the border.

That bright morning, we had hidden sausage, cheese, butter, elderberry juice and "Krowki", Poland's traditional caramels, to exchange for Czech clothes.

I stood quietly in the customs hall. The soldiers looked enormous to me and I eyed the captain on duty in his imposing green uniform and cap with a golden eagle, the symbol of Poland.

The lady in front of me was dressed in the traditional clothes of the mountains and was forever straightening her red and green floral skirt and the lacy white petticoats underneath it.

"Next?" the officer said. She stepped forward, nervously pulling at her white, embroidered blouse and the young customs officer looked at her with disapproval. The government did not like to see these costumes except on festive days. They wanted us to wear plain workers' clothes like those on the Russian posters in our streets.

"Anything to declare, Pani?" the soldier asked, harshly.

Flustered, the old woman placed her bag on the dirty, laminated customs counter. As she leaned forward, though, we heard a resounding crash.

The customs officer barked a command and rifles clicked in trained response. I was terrified.

As suddenly as it began, though, the tension broke as first one, then another soldier began to laugh. I stared up at Mamuska and followed her amused gaze to the feet of the old lady, where a puddle of alcohol was spreading over the floor. Clearly, her copious skirts had been hiding a bottle of home-brewed vodka on a string.

We laughed along with everybody else, although we felt sorry for the old mountain woman when a search revealed several more bottles hanging under the wonderfully embroidered petticoats. Now she would have nothing to barter.

Giggling was Mamuska's weakness and, in that moment, she laughed so much that she forgot to be cautious with her own bag. It landed with a thud on the counter and I flinched. I knew she had put home-made elderberry juice in the bottom and sewn its vinyl fabric with a false seam. The border guard looked suspicious and Mamuska, red-faced, bent over to her foot.

"Oh this stupid shoe, sir. It's always falling off," she said.

I peeped up at the officer, afraid. She didn't sound very convincing to me.

He scrutinised her for an uncomfortable moment, then searched the inside of the bag carefully. Mamuska had cut the sausage into small pieces and packed it with chunks of bread, making it look like food for our journey. I held my breath. Her sausage trick had apparently fooled him.

He fished his way through the clothes and found some Krowki caramels. They did not raise suspicion either as Mamuska had divided them up, too. Some were in my bag and some she had sewn into the lining of my sleeves. The cheese was in our pockets.

"Anything else to declare, Pani?" the soldier asked when, at last, he was satisfied with his search of her bag.

In Silesia, our southern region of Poland, we have an idiom with which to tease one another when travelling. "You've packed so much," we say, "hadn't you better carry butter on your head?" In much the same way, English-speaking people refer to taking "everything but the kitchen sink".

For this border crossing, it so happened that my mother had in fact placed illegal, farm-fresh butter in a bag under her home-made felt hat. Czech people would give a great deal in exchange for butter. Speaking utter truth, therefore, Mamuska raised her dark brown eyes to answer the border guard's question.

"Well, there is the butter on my head, officer . . ." she said.

I stifled a gasp, but it never occurred to the soldier to take her seriously. "All right, Pani! On your way!"

"Mamuska, what did you say that for?" I asked, as soon as we were out of earshot.

"Pan Jezus says to tell the truth, Jasia!" she said, giving me a big wink. "What did you want me to do? Lie?"

Excitement filled our early days in Czechoslovakia. Aunty exchanged our sausage, Krowki, butter and cheese for money enough to buy all we had planned. We all went shopping together and they bought me five pairs of tights, each a different colour, together with new shoes that had smart bows at the front. In Poland, even in winter, many children who had grown into larger-sized footwear went to school with their shoes cut open and their toes sticking through because needed sizes could not be found in the shops.

Mamuska stocked up, too, on sewing needles and thread for herself and drawing pens and quality paper for my Tatusiek. He was an industrial designer and these were the tools of his trade. She bought him nails and screws as well. He was often called upon to make models of his designs in the cellar of our house, yet these basic items were also unavailable in our shops.

Mamuska had a secret motive in taking me to Czechoslovakia. My cousins attended special children's lessons at their church on Sundays and no such class was available for me in our home town. To Mamuska's sorrow, she had never been able to pass on her indomitable faith to me. In Czechoslovakia, she hoped I would find it.

She knew I was far from enthusiastic. Religion at home meant opening a huge, metal-clasped family Bible with elaborate Gothic lettering. The words were written in an older style of Polish and I found it heavy, solemn stuff. Mamuska had taught me to read on this Bible and, whenever guests came, called on me to demonstrate. I enjoyed their praise but the message remained lost on me.

Here in Czechoslovakia, though, the Bible was presented differently. The teacher did not have a Gothic Bible. He had a board covered in felt and placed on it a set of rainbow-coloured figures which moved under his deft fingers. I had never heard of television and I found myself intrigued by this moving picture show.

He spoke of a sower who threw seed on to all kinds of gardens. Some fell on shallow soil, some on rocky ground, some among weeds and thorns, but some fell in rich, good soil. "Pan Jezus needs our hearts to be like the good soil," he said. "We must give Him our lives for ever."

I wanted to think I was like the good soil, but although people generally told me I was a good little girl I knew it was not true. For one thing, I liked showing off because I liked compliments and Mamuska had called this pride. For another thing, I played with the truth on occasions, if it made people admire me more, and I knew lying was a sin. I became jealous, sometimes, too, especially if others received more attention than I did, and Tatusiek had shown me that envy was wrong. No, without doubt, I was not a very good little girl at all.

I was more like the soil with weeds. My parents took me to church on Sundays and there I listened to nice words about God. Then I came home and let bad things grow in my heart and choke the good seed. I understood why the teacher said that going to church did not make a person a Christian.

As the lesson drew to a close, I was on the point of making the most solemn decision of my few years. I wanted my life to become "good soil". I was ready, poised on the edge of my chair, to become God's child, when the unexpected happened. The lesson finished.

I felt strangely let down. I wanted to protest. "Wait! You've told us what we have to do, but you haven't told us how to do it!" I could not, of course. I stood up, along with the others, but inside I was deeply disappointed. It was as though I had been watching a wonderful movie and someone had switched it off before the end.

I walked away from the lesson in silence. We would not be back in Czechoslovakia for a long time and I knew of no one in Poland who could explain how I could become God's child.

In the months that followed, it was religion as usual in our house, but nobody could explain to me about the weeds. Loving, faithful Mamuska never missed a day in reading to me from our huge family Bible, but it seemed as old-fashioned and remote to me as before. My whiskered, olive-skinned Tatusiek was equally devout. Each night, he read the Bible for an hour or two before bed, but he was very shy about his faith. From him I learned much wisdom, but I never discovered how to become like the good soil. An individual relationship with God was too personal for him to discuss freely. In time, I forgot all about the different kinds of soil.

Instead, I found myself pulled in another direction altogether. In the Poland of the fifties, religion was usually conveyed to children as something dull, dreary and somehow irrelevant. The ideology of Communism, however, was presented to us in a colourful package which I grabbed eagerly.

I did not understand the suffering which the adults in my world were undergoing. Stalin had said that imposing Communism on the Poles would be like putting a saddle on a cow and, had it not been for his ruthless cruelty, he would never have been able to break in the free-thinking Poles. Those were tense days. No one dared trust another. A careless word or misinterpreted phrase was enough to bring the secret police to one's door. People were taken for questioning over the slightest issue. Some came back with such severe emotional damage that they needed psychiatric care. Others never came back at all. Thousands went to prison. Thousands more went to camps.

I could see the worried faces of the adults around me, but I knew little of the dark forces which threatened their lives.

On May 1st, therefore, I could not understand my parents' reluctance to attend the Labour Day parade held in our town. Tatusiek and Mamuska went because they were forced. I went because I loved it.

Poland turned into paradise for this celebration. Miraculously, our government made all kinds of meat available. My outspoken Mamuska said it was because they held secret stocks that should have been put in our shops anyway, but I didn't question it. This was the only day of the year I got to eat sausages of such good quality and I crunched into their spicy contents gratefully. Wonderful chocolates made a guest appearance on Labour Day too. So did a huge range of books and I loved nothing in the world more than reading. Labour Day was a dream come true for me.

It began with a colourful procession. Our town's best worker led the parade, carrying an enormous red flag. The Party members came next. Then came rows of workers, proudly wearing their work clothes and bearing huge banners.

The iron factory workers' banner read: "We pledge to serve our country with an iron will!" "But all that iron is going to Russia!" said Tatusiek in a very quiet whisper to Mamuska. "Their factories produce parts for Russian tanks so they can come and point their guns at us if we step out of line!"

Mamuska nodded and placed her arm through his. Dairy farmers came next, prodding their cows and distributing tiny pieces of cheese, something we saw only occasionally. Many people said, however, that Russia was getting more of Poland's dairy products than we ourselves were. "Do you know why Polish cows are such a funny shape?" Tatusiek asked Mamuska. "It's because they're fed in Poland and milked in Russia!" She giggled so loudly that he had to stop her with a funny sound he often made in his throat. I called it his teddy bear noise. He always made it when he was embarrassed.

I turned back to the parade. The farmers adorned their trucks with spring blossom and pine branches and, on the back of each one, recreated a typical farm scene for the onlookers to enjoy. Some families kneaded dough for bread, sending flour all over the laughing spectators. Some threshed wheat, moving their wooden implements in practised rhythm. Others went through the motions of shoeing a horse, a fiery furnace ablaze on the back of their trucks.

One special truck was my favourite and Tatusiek put me on his shoulders to see it better. It bore a map of Poland made out of flowers, wood and seed, a kind of art I loved.

"I'll tell you what's what, Jasia," Tatusiek said, always ready to seize any opportunity for me to learn.

The country was shaped like a flattened heart, with Germany to the west, Russia to the east and Czechoslovakia underneath.

"We'll do it by colours. At the top you can see the golden beaches of our Baltic coast; the only place Poland meets the sea. In the right hand corner, there are the crystal-blue lakes we call Mazury. In the middle you can see the 'Great Green Carpet' where wide, rich plains sweep across our country. Underneath that is our part of Poland, Silesia. It's brown near the middle of the country because there are many dirty chimneys from the factories there. But the further south you go, the greener it is, specially here in our beautiful mountains on the Czech border. Near our Beskidy slopes, you can also see the rocky Tatry mountains, the highest Poland has. Through it all, like a great blue ribbon, you can see the River Vistula, flowing like the letter S, from south to north." I did not get it all, of course, but I managed to repeat a few of the terms before clambering down from his shoulders to play.

The girls on these floats were dressed in Silesian regional costume. They wore floral skirts, red-laced vests, embroidered blouses with puffy sleeves and rings of flowers in their hair. The boys wore black vests with bright red pom-poms. I heard members of the Party making fun of these costumes, but I didn't care. Regional clothes were my favourite.

Mamuska had sacrificed a dress of her own to make me a similar outfit and, as they passed, I danced with my teddy bear, Miszek, on the side of the street.

A few people smiled and I performed a little more until I noticed one woman staring at me with particular interest.

"Hullo, kochana!" she called, when our eyes met, and I flinched. "Kochana" is a term of endearment, but I thought it too friendly for someone who was a stranger.

I turned around to watch the parade but every time I looked back found the woman's gaze still fixed on me.

"Who is that lady?" I asked at last, tugging on Mamuska's sleeve.

Mamuska followed my gaze and her smile faded.

"Never mind her," she replied, looking a little flustered.

"She's just a neighbour from the town where we used to live."

"But who is she?" I insisted, intrigued all the more by Mamuska's reticence.

"Oh, you could call her Aunt Mila," she said. "But, look, someone else is smiling at you. He's up on the Tribune."

The Tribune was a specially constructed wooden platform near the town hall, decorated with beautiful red cloth, balloons, flags, slogans and enormous photographs of Stalin, Lenin and Gomulka, Poland's leader. The most honoured people in our region had gathered there to address the assembled village.

Tatusiek lifted me again on his broad shoulders and I gave a squeal of joy. Seated among the rows of soldiers and Party officials was the man whom, after my beloved Tatusiek, I loved best in all the world. His name was Gustaw Morcinek, a widely-read author in the Poland of my youth, but also, as it happened, our former neighbour. I loved Uncle, Wujek, as I called him.

"What is he doing up there?" whispered Mamuska loudly.

Tatusick shrugged. "No doubt he has to be part of these things if he wants his writings published."

I waved eagerly at Wujek Morcinek and he threw down two red carnations, one for me and one for Miszek, the bear. I blew him back a kiss. Somehow, he often managed to look happy and sad at the same time.

"He co-operates with the government too much," Mamuska continued in a fierce whisper.

Tatusiek whispered back to Mamuska. "Don't forget that he spent five years in Dachau prison camp during the war. He has suffered terribly. Who are we to judge him?"

At that moment, a hush fell over the crowd. A man in uniform came to the microphone, wearing more medals than I had ever seen and leaning on a walking-stick. I didn't like this rather sinister-looking fellow and I specially disliked his daughter, Iwonka, who with her blonde hair in ringlets stood near the platform preening herself in a foreign dress.

"The Moskal!" said Mamuska.

"Ssshhh!" said Tatusiek. "Moskal" was a disrespectful term for Moscow residents. In our language, it is also a play on words since *moskal* is our word for herrings which have been pickled in sharp vinegar.

Nobody knew where the Moskal had come from. He had moved to our area just after the war and he was given the best house in the town. He said he came from eastern Poland, but he spoke with a heavy Russian accent. It was whispered that he was in charge of the secret police.

After the Moskal's speech, other military men followed, their many medals winking in the sun. I was bored until it was Wujek Morcinek's turn. The son of a poor coalminer himself, he had countless tales to tell about the hardship of workers in the old days and the improved conditions under Socialism. Everybody clapped for my Wujek.

When at the end of the parade he drove us home in his beautiful Wartburg car, I hoped everyone there would notice. He was a famous man. I felt very important being his friend.

Gustaw Morcinek was to shape my childhood in more ways, perhaps, than even he realised. Entering his home was, for me, like being transported to another world. Wujek's house had plush velvet armchairs, Persian carpets and expensive tropical palms and ferns from abroad. His sister, Tereska, kept everything spotlessly clean and baked delicate biscuits to serve in their expensive crystal bowls. To my amazement, she often served me German chocolates, tropical bananas and oranges as well. Every detail in Wujek's life made what we called in Silesia a "postcard" of his status.

Wujek's garden was different too. It was full of beautiful flowers and ornamental trees, unlike the vegetable plots of most homes, and seemed to me a little like fairyland. He helped me think that way.

"Listen to the earth. It makes secret sounds. There's a whole world hidden down there," he would say, his ear to the ground. I would put my ear to the grass, too, and listen for ants, worms and other creatures until I thought I could even hear the grass growing.

Morcinek, the master storyteller, would weave a story

around whatever noises buzzed in the garden on any given day. Soon, I too "heard" as he did until, at last, he would say, "Now it's your turn. You tell me a story." He would listen seriously as I spun a little tale and told me always: "One day, my girl, you'll be a writer too."

Wujek became my teacher as well as my friend. When he introduced me to stories in books, I became frustrated that I could read only the Gothic lettering of our ancient family Bible. Wujek patiently taught me to read modern Polish, while Tereska plied me with her gourmet biscuits.

He also showed me how to recite poetry, an art-form traditionally loved in Poland. Once I had mastered both, I became his little companion on many of the appointments in which he addressed local groups in the community.

Why did a man of his stature seek the friendship of a little girl? It never occurred to me to ask. I had no idea that he was lonely or shy. Nor did I guess the pressure he was under from the Communist Party. I had heard that some people were angry with him for renaming the Silesian industrial city of Katowice after Uncle Stalin, but since Uncle Stalin was such a nice man, I didn't understand the problem.

I simply loved Wujek Morcinek and, the more time I spent in his world, the more I wanted my own future to be just as grand.

Wujek could call for me at any time, even if I felt quite unprepared for an important event.

"But I'm dressed only in my playclothes!" I protested on one occasion, when he invited me to a meeting.

"Never mind, just come as you are!"

At the meeting, Wujek entertained the students with tales from his writings and then introduced me to the assembled group.

I stood, looking out at the audience members in their uniforms; navy blue skirts, white blouses and red scarves. One day, I would wear the same, I thought. I recited for all I was worth, choosing Wujek's favourite poem. It was called "The Boaster" and written by a Polish poet, Jan Brzechwa.

The boaster stood in a corner
She was talking all the time:
"I am more clever than anyone,
And the nicest dress is mine.
My face is glowing with health,
If I speak, I am always right,
My answers are simply brilliant,
At school, they say I'm bright . . .
I'm smart, I'm shapely, I'm very sweet,
I'm beautiful as can be . . .
Who am I? I think you've already guessed . . .
I'm the boaster! Yes, that's me!"

I hammed this poem shamefully. I pouted, flounced and curtsied, making the most of every line. Under Wujek's coaching, I had recited it in many places in our village, and it had already brought me a certain amount of renown. Today, the applause was deafening. As I bowed, I made a decision.

My life would be lived on a stage too. I would make sure people noticed me and, since that meant joining the Party, I would do so.

At five years of age, I was skipping blithely into the very trap that Communism had set for the children of Poland.

2

UNCLE STALIN

I lost no time. Soon after I was enrolled in elementary school, I joined "Zuchy", a Scout group some called "the kindergarten of the Communist Party".

Scouts, a neutral enough movement in other parts of the world, had became a tool for Socialism in Poland.

"Atton . . . tion! Left . . . right . . . left . . . right!" I marched to Russian military music with shoulders squared and head held high.

"Be prepared, Zuchy! The enemy may return any time!"

Enemies. Both inside and outside the classroom, Polish children were always warned about the enemies of our liberation. In a way, we lived in a constant state of war.

We stood to attention in the beautiful forest of our mountain range as our teacher explained who our enemies were. We felt terribly important, we young soldiers of the revolution.

"There are three kinds of people you must fight," said Pani Natasza.

"You must be on the lookout for *kulaks*, private farmers, who do not join the collective farms Uncle Stalin designed for us. Some of them do not give their goods to the State, but sell them privately." Pani Natasza scrutinised us and I squirmed. The butter Mamuska carried at the border was bought privately from a widowed friend, Aunt Ela. Was Aunt Ela an enemy of Poland?

"You must be on the alert for imperialists too, people loyal to the wicked Czar. I can tell you how to find them!" She explained that the eagle, our country's symbol, had worn a crown in the bad old days. Now it no longer bore one because that was something the Czar used to wear. "So, Zuchy, if you see any eagle with a crown in your house, I want you to bring it to our meetings." I felt uncomfortable again. The one part of Tatusiek's Polish uniform that had survived the war was his cap. It bore an eagle wearing a crown.

"The third kind of enemy is the worst," said Pani Natasza, raising her arm in revolutionary stance just like the people in the Russian-style posters in our town. "We must protect Poland from the Germans! Who knows the name of the Germans we fought in the war?"

"Nazis!"

Every family in our part of Poland had lost relatives or friends during the German occupation and our teachers had never let us forget this fact. They regularly showed us movies about the terrible suffering of the war years, though during the most violent parts I covered my eyes and ears with my hands. At this early stage of my young life I had already been taken to Auschwitz, the concentration camp which had seen millions slaughtered. I had vomited during the visit and woken up screaming in my sleep for nights after it.

"Yes, Nazis! I'm sorry to say that some Polish families get packages from Germans! What would you think about such people?" Here again, I felt uneasy. Mamuska had a German friend who sent us packaged soup and other treats. I loved the soup. It had special herbs which made green edges around your plate. Mamuska kept it for Sundays only. I wondered how soup with green edges could be bad for Poland? It was going to be harder than I thought to be a good little Communist girl.

"You don't think the Nazis would give up on Poland so easily, do you? Germans have been fighting our country for centuries! No, Zuchy, we must be on the alert. They might return at any time. Are we prepared? Atten . . . tion! About turn! March!"

Military-style activity followed. Pani Natasza gave us a junior reconnaissance game in the magnificent woods high above our town.

I loved the forest world with its rabbits, squirrels and deer scurrying about us as we moved into their domain. Stealthily,

I set out among the conifers and beech trees. I had two team-mates. One was Jurek, a neighbour's son, whom we had nicknamed Big Ears. He had a plain, freckled face that was somehow a little too large for his thin body, and his head was dominated by two large ears. My other team-mate was Iwonka, the Moskal's daughter. She had blue eyes, pink cheeks and golden hair set in ringlets, and she wore beautiful clothes underneath her Scout tunic.

The three of us had a set of secret messages which we were to leave behind us. Those following would interpret them according to our platoon's little code.

"Over here, Jasia!" Big Ears had become quite bossy in this role. "Make a bend in the twig here!" I made a half-break in the branch of a spruce tree and he pointed it in the direction the next person was to follow.

"Oooh, that'll fool 'em Nazis!" he whispered gleefully.

"Come on, we have to hurry!" Iwonka liked to give orders too. Together we gathered stones to hide a secret message.

"Them Germans'd never guess our code! I wonder if even our platoon can work it out?" Big Ears boasted.

I had always thought these two children were show-offs. It never occurred to me that my behaviour mirrored theirs.

With our task almost done, Big Ears and Iwonka returned silently along the track to see whether our friends had succeeded in following the trail.

Alone in the dark shadows of the forest, I suddenly felt afraid. It was one thing to think about Nazis in the sunshine, but quite another here in the sunless interior of the woods. I placed my last clue in the branches of a giant chestnut tree and, in that moment, thought I heard the crack of a twig. I swung round. Was there a monstrous Nazi watching me? Images of Auschwitz floated back to me. I remembered seeing dolls of little girls my age who had been tortured and died there. I had even seen the hair of the dead inmates and been told it used to be made into blankets that warmed German soldiers. I stood still in fear, half-expecting to find a bayonet pointing from behind a nearby trunk. When, a moment later I heard a plane overhead, I bolted, certain it would bear a swastika on its belly.

I raced into the safety of a nearby sunlit area. It was huge and the light streamed easily through massive beech trees which formed a canopy overhead. Something about this place intrigued me. It looked as though someone had deliberately cleared it.

I stepped over the uneven stones that formed its floor and, to my amazement, came upon rows of seats. Each was made out of rounded, grey-green beech trunks. Why? I walked between the benches and stopped in surprise. A huge wooden cross stood at the front. Beside it was a large rock over which ran a tiny stream that might have been used for baptism. Had this once been a secret church?

The clammy damp of the forest air was almost wet against my face as I reached through the ferns to touch the "font". It was very different from that in the church our family attended, but recognisable just the same. Near the cross, a plaque stated that this place had indeed been a church, from 1654 to 1709. The same sign also had words from Exodus 2:3 and said something about "holy ground".

I sat on one of the hand-hewn pews, thinking. "Holy ground" sounded a bit like the good soil I had heard about in Czechoslovakia. That issue was still an unsolved problem for me.

Birdsong filled the quiet sanctuary as I lifted my face to the rays of sunshine that shone through that forest cathedral. The light was so bright that I had to squint and, through my half-closed eyes, the rays diffused into lines that took the form of a great golden cross, beaming through the branches. Perhaps it was my fanciful mind, but in that moment I had the feeling that God Himself was trying to reach out to me, that He wanted me to become His child.

I hardly dared to breathe. "God . . .? God . . .?" I half-whispered. "Can you turn my heart into good soil? Can you make me holy ground?"

I waited in the forest stillness.

"Where do you think Jasia's got to?" Iwonka's harsh voice broke into the crystal moment and it was shattered.

"She's gotta be round here someplace," I heard Big Ears

answer and I bolted into the cover of the nearby foliage. They were the last two people I wanted to catch me praying. I could just imagine how they would mock me.

That night, we sat around a bonfire cooking food on long sticks under the shelter of the red-leaved beech trees. The pines murmured in the wind behind us. Big Ears gave me a dig in the ribs.

"Look at Iwonka," he whispered, pulling a face. "How come she gets all them treats?" Through the smoke, I caught a glimpse of Iwonka brandishing a fat, juicy sausage on her stick. We had all been required to bring food from home, but the rest of us had only potatoes to roast. Iwonka gave a smirk of satisfaction as we eyed her sausage longingly. Her family, like all Party people, was allowed to go to the yellow-curtain stores. There they could buy unlimited supplies of goods behind the shelter of heavy yellow curtains that hid the shops' contents from the eyes of other people.

I never liked it when Iwonka got all the attention so I seized the moment to ask Pani Natasza about the place I had found in the afternoon. Immediately, I regretted doing so.

"Oh, that useless old relic! It was once used for religious purposes, but it's more of a museum piece now. Boys and girls like you know that in our modern Poland we don't need the superstitious ideas of the past. We will use science to rebuild our country!"

Pani Natasza's dark eyes scanned my face and I was glad that she could not read the secret thoughts I had entertained that day.

She went on, fiercely condemning religious people. "Maybe you have heard older people talk about God, but you know better than to believe them." At this very moment, I was certain, my loving Mamuska would be kneeling on her stiff knees and praying for our Scout meeting, our family, our village, and, quite probably, our whole country. My Tatusiek, too, sat every evening beside the bed, reading our ornate family Bible as though his life depended on it. The picture of them both brought a warm, cosy feeling to me and, despite the fire, I shuddered in the pine-scented cold of the forest.

Pani Natasza continued to observe me. "Don't let that old-fashioned religious nonsense inside heads as clever as yours! You young ones are the future hope of Poland!" Her harsh, mocking laugh filled the forest evening.

I quickly turned my mind from God and, feeling nasty, gave Iwonka's stick a good bump.

At our campfire concert that night, I decided I had better do something to regain Pani Natasza's favour and volunteered to give a poetry rendition.

I chose a winner. It was a eulogy to Uncle Stalin.

> The train of history ran so fast,
> Signalled by the light of the ages;
> The revolution needed no acclaim,
> Nor flowery words from the sages.
> It needed only an engine driver.
> Who was that? I'm eager to tell:
> Leader! Communist! Our own Stalin!
> His name resounds like a great bell!

Afterwards, I was applauded and given a bag of sweets for my performance. With relief, I knew I could now bask in Pani Natasza's approval. Deep down, there were still doubts over many of the things she was teaching us, but I kept quiet about them.

Perhaps, that day, I had subconsciously learned the first rule to success under Communism. To gain favour, you had to tell the leaders what they wanted to hear.

In the following weeks, I searched for Tatusiek's army cap but was unable to find it. When I asked him about it, he seemed as mystified by its disappearance as I, but broke into German to discuss the matter with Mamuska. I hated it when they did that. I couldn't understand German so I always felt left out. Besides, I would inform them in an important tone, they shouldn't be speaking German at all since Germans were our enemies.

To that they would protest, but afterwards Tatusiek's eyes would soften and he would stroke my cheek and say,

"Kochana, one day you will understand!" Then, with a hug, the subject would be closed. Increasingly, though, I realised that I was coming to believe one thing and they another.

In the months that followed, my confusion deepened.

"Come on, you two, it's time to take the baby for a walk!" Tatusiek announced after school, one autumn day.

He came up from the cellar bearing the pram I had used as a baby. My parents liked to use it to distribute Aunt Ela's meat to her private, illegal customers. I had always loved my pram. At a time when others had needed to pull their babies around in a simple wooden box, my gifted Tatusiek had used scraps to create an elegant pram, similar to those he had seen in Germany. I fingered it, reminiscing.

"Kochana, are you not helping Mamuska?" Tatusiek said reproachfully.

Mamuska was weighing out customers' orders on her brightly polished brass scales. She wrapped each separately and then Tatusiek arranged them all inside the pram in the shape of a sleeping child.

I shrugged, uncertain. "Pani Natasza told us it is wrong to sell meat privately."

"Pani Natalia!" said Mamuska. "Your teacher is not Natasza! I have known her family since she was in a pram herself!"

"But she has changed her name to Natasza!" I replied.

"Has she indeed! So now we are all to go by Russian names? God bless Poland!" Mamuska was vehement.

"Hush Mania!" Tatusiek admonished quietly. He always called her by this affectionate form of Maria. "Someone may hear outside the window!"

"Let them hear!" she said, but dropped her voice all the same. "Aunt Ela struggles, month by month, to keep her family alive. If she didn't sell meat privately, she and her boys would starve!"

"But my teacher said the other people in Poland need food as well!" I whispered.

Mamuska put her hands on her hips. "And they'd have it

too if it weren't for Pani Natalia's" she spoke the name with emphasis, "friends in Moscow!"

"Sshh Mamuska!" I looked anxiously out of the window. Sometimes, Big Ears' parents picked fruit from the trees in our garden while listening to our conversations. We knew they were somehow connected with the Moskal.

"Your mother speaks the truth, kochana," said Tatusiek, his deep voice low. "In the past, Poland had no trouble feeding itself. If, today, our meat was not sent to Russia, Poland wouldn't be hungry!"

Mamuska covered the "baby" in the pram with one of her beautifully crocheted baby blankets and, with a wink at Tatusiek, put a bonnet on the "head". Tatusiek pulled up the hood of the pram so that others could not easily see inside.

Our little family pushed the baby carriage proudly along the streets of our town, sheltered by the golden branches of chestnut trees. The plan was simple. We would go from house to house delivering each order as requested, and would return the baby to its proper shape before moving on. We were not the first to think of distributing meat in this way. Many Poles did the same. Tatusiek told us they even did this in the Soviet Union.

"Did you know that Khrushchev's wife delivers private meat too?" he asked, his eyes serious.

"No!" I was amazed. Why would Russia's new leader need to, I wondered. Didn't they have yellow-curtain shops in Moscow?

"Oh yes. One time she had a baby pig in her pram, wrapped up in a blanket and bonnet, when she met a member of the Central Planning Committee of the Party!"

"Did she get caught?" Mamuska gasped.

"No, kochana. The Party man looked at the snout poking out under the frilly hat and said, 'Lovely baby, Pani Khrushchev! Looks just like his father!'"

That afternoon Aunt Ela's delighted customers were also full of fun.

"I'm so glad you've brought me pork," laughed one. "You know we can't buy it anywhere these days. They say it is because all the pigs have joined the Communist Party!"

For all their humour, though, these people were sincerely grateful to have help in feeding their families. The depth of their need was evident, even to me.

I was silent as we pushed the empty pram home over the town's carpet of orange and red leaves. Whom should I believe? Pani Natasza? Or Tatusiek and Mamuska?

Had I understood more of that turbulent period of Poland's history, it might have been easier to make up my mind. I had been too young, however, to know of riots in Poznan, a town in central Poland, that had seen scores of people killed and hundreds more wounded. "Give us bread!" frustrated housewives had shouted. "Down with dictatorship! Down with Russians!" Pani Natasza never mentioned these elements in her portrayal of our bright new Socialist Poland.

Admittedly, I had noticed a little tarnish on the gilt-edge of progress in our country. We were cleaning our teeth by putting salt on an old crust of bread. Tatusiek was splintering matchsticks into four long quarters, with a little of the match-head remaining at the top of each sliver so it could still light when struck. Mamuska was spinning wool from Aunt Ela's farm and Tatusick had built a loom on which to weave it for our clothes. He had even managed to make a rudimentary camera as well, since the shops had none for sale. He used it to record my growing years and the little black and white photographs he processed himself never faded.

Without question, my parents doted on their strong-willed daughter and it was no doubt out of love that Tatusiek set himself the task of teaching me the true story of Poland, past and present. In the confusion of those times, however, I proved a recalcitrant student.

"Did you know that Stalin and Gomulka have not been the best of friends?" he asked.

"That's not true!" I protested, thinking of the portraits of both my uncles hanging, side by side, in our classroom.

"It is, kochana," said Tatusiek quietly, lest anyone hear

outside our window. "For some time, Stalin even imprisoned Gomulka."

"Why would he do that?"

"Because Gomulka wanted what he called 'a Polish road to Socialism'. That means he wanted to run our country the way Polish people wanted, not the way the Soviets wanted."

I said nothing, but remained defiant.

"Only after Stalin's death did Gomulka lead the country again. But Pan Khrushchev was not happy about it so he brought tanks to Warsaw while they had a chat." I knew about Soviet troops, untold thousands of which had remained in Poland after the war. Sometimes I saw them in our woods, near the border.

"Khrushchev could not stop Gomulka, though, and he had to send the troops away and go home again himself. But," Tatusiek went on, "after a while, Gomulka became scared of Moscow. That's why he expelled 200,000 members from the Party. As well, although he released many priests, including the head of the Roman Catholic Church, Cardinal Wyszynski, people say there are still priests in prison." We were not Catholic ourselves, but I was sure my godly Tatusiek prayed for this widely-loved Cardinal and those priests. I knew Pani Natasza didn't.

It was all very difficult. I felt my parents' love and, knowing them to be the very best people in the world, I wanted to believe what they taught me. At the same time, though, I continued to crave applause and realised that becoming a Socialist star was the only way to get it. So I resolutely turned my face away from the disappointment in Tatusiek's sad eyes and insisted on Pani Natasza's teachings. If it hurt me to hurt them, I tried not to admit the fact.

When reality got too much for me, I turned to fantasy. I would disappear for hours at a time in the highest branches of our apple tree to read. Alternatively, since I adored children, I often played pretend by holding school.

I did not mind whom I taught. I found pupils in our backyard in the form of chickens and rabbits. Sometimes, I gathered our chickens and, with a line of grain, coaxed them under our apple tree for lessons. I told them the story of the Ugly Duckling who couldn't find his true family, a story I had read on Wujek Morcinek's knee. I wept as I recounted it, though the pathos was lost on the unfeeling creatures. At other times, I put rabbits on our rickety wooden bench, two by two, and gave them a little grass to eat while I taught them history. Their big eyes would watch me perform while they munched contentedly. I was in my element.

Best of all, though, were the classes with live children of the neighbourhood. Big Ears attended with several others from nearby homes. Usually, I made up the numbers by including Miszek the bear as well. I never planned the curriculum. Teaching was pure joy for me and there always seemed something at hand to serve as a lesson.

One unforgettable day, at twelve o'clock, I turned on the radio so they could hear a trumpet melody which is one of Poland's most loved traditions. Every day, at midday, this melody is broadcast from Krakow on all the radio stations of our country.

"Do you know why?" I asked my little class.

None did so I settled into teacher mode.

"Long ago in Poland, during the twelfth century, enemies were invading our country. They were called Tartars and they were very nasty and cruel. They attacked Krakow because it was the capital city of Poland!"

"But, teacher, Warsaw is the capital, not Krakow!" protested Big Ears.

"But Krakow was the capital in the old days!" retorted Iwonka, with a flounce of her golden curls. "Oh Big Ears, don't you know anything? You're so dumb!"

"I am not!" His bottom lip was trembling.

"You are so! You're stupid. No surprise you're *za swe*!"

A shocked gasp went through our little class. *Za swe* was a term never to be used. It was time for the teacher to take control.

"Apologise, Iwonka!"

"But it's true! He is *za swe*," she insisted.

By now there were tears on Big Ears' pale cheeks.

The phrase *za swe* is a derogatory way of referring to an adopted child. Mamuska had once told me Big Ears was adopted, but I had never spoken of it. In the Poland of my youth, if people could not have a child themselves, they would go to almost any lengths to hide the fact. The phrase *za swe* meant, literally, "to get for oneself" and was, in our region, a very insulting way of referring to the adoption process.

"If ever you need to speak of a person's adoption," I told the class, "you should use the right word: *adoptowany*. Never, ever say *za swe*!" Mamuska was nodding approvingly as she overheard me faithfully parroting her teaching on this point.

Big Ears shot me a grateful look and, although he always annoyed me, I tried to think kindly of him. After all, being *za swe* was the worst thing I could imagine.

"Sit still!" My class had grown restless. "Yes, Big Ears, Warsaw became Poland's capital at the end of the sixteenth century, but Krakow was the capital before that. So when the Tartars attacked us, it was Krakow that they wanted to conquer." The facts were easy for me to recall, thanks to the reading I had done in Wujek's luxurious mansion.

"There was a brave Polish trumpet player who wanted to warn the people of the city. So he climbed into the beautiful tower of the church in the Krakow Square and played a tune called 'The Heynal' to tell them about the Tartars. He never finished because the Tartars arrived and shot an arrow through his heart. But the people of the city heard his warning! Ever since then, a trumpeter has played the same music in the same tower, stopping 'The Heynal' at the very same moment."

"So that's why, at midday, them radio stations are always playin' it!" Big Ears wanted to restore a little of his injured pride.

"Yes, Big Ears. The trumpeter of Krakow is very important to Polish people!"

"But it was sad he died, just the same!" said Iwonka.

"Oh yes, many Polish people have died for love of their country, but deaths are always sad!" I replied, trying to sound wise and ponderous like a grown-up teacher. Her words, however, gave me an idea.

"I'll tell you what we'll do for the rest of our school time! We'll have a funeral ourselves!" I announced.

"Who we gonna bury?" asked Big Ears, wide-eyed. "No one's died!"

"We'll use Miszek!" I said. "He's a good bear. I'm sure he won't mind."

I had been thinking it might be fun to organise a play funeral since recently I had attended the burial of Mamuska's old, whiskered father.

The group went home to dress for our solemn occasion. The correct thing to wear was Silesian regional costume, and all the girls returned with white blouses and colourful skirts of one kind or another. Iwonka and Big Ears, coming from the wealthiest families, looked best. Iwonka had a beautifully embroidered blouse over which she wore a dark jacket that matched her flowery skirt. Pretending she was a married woman, she also wore a headband across her forehead, covered by a floral scarf tied under the chin. Big Ears strutted in wearing an old suit he had found in his attic, together with an ancient black hat. The others, coming from simpler homes, had made do with the best they could find.

I led my motley congregation out into the fields carrying Miszek. There I preached a sombre sermon about God, using phrases I had heard thundered from a man in a long dress who preached weekly from the high pulpit in our church. I knew clerical language because my pious parents never allowed me to miss a Sunday. I knew the hymns too and sang a couple loudly as the children dug a hole and buried my beloved teddy.

When it was all over, I came home and all at once realisation hit. Miszek was gone.

"Where is he?" Mamuska asked, astonished.

I was suddenly frightened, "He died, Mamuska!"

She was bewildered. "What do you mean? Where have you put him?"

"We buried him!"

I burst into a wail of grief, utterly inconsolable by this time. A family conference followed. My parents gathered all the children of the neighbourhood and began a search for the grave. It could not be found, however. In the excitement of the funeral, we had forgotten to erect a headstone. Miszek, the honey-coloured bear, had gone for ever.

Our home was in grief for some time after that. My mother missed my grandfather, and I missed my teddy. Death, the mystery, had suddenly become clear to me. When people died, you were separated from them. You could not see them any more.

"You won't see Grandfather again, will you, Mamuska?" I asked one day, when we were taking flowers to his grave.

"Not on this earth, kochana," she said, sadly.

"And I won't see my teddy bear either." I knew, deep down, I grieved rather more for the bear than for Grandfather.

A sudden thought struck me and I looked at her anxiously. "You won't die, will you, Mamuska? It would be such a dreadful thing for a mother to be separated from her baby!"

She opened her mouth as if to speak and then shut it again and reached out her arms to hold me.

"I don't understand you, Jasia. You're always afraid I will go away. Why would I ever leave my little girl?"

For some reason, the fear of losing her overwhelmed me and I burst into tears. She thought my grief was for her father and sought to comfort me. "Kochana, we will see Grandfather in Heaven," she said matter-of-factly.

"But how can you be sure he's there? And how do you know you will go there? Is it because you are never naughty?"

She kissed my forehead and wiped my tears. "No, kochana. Sometimes I am quite naughty, even at this age. But Pan Jezus died for my sins and He is my Saviour so, the Bible says, I will go to Heaven."

I was still crying, my head buried against her shoulder.

"Hush, my Jasia. You will go to Heaven too. You want to be Pan Jezus's little girl too, don't you?"

Did I? I wasn't sure. That was the problem.

3

INFLUENZA VERSUS TUBERCULOSIS

"Whom shall I marry? The hairy one? Or the handsome one?"

I stood before our full-length mirror, hands raised in what I hoped was regal bearing. I was alone in the house. Tatusiek and Mamuska were out Christmas shopping. Today, I was Queen Jadwiga, a beautiful Polish sovereign who had been married at just ten years of age. Being seven years old myself, I loved her story and had read it so often that I could say some of the lines.

"But mine is only a paper marriage!" I wailed, straightening Mamuska's nightie which I was forbidden to wear but which, today, had become my royal gown. It was a long way from the ermine and silk the queen would have worn, but it served its purpose.

"And, although I adore my Hapsburg prince, I may have to sacrifice that love, now that I have come to maturity!"

Queen Jadwiga was famous for this. Poland lies between Russia and Germany and, with no natural boundaries, has often been caught between the hammer and the anvil of its neighbours. Jadwiga was therefore asked to renounce her childhood betrothal and to marry a Lithuanian prince, Jagiello. By her doing so, Poland and Lithuania could forge a commonwealth strong enough to stand against its enemies.

"Must I really give up my Austrian love? Must I marry the heathen Jagiello?" I wailed, giving a little shudder, as I examined my reflection in the mirror.

I bent a royal ear to heed the wisdom of the wise men in

my court; our grandfather clock served as one and a long, wispy asparagus plant the other. I imagined their gruff voices pointing out that the dreaded German Crusaders would attack Poland unless it merged with Lithuania.

I folded my hands in prayer and peeped back at the mirror. All the books said Jadwiga was religious.

"Oh God, I am afraid!" I whispered. "It is best that I marry the Lithuanian, but it is said that the heathen is hairy and I know not if he be man or beast!"

I was wiping a tear from my royal cheek and revelling in the pathos when, suddenly, I heard someone at the door.

I panicked. Could Mamuska be back already? If she found me wearing her nightie, I'd be sure to get a spanking.

"Is anybody home?" I stopped short in my rush. That was not Mamuska. "Hullo! Hullo!"

I knew that voice. It belonged to Aunt Mila. She had visited us, from time to time, since that first occasion when I had seen her.

"Yes, I'm here," I said.

"Jasia! Kochana Jasia!"

"What would you like, Aunt Mila?" I asked in polite but cool tones.

"Well, to come in, kochana! Open the door!"

"But I'm not allowed to!"

"Whyever not?"

"Because Mamuska is out and I am not to allow strangers in when I am alone."

There was a pause. "But I'm not a stranger, kochana. I am your Aunt Mila."

"I know, but I'm only to open the door to my own Mamuska! Otherwise I won't get a surprise when she comes home."

There was again quiet on the other side of our white, panelled door. I felt a bit awkward. Something about this lady's strange attitude continued to trouble me.

"Well, why don't we have a nice chat through the door, then," she said at last. "What are you doing, child?"

"I'm playing pretend!"

"And who are you pretending to be?"

"Queen Jadwiga," I said, hoping she would be impressed. She was. "Fancy knowing about Jadwiga at your age!"

Nothing could have pleased me more than a live audience, even one the other side of a door. I told Aunt Mila how Jadwiga married Jagiello, how he had been baptised a Christian and the dreaded German Crusaders had to leave Poland alone. "So Jagiellonian children and grandchildren and great-grandchildren ruled Poland and kept it safe for generations! And it was all because good Queen Jadwiga gave up the handsome man and married the hairy one."

Aunt Mila was as complimentary as I'd hoped she would be.

"You know so much, child!"

"Of course. My Tatusiek tells me all these stories. I have the best parents in the world, you know!"

Again there was silence, and again I felt awkward.

"Well, I should go now, Aunt Mila."

"I'll visit again soon, Jasia. You'd like that, wouldn't you?"

"Of course!" What else could I say?

"*Z Bogiem!*" I said, hoping that would conclude the episode. This phrase means "Go with God". It is a traditional form of goodbye in Poland.

"*Z Bogiem*, little Jasia. *Z Bogiem!*" At last she was gone.

I looked outside. Through ice flowers forming on our windows, I could see the moon rising over the white mountain peaks. The snow on our barren apple tree had already begun to reflect its light. It was getting late. They would be home soon.

I returned Mamuska's things to her immaculately tidy cupboard, hoping she would not notice they had been disturbed.

I was in luck. When she returned, she was much more concerned about Aunt Mila's visit than anything else.

"Did you let her in?" Mamuska asked as she blew the snow from her grey felt hat and matching home-made scarf.

"No, of course not."

"What did she talk to you about?" Mamuska's tone remained uncertain, but Tatusiek said something to her in German and made his teddy bear noises. He bent to kiss my cheek and there was wet snow on his prickly moustache.

"Because you were a good girl, you can have your surprise now," he said, and placed a little book into my hands. "It's about another Polish king and queen."

Mamuska protested. "Pavel, the child already reads too much. Her head's already full of dreams and palaces! I think she believes she was born a princess!"

Tatusiek answered only with more teddy bear noises and carried me into the kitchen.

"We're going to bake Christmas treats!" he declared. "And we'll start with *kolacz*. To work!"

Tatusiek was the best cake-baker in our house and took charge, every year, of the Christmas delicacies. Kolacz, a form of fruit pastry, was my favourite.

"Did you know it was Queen Jadwiga's favourite too?" he asked, rolling out the pastry.

"When Jagiello was baptised, the ladies of Krakow baked Jadwiga the biggest kolacz in Polish history. It measured one square mile. A piece of it still stands in Krakow today," he concluded. My learned Tatusiek never missed an opportunity to increase my education.

"If you tell the child stories of baptism, you'll get her in trouble at school," said Mamuska, with a wink.

Tatusiek answered her solemnly. "While I am alive, Mania, I vow my daughter will be taught the true story of her country!"

We began to spread blueberries over the pastry base.

"She'll only ever hear half the story in her classroom," he continued. "She's still drawing pictures of Gomulka as the saviour of our nation."

Mamuska had another fit of giggles. "Saviour?"

I turned to face them both. I was not my teacher's little Socialist star for nothing. "You shouldn't laugh! My teacher said that Uncle Gomulka is going to make life in our country as lovely as it is in the Soviet Union!" At this they both burst into laughter.

"Kochana!" said Tatusiek gently when he had controlled

himself. "It's true that Gomulka started well, but you know what I told you! After Gomulka was threatened by Moscow, he changed. He told the nation that while he was against the old ways of Stalin, he was not supporting the new ways of the reformers either."

"Whatever are you thinking of, Pavel?" Mamuska interrupted. "She'll never understand such talk!"

"We have to make sure she understands, Mania." I loved that in Tatusiek. He always made me feel grown up.

"I'll give you an example, Jasia. Gomulka said that, while influenza is bad, you can't cure it by catching tuberculosis. In fact, TB is worse than flu. Isn't that true?"

"Yes." My childhood had been plagued with sickness and I had already contracted both of these ailments.

"What Gomulka means is that you can't cure the old problems left by Stalin by allowing the reformers to bring new democratic change. So you ooo, while Gomulka is better than our last leader, he's not as good a leader as our country needs."

"He's a coward," said Mamuska forthrightly. "If he'd stuck to his promises, I wouldn't be getting up at dawn to queue for hours, only to find the shop's out of meat when it's my turn to buy!"

Tatusiek patted her hand and turned to me. "Tell me, Jasia. Is life getting easier for us? Or is it getting harder?" he asked.

I was silent. There was no denying life was still very hard. I had heard enough talk in our house to know that. People were waiting up to fifteen years to get a tiny, poorly-built apartment with thin, plywood walls and miserable facilities. The tinny cars on our roads hardly ran. Food was in short supply. So was clothing. My shoes from Czechoslovakia, though beautiful, had not proved warm enough for winter and the shops had none. Each day, Tatusiek bound my feet with newspaper for insulation, yet when I arrived at school they hurt so badly I could hardly bear to put weight on them. It took an hour of pain for them to settle down.

"Ach, but it's Christmas!" Tatusiek said, with a floury hug. "The country might not have improved, but God has provided for our needs. We have butter from Aunt Ela's farm and raisins from our German friends to make our kolacz extra special. Come on! Let's finish it!"

Together we rolled little chunks of pastry in sugar and dotted them here and there over the blueberry topping. I opened the cast-iron door of our coal stove and the kolacz went in to bake.

"Not as big as Queen Jadwiga's, but just as beautiful," said Tatusiek.

Mamuska placed saucepans of beetroot on top of the stove to make borscht. If the oven had to be heated for the kolacz, the elements above it must be used as well. There was too little coal for any heat source to be wasted.

While the stove was hot, Tatusiek also made the other traditional Christmas fare. He baked bread braided from three strands of dough, representing the three parts of the Trinity. He made *piernik* as well, rich, golden gingerbread which would be cut in chunks and hung on the Christmas tree, filling our two-roomed flat with the scent of spices.

Winter deepened with the final days before Christmas. The powdered-sugar snow on our pine trees froze and hardened until their branches bowed with the weight. Our mountain houses, always resembling cuckoo clocks I thought, were iced in a thick layer of pure white snow. Our town looked like a life-sized Christmas card.

The truth was, however, that the Christmas message was not welcomed in Socialist Poland and as a result I found myself living a double life.

At home, I helped Mamuska as she scrubbed the place spotless "in preparation for the Christ Child". At school, I helped Pani Natasza decorate our classroom with political slogans, flags and pictures, celebrating Socialism's plan for progress in the new year.

"Whenever we have a Christian celebration to enjoy, they set up some political event in competition to it!" Mamuska protested. "They behave like spoiled children!"

Perhaps it was true. I didn't know for sure. I simply tried to please everybody. At home, I cut and pasted the paper snowflakes, angels and birds that have come out of Poland's rich folk tradition. At school, I celebrated the country's progress by cutting and pasting pictures of the plain new apartment blocks built according to the Russian style and the factories whose black smoke was filling our skies. At home, Mamuska used her powerful voice to teach me the carols of our heritage. At school, I sang only about the Socialist train of progress and how rapidly it was chugging forward. At home, the green of fir branches dominated our beautifully decorated room. At school, the red of Socialism was everywhere. At home, dear family members came for Christmas treats. At school, Iwonka's father and Wujek Morcinek visited to inspire us with Socialism's progress.

Our home was typical of most in the area. "You haven't experienced Christmas until you've had a *Polish* Christmas," Poles always say, and there was no way our stubborn people would allow the season to be spoiled.

It was true of me too, budding Socialist star or not. By Christmas Eve, I, along with every other child in the village, was sick with excitement. Mamuska called us to the table and Tatusiek stood to pray.

"Before we start, we will bless one another!" he began, lifting from his plate a paper thin wafer moulded into the shape of the Nativity scene. The church produces these each Christmas and, with them, every Polish family member has an opportunity to speak out a thought or prayer for the others gathered around the table.

We spoke out our prayers for one another and when my Socialist conscience troubled me I quietened it. This was too sacred a moment to spoil. Afterwards, Mamuska read the Christmas story from our metal-clasped Bible and then it was time to eat.

She set steaming borscht on the table, together with brightly-coloured vegetables set in aspic. Normally, we never ate such a luxurious salad. Nor, at any other time of year, did we see the glowing golden oranges she had arranged on a gleaming white plate. The braided Christmas bread stood beside them along with a bottle of fruit wine my parents had brewed in our cellar.

It was a huge carp, however, that provided the central element to every Polish Christmas meal, "because the fish was used by the apostles of old as a secret sign of their faith in Jesus Christ," Tatusiek explained solemnly. "It reminds us that the early Christians, though oppressed, stood faithfully for their Lord."

As he served the beautiful fish, he went on to say that, in the old days, if Poland had no king in office, it was ruled by the leader of the Catholic Church. "So you see, kochana, God is very important to Polish people! Poles will never give up their faith, no matter how hard today's government tries to instil atheism."

I ate, for a moment, in silence. "I wonder what Pani Natasza and our uncles in Moscow will do tonight? It must be horrible to miss out on a lovely Christmas dinner."

My parents looked at one another for a moment and then burst out laughing.

"Kochana, what do you suppose your 'uncles' in Warsaw are doing right now?" said Tatusiek, moustache aquiver.

"I don't know," I shrugged defensively. I hated it when they laughed at me.

"They are, without doubt, celebrating Christmas and far more extravagantly than in our modest home. We will have only four courses tonight. Wealthier families have seven, nine or even twelve! But it is our Warsaw leaders who will have the biggest meal of all!"

"But my teacher said . . ."

"Kochana, your teacher will have twelve too! I've seen her shopping!" said Mamuska decisively and stood up from the table.

She went to open the kitchen door into our second room. This was never heated, even in deep mid-winter, as our coal rations were sufficient for one room only.

"Excuse me a moment," she said. It was minus twenty-five degrees and her breath made puffs of steam in the unheated air. "I need to open the window beside the Christmas tree!

Otherwise, the angels won't be able to fly in to leave us their presents." She shut the door behind her and was gone rather a long time as Tatusiek and I laid our kolacz and other Christmas goodies on the beautiful table.

"Do you want to see if the angels have come?" asked Mamuska, smiling secretively, when she returned.

I flung open the door and gave a squeal of delight. There were gifts everywhere, bathed in the rainbow colours of the lights on the branches. The three of us sat by the tree to open the presents and I hardly knew where to begin. The angels had made everything look so pretty. They were wrapped in the brown paper we normally had in our stores, but each had red ribbon around it, together with a green sprig from a pine tree.

Tatusiek chose one for me. Inside was a red knitted hat with a border of white rabbits. "Look Mamuska, it is exactly the same design as the outfit you knitted me. The angels must have peeped into my cupboard and seen it there. Aren't they clever?"

Mamuska, twinkling all over, agreed and Tatusiek, looking softly at her, said that one of the angels was very clever indeed.

More wonderful packets unfolded their surprises. The angels had chosen all our favourite things. I had just sat down contentedly to turn the pages of a new book when Tatusiek and Mamuska said mysteriously, "Jasia, what is this?"

They handed me a bulky parcel which the angels must have hidden behind the curtain. I opened it in a rush and then stopped, speechless at its contents. Inside, there was the most beautiful doll in the whole wide world. I picked her up in wonder. She had honey-coloured hair that framed an exquisite baby's face. I tipped her towards me and gave a squeal of astonishment. The blue eyes in her ceramic face opened and closed again. I had never seen anything like it. I held her close and she felt as soft as a real baby. She seemed almost alive.

"Mamuska, the angels didn't bring her from Poland, did they?" I asked, eyes moist with joy. I had seen Polish dolls in the few shops that sold toys. They were moulded entirely out of hard plastic, body, face and hair. Their eyes were put on their ugly faces with cheap paint. I would rather have had no doll at all than own one of that kind.

"Where is she from?" I stared down in wonder at the little miracle in my arms.

"What kind of dress does she have, kochana?" said Tatusiek, gently.

I held her at arm's length. Her outfit looked like a national costume I had seen somewhere. She had a red and green striped skirt with flowers printed on it and a pretty white apron over the top. Her blouse was of white embroidery with puffy sleeves peeping out from under a black vest that laced up in front.

"I remember now! She is like the girl on our calendar from Germany!" I cried. Tatusiek smiled.

"That's right. She is Bavarian!"

"So the angels brought her from Germany!"

"They did!"

"Oh, but . . ."

I could not finish the sentence. As I looked down into those beautiful blue eyes, they seemed to return my gaze. Yes, she had come from Germany, but no matter what my teacher said I could see nothing bad for Poland in this sweet baby.

"I will call her Ania and keep her always," I whispered. It was my favourite name and nothing but the best would do for my baby.

When, a little later, my parents gave me a pram the angels had brought for her as well, I was beyond words. It had a pink pillow with roses and a matching sheet and blanket. I put Ania in it and wheeled her excitedly round the room. Finally, exhausted, I sat down beside the tree and fell asleep under its beautiful lights.

Tatusiek tucked me into bed. He put out the lights on the tree and the room felt colder than ever as I snuggled under an enormous eiderdown. Tatusiek kissed me and joined Mamuska in the warmth of the kitchen. I put just one hand out to rock Ania's pram.

"I don't care that you are German," I told her before falling asleep. "I won't ever leave you. Mummies don't leave their children!" Hours later, my parents found me sleeping soundly but still rocking the pram.

Next morning, we woke at 4 a.m. and trudged through the deep snow, past little homes with a golden light in their windows, to attend church. The stone building had no heating and I sat snuggled between my parents to keep warm. All kinds of people from our village had gathered to worship. We sat near the aisle and I watched as they filed in, wearing coats and newly knitted hats and gloves. The place was ablaze with candles and a great golden hue lit each passing face.

Hundreds of voices burst into a carol and I turned to stare at the congregation, each member gazing heavenward and singing with zeal.

As I did so, the door at the back of the church opened and a late-comer scurried out of the whirling snow. She looked about, as though reluctant to be seen, and then stood against the back wall to sing, loosening her scarf. In that moment, I saw her face and let out a gasp.

"Ssshhh, child! What are you thinking of? Turn around and stop staring. It's rude!"

"Mamuska, look, look . . ."

She turned, reluctantly. Then she started to giggle.

"Ssshhh Mamuska!" Now it was my turn to admonish. I could not stop her laughter, though. For there, huddled against the back wall of the church, was Pani Natasza, my card-carrying Party member teacher.

I turned back quickly and stared at the huge, lighted Christmas tree at the front of the church.

How could Pani Natasza explain her presence? Did that mean I could believe in God and still be the star pupil in her class? I did not think so. Nor did I think I could ever tell her that I had seen her in church.

The national schizophrenia that marked Poland had begun to reach deeply into my little life and I didn't know what to do.

I struggled through the remainder of the school year, trying to please all the adults in my small world. Summer holidays brought a welcome break from the tension between classroom and home. When Mamuska told me we would help Aunt Ela with her harvest, I looked forward to it and climbed happily into the child's seat on Mamuska's bicycle to set out through the fields. The summer wind felt warm against my face and it turned the birch leaves so that their silver undersides caught the sun as we passed.

We rode down several tree-lined roads but when we rounded a corner a sudden chill came over me. We were passing a white-walled farmhouse which I thought I had seen before.

"Can we stop, Mamuska?"

She stiffened a little.

"Mamuska," I persisted, "haven't we been to this house once?"

"Your imagination, child! It'll be your undoing! Look at the scenery."

Her response puzzled me, but I became dutifully silent and gazed about me. Foxglove was everywhere in the gardens and dog-roses grew wild alongside the fences lining the road. Behind them, wheat fields of burnished gold stretched all the way to the foothills of the dark green mountains.

Some of the hay fields had already been cut and I loved looking at the mounds of hay that had been gathered on to spiked, wooden stands, according to Silesian tradition. Their tall, rounded shapes made me think they looked like proud old men, standing side by side across the pasture, on the alert to protect their homeland.

Aunt Ela's farm was teeming with villagers who would help harvest her wheat fields. The farmers in our area always teamed up to assist one another on harvest day. Of course Aunt Ela could not afford hired helpers, but she could pay these villagers with illegal pork, sausages, white cheese and butter. She kept all of these in a stone cellar that could be reached only by means of a hidden trapdoor.

Her son, Marcin, had taken me there once. He had explained how, without this clandestine business, their family could never have met its daily costs. I liked Marcin. He was blue-eyed, intelligent and friendly. He told the truth too. I was sure of that. The trouble was that I did not know whose truth I should believe.

In Zuchy, I had won points insulting the kulaks of the old system, but now that I was face to face with the farmers, I suddenly felt ashamed of myself. We had been taught that these people were lazy, self-seeking aristocrats, but their weathered faces and rough hands were proof enough of a very different story.

The air shimmered with summer heat as the villagers sweated over Aunt Ela's wheat fields. The men laboured in rows, bent double, one hand behind their backs as they worked their sharp sickles with the other. The women followed, scarves tied at the back of their necks, gathering large bundles of wheat. They bound each at the middle with a single strand, giving them the appearance of a waist. The villagers called such sheaves "missies" and that long morning saw countless numbers of them take their place across Aunt Ela's flattened wheat fields.

Lunch was served under a huge chestnut tree. Marcin and I carried out baskets of freshly baked bread, displayed in crisp white linen. Aunt Ela brought her beautiful butter too and large pots of tea she had flavoured with strawberry juice. A tall, muscular farmer lifted Aunt Ela's huge round loaves and, taking a big knife, cut the sign of a cross in the brown crust of each one. Few people in Poland respect their Creator more than those who work the land. Reverently, the men removed their hats and bowed their heads under the blue sky. In a deep voice, the farmer quoted a Bible verse:

"Land that drinks in the rain and produces a crop useful to those for whom it is farmed receives the blessing of God. But land that produces thorns and thistles is worthless and is in danger of being cursed. In the end it will be burned. So says the Good Book in Hebrews chapter 6, verses 7 and 8."

He closed his eyes. "Thank you, Pan Jezus, for the fine crop on this land. May that verse be true not only of our farmlands, but of our souls as well. Amen!" His verse disturbed me.

Thorns and thistles sounded uncomfortably like the weeds I had heard about in my earlier years. I opened my eyes and stared miserably as the man prayed. I wanted my life to be filled with good things, not ugly weeds. I wanted to have a bright, shiny face like this farmer's and Marcin's, their expressions radiating honesty and faith. Since joining Zuchy, though, I was having to behave more and more as though God did not exist.

The golden afternoon wore on and the missies began to cast long shadows over the newly harvested fields. The reapers' backs were bent with the weight of the day, but as they returned together from their toil they burst into happy song. The lilt of old Silesian tunes filled the air, followed by traditional hymns of our region.

"You will never be sorry if you choose to walk with God," said one line and the harvesters nodded with conviction as their rich voices repeated it.

"And it's a good thing God can be relied upon," muttered one sweaty farmer quietly to an old friend. "We certainly cannot count on the government!"

"That's a fact," said his wizened companion. "These new boys in Warsaw might know a lot about Communism, but they don't know a thing about farming."

I didn't understand their talk but Marcin explained it to me. "The government made all the farmers plant their crops according to the plan on the Warsaw calendar. That was a mistake. They should let the farmers be guided by Mother Nature. Many farms have lost their crops because the government made them sow much too early and a late frost destroyed them. But you can't tell those government people. They've got their Six Year Plan to fulfil and they'll make you work according to their schedules."

"Those boys in Warsaw have never had dirt under their fingernails. That's the problem," the old man continued, cleaning his hands at Aunt Ela's stone well.

"But at least we can give thanks that Gomulka kept one of his promises. He has given up on collectivisation!" said his friend.

"He had no choice! The country would have been in ruins if he'd tried to keep it going!" said another. The previous government had attempted to force Poland's farmers into collective farms. Even I knew of that from school and Zuchy. It had met with staunch resistance, however, and now 80 per cent of Poland's collective farms had been dismantled, leaving the farmers free to work their own, individual land.

"But," Marcin told me solemnly, "it's still hard for farms like my mother's. The collective farms are the government's favourites. Our country has a shortage of farm equipment and private farms are always last on the list to get any. But we are still expected to fulfil our production quota. We are supposed to report every chicken, baby pig and newborn calf to the Town Hall. If we kill a pig without first meeting our quota, my mother could face up to five years in prison. But if we give them everything we produce, we'd starve because they pay so little. Do you see now why Mamuska sells her meat secretly?"

"Oh yes, we wealthy kulaks . . ." laughed Aunt Ela, over-hearing her son as she arrived with huge plates of crisp, browned potato pancakes. "They want the whole nation to believe we are so rich we are like aristocracy!"

Joyful after her successful harvest, Aunt Ela clowned around, offering her food as to royalty.

"Your pancakes, my lord. Your sauce, my lady . . ." she said with an exaggerated bow to each. Mamuska had told me that many of these men and women were battling bankruptcy, but they roared with laughter and returned the honours.

Another farmer, returning from the field, observed their fun. "And my royal sceptre!" he boomed, brandishing his sickle in the air before placing it with the rest.

The full extent of their satire was entirely lost on me, at my eight tender years, but I loved playing princess at any time and went along with them. Their jokes continued until the heat went out of the day.

"What are the four things wrong with Soviet agriculture? Spring, summer, autumn and winter."

"What would happen if Communism took control of the

Sahara? They'd mismanage their resources so badly that, within four years, they'd have to import sand!"

The old comic farmer who had spoken first now stood on a tree stump, one hand raised in the air, shaking his head in mock admonition. "Dear me, gentlemen. I think you should all be ashamed of yourselves! If I didn't know you better, I'd think you were members of the dangerous new group, the reformers!" he declared, melodramatically.

"And we all know you can't cure influenza with tuberculosis!" shouted another. At that, one of the farmers started to clear his throat. Another followed, then a third, until the whole group gave way to a mock fit of coughing.

When at last the laughter subsided, their singing resumed. In time, the chestnut tree became a great black silhouette against the red and gold heavens and a blazing fire was lit. I was asked to recite a poem as the villagers sat drinking warmed herbed beer, a favourite of the mountain region.

"Don't recite about Uncle Stalin tonight!" whispered Tatusiek as I stood, adjusting the large bow Mamuska had put in my hair. I performed "The Boaster" as it had become a kind of trademark for me.

The farmers raised their beer glasses and requested another poem. I, never needing to be asked twice, quickly obliged. I recited an animal fable by a much-loved Polish children's author, Maria Konopnicka. She wrote about a group of flies who met in a bar and spent their time boasting about their cleverness in escaping the wiles of hungry spiders. Each one told a story that outdid the others, but none noticed the danger his pride was placing him in.

Unseen, in one corner, though, "something" was lurking,
And, as the flies talked, it was moving ahead.
That "something", a spider, was busily working,
And spinning around them a strong, silver thread.
He spun while the flies told their tales so tall,
And they never noticed till he'd caught them all.

Afterwards, I settled down between my parents and stared

at the rising moon. Tatusiek was pleased with my recital but, holding me close, whispered, "And you, kochana? Will you take care that you yourself are not caught in a silver web? I don't want my little daughter to get trapped by any spider."

I didn't have to ask what he meant. My parents were certain I was being duped by Pani Natasza and the Scout movement. Soon I would have to choose which of the grown-ups around me I was going to believe.

For the moment, though, I shut my eyes on the whole confusing adult world and did the best thing I could think of. I fell asleep.

4

THE DOG AND THE WOLF

> Once a scrawny Wolf set out
> In search of food to eat.
> Shivering, he sought a way
> To warm his frozen feet.
>
> All at once, he saw a Dog
> Whom, as a pup, he'd met;
> A well-groomed, fat St Bernard,
> Now grossly overfed.

A dream had come true. I was performing in front of our school, its podium draped in red flags and banners, with Wujek Morcinek beside me. It was September 1st, a day set aside in remembrance of Hitler's invasion of Poland. My Wujek had been invited as our guest speaker and I had been asked to recite poetry. The Moskal was on the platform too. As usual, his chest was bedecked with so many medals I wondered how he did not topple over.

With my head held high above my Communist red scarf, I growled and barked and pranced my way through this poem, a famous if controversial one loved by Poles.

Pan Wolf, I explained, asked how his friend had become so fat. Pan Dog replied that he had simply learned to bow to his master and protect him from "undesirables", like the poor, for example, or Jewish people. Pan Wolf could be fat and warm too, the dog suggested, if he did the same.

The idea appealed to the hungry wolf until he noticed something that disturbed him.

"What's that upon your neck, friend?"
The hungry Wolf inquired.
"Just my collar! Useful when
A leash may be required."

"But why did you not mention
This important matter?"
"Why should I when my lifestyle
Makes me warm and fatter?

"Wait, Wolf, why are you leaving?"
The Dog said, mystified,
"Aren't you coming with me?"
The Wolf turned round and cried:

"I'd rather live in freedom
And eat whene'er I can
Than feast myself in slavery!"
And off the gaunt Wolf ran.

"Well done, Jasia! Let's have a round of applause, children!" My school principal looked approvingly over his half-spectacles and placed his arm around my shoulder.

"Of course, children, you can tell me the author of this poem?"

"Mickiewicz!" the assembled body chimed as one. We all knew him. This eighteenth-century writer was Poland's answer to Shakespeare.

The wizened principal eyed us carefully. Most of us were too young to realise the controversy Mickiewicz could evoke, but he was taking no chances.

"Mickiewicz never wanted Polish people to be slaves like Pan Dog. Neither do our present government leaders. We could, for example, be living in captivity to the United States, or to Germany, but our Russian liberators have made sure we are free!

"Today we have been honoured with a visit from a famous author of our own times: Pan Gustaw Morcinek." I nearly burst with pride when Wujek came to the microphone and told stories. Although he had suffered terribly at Dachau prison camp, he spoke without bitterness that day. Preferring always to be positive, he told, instead, stories of brave Polish freedom fighters who could inspire us all.

When he was finished, the principal resumed the microphone. "These days, we face new enemies as well as old. Germany is still our foe, but so is the United States. Americans are jealous of the progress we have made under Socialism!"

We had learned about this. Our teachers had explained that American Capitalism had resulted in great suffering. We had been shown pictures of dirty slums and knew, without doubt, that every American lived in dreadful poverty.

"Today, our government has asked for your help in dealing with a secret weapon the Americans have sent to Poland. A terrible thing has happened. They have dropped a plague of beetles on our potatoes!"

A shocked hush fell over the school. "How do you suppose they got them here?" he asked.

"In a boat?" said Big Ears, always eager to be heard in school meetings.

"No, the beetles would have died in a boat," the principal replied. "The Americans dropped them, secretly, at night, from their aeroplanes." He went on to explain that the CIA had master-minded the entire conspiracy.

Another student, Joanna, raised her hand. Joanna was the daughter of a man whom we had never seen. It was whispered that he was in prison for his political beliefs.

"Please, Pan, I don't understand. Why would Americans want to hurt Polish people when they give us free milk to drink?"

At school, in those post-war years, all Polish children drank American milk. We saw the US flag on every box.

The principal's voice became icy as he looked at Joanna. "It's all part of their clever plot, Joanna, but," he looked at her sharply, "we have no more time for questions. You will see me later!" Joanna would definitely be in trouble.

"Now Jasia will express our thanks to Pan Morcinek and you will be dismissed from classes to help save the potatoes."

I recited a revolutionary poem and presented Wujek with a huge bouquet of roses. As I did so, he whispered that he would pick me up after school and take me for a ride in his beautiful car.

I led our school students out into the street. Marching two by two, we sang a popular Socialist song: "We are building a new home, Poland . . ." We paraded past a heavy Russian-style poster of a worker with a scythe and I tried to flex my muscles and look the part.

The late summer fields had a deep-gold toasted look at that time of year. There was a tired feel to them, as if summer had burned itself out and the earth longed for the cool of autumn.

It was hot work checking for the orange and black beetles. A congenital heart problem plagued me on occasions like this and as the day wore on I struggled not to tire. It would never do to show weakness if I were to lead the others in battle against the Americans. I was bent double, hard at work, when I heard Joanna call softly.

"Woof, woof! I've found a dog over here!"

"What are you talking about?" I asked, straightening and wiping the perspiration that trickled down my neck.

She chuckled. "You, Jasia! You're just like the dog in the poem! You're even wearing a red collar!" She gave my prized red scarf a tug and I pulled away, blushing.

"Here doggy! Nice doggy! Don't bite now!" she said, laughing the harder.

"Maybe the dog's sniffing out them beetles. Dogs have good noses, don't they?" Big Ears lost no time in joining the fray.

The two of them laughed out loud, and Joanna looked around, hoping other students would be brave enough to do the same. Iwonka's presence inhibited the rest, however. They stopped work to watch with interest, but they said nothing. For once I was almost glad to have Iwonka around.

"Know which way the doggy's facing?" Joanna continued.

"East of course! That's why it's on all fours! Our government may be against the West, but it's quite happy to bow to the East!" She gave me a withering look. "What our school doesn't tell us, Jasia, is that Mickiewicz hated the Russian control over Poland. Poland hasn't changed much in all these years has it?"

Groups from other schools were working nearby and, to my horror, I saw Marcin was among them. I bent closer to the earth, hoping he would not spot me in this humiliating moment.

Only when I was sure Marcin's group had moved elsewhere did I stand to my full height and, blinking back tears, shout in my most commanding tone: "Get on with your job! Anyone who doesn't collect enough American beetles will be reported by me. You have been warned!"

At that, they all got back to work. I stood, welcoming the afternoon breeze that blew down from the pine-clad Beskidy slopes and allowing it to dry the tears on my cheeks. I was the most important student here and, even if others were nasty to me, I could shut them up. I liked that. It quietened any private misgivings that such questions raised for me.

When Wujek Morcinek met me later that day, I stepped proudly into his elegant brown Wartburg. It was a German car, but I never heard anyone comment that these were enemy vehicles. In fact, only the most important people in the Party used them. Wujek stopped in a shop to buy me a new book and I revelled in the attention of the bookseller when she saw me with my famous uncle.

He drove me to the Vistula river for afternoon tea. With the eye of the artist, he chose a picturesque location where the mountain slopes came right to the water's edge. I sat drinking in the beauty of the scene. Wujek seemed to be in love with the Beskidy mountains and often set his writing in this region so others would love it too.

"You must be hungry, Roztomila," he said, calling me by a Silesian term of endearment which, likewise, featured in his books. From his luxurious car, he produced kolacz, the fruit slice we usually saw at Christmas only. For Wujek, it was daily fare.

"Wujek, was it hard for you to talk about the war today?" I asked.

He lowered his blue eyes over his long, aquiline nose, and for a moment there was deep pain etched in his face.

"There is a wound, still, Roztomila. But German people are suffering deeply themselves as they rebuild their country. How can I not forgive them?"

"So you are not angry with them, Wujek?" I asked, surprised. I was still angry with Big Ears and Joanna for their nasty words that day.

"We must always look for the good in a man," he answered quietly.

He brushed away a bee and picked a nearby dog-rose. "As I journeyed home after those years of sadness, Roztomila, I filled my heart with honey from the flowers beside the road and let the white summer wind blow through my soul."

I looked up at this poetic man in amazement. The Moskal and all my teachers spoke of Germany with great hatred, but Wujek Morcinek had not let himself become sour or bitter, even after the nightmare of Dachau.

In time, we wandered beside the Vistula river, listening to the music of the water. Wujek stopped in front of a tall spruce on to which someone had nailed a tiny wooden house, built in the triangular style of Polish mountain homes. Inside, there was a carving of Pan Jezus's crucifixion. In Polish, we call these *kapliczkas*, little chapels, and, large or small, they can be seen all over the country. I was surprised, though, to see Wujek cross himself and look up reverently at Pan Jezus.

"Do you believe?" I whispered to him.

"I believe in the newborn heart, Roztomila," he said quietly, placing fresh flowers underneath the kapliczka.

I had never heard Wujek refer to his faith before. What else, I wondered, did my uncle believe that he could not voice? A sudden thought struck me. Might Wujek too have been called the dog in Mickiewicz's poem? Was he wearing a kind of collar, just as Joanna had said I was?

Wujek spoke little more that day, but I went home heavy. It was the first time I had realised that this man, who seemed to have all that life could offer, could also be very unhappy.

All the adults I knew, it seemed, were troubled during those years. Tatusiek spoke often of his worry at the nation's lack of progress. Mamuska talked, usually, of the shortages and high prices. If I needed a new pair of shoes, the topic was discussed for weeks before the decision was finally made. Every zloty was accounted for in Mamuska's neat handwriting on the pages of the family accounts book. There were too few of them to waste.

The zloty was buying less and less, however, and people around the country were beginning to laugh about the Polish road to Socialism promised by Gomulka. In Mamuska's words, the honeymoon with our leader was well and truly over.

"Why can't we get enough eggs?" some joked. "Because the nation is going so quickly along Gomulka's road to Socialism that the chickens can't keep up with us."

"Heard about the latest issue of postage stamps?" laughed others. "New ones came out with Gomulka's picture, but they have been recalled because the stamps did not stick to the envelope." "Was anything wrong with the glue?" the listener was supposed to ask. "No," came the answer. "The problem was that the people were spitting on the wrong side of the stamp!"

I did not know it at the time, but statistics issued during those years showed that the people of the nation had good cause for concern. Two out of every three homes had no running water, four out of five had no toilet and six out of seven had no bath or shower. In our own home, we had the luxury of piped water in the kitchen because the house was, as it happened, commandeered by Nazis during the war and they had insisted upon it. We did not have our own toilet, though. We shared a communal one outside. We had no bath either. Every Saturday night, Mamuska boiled water and filled an iron tub for each of us to use in turn.

As difficult as life was, these physical hardships might have been bearable for the Polish people had they not faced assault on their religion as well.

During Gomulka's honeymoon period, he had permitted parents to choose whether or not they wanted their children to have religious instruction at school. When 95 per cent of parents chose in favour of it, however, the Party had been displeased. Gomulka therefore placed the decision into the hands of the head teachers, most of whom quickly cancelled religious instruction. The churches then offered to teach children on their own property, but the Party tried to control this too.

At that point, Cardinal Wyszynski urged his people to obey God rather than man.

The Church was on the offensive. Throughout the country, people turned up determinedly for worship and brought their children with them. Colourful kapliczkas and crucifixes increased in number and, adorned with flowers and ribbons, made a delicate but determined statement to the authorities.

In my own small world, while I understood little of the broad picture, I nevertheless found life very confusing. I could see that Uncle Gomulka's promises were not coming true. Yet I could not bring myself to turn from the Party and believe God's promises either. There was too much to lose.

I teetered through those uncertain times, hovering between home and school, Party and religion. It was in my ninth year that a journey to Czechoslovakia finally tipped the scales.

The trip began innocently enough. Mamuska took me across the border with her unique combination of prayer, humour and smuggled goods. We bartered our Polish products and shopped excitedly in the comparatively well-stocked Czech stores.

Just before our scheduled return, my aunt sent my cousin on an errand and suggested I accompany her. A neighbour's book needed to be returned.

"How kind of you to bring it," the lady said as we stood at her front door.

She disappeared for a moment and returned to hand us each a piece of piernik, the golden gingerbread I loved.

"Aren't you going to introduce me to your little friend?" she asked, looking at me with interest.

"Jasia is my cousin from Poland, Pani."

"From Poland? But you don't have a cousin . . ." she began, then half to herself added: "Oh, now I remember. She must be the *za swe!*"

What had this woman called me? My heart started to thump and my head swam until I could almost feel the blood pounding in my temples. I stared at the woman in horror, too shocked to move.

My cousin's eyes were wide with fear as she looked from the lady to me and back again. No one knew what to say next.

"I, uh, I . . ." the woman faltered, a strange look coming over her face. "I must have made a mistake. Uh, come inside. Come and have more piernik!"

"No!" I stood like a statue on the lady's doorstep. It didn't matter that we were in Czechoslovakia. *Za swe* meant the same in both countries. She had said I was adopted.

"No! No!" I choked on the word.

"No piernik, dear?" She spoke gently enough, but her face looked anxious.

"No!" I wanted to shout it. No, I wasn't *za swe*. No, I wasn't adopted. What right had some total stranger to come into my life and say I was?

We left immediately and I ran towards my aunty's home as fast as my legs would carry me.

"Jasia, don't! It's not good for you!" My heart condition had prevented my participation in sports and my cousin knew running was strictly forbidden.

I ignored her warning and ran on. I had to get to Mamuska. I had to find out it was all a stupid mistake, a terrible lie. When I burst through the door of their apartment, Mamuska took one look at me and then leaped to her feet, concerned.

"Jasia, are you sick?" she asked.

I did not know what to say to her. Now that we were face to face, I suddenly found I could not voice the question. I was too frightened of the answer.

"Nothing's wrong. Nothing at all!" I said miserably.

Mamuska turned to my cousin. "Did Jasia run? Is it her heart?"

"Well yes, Aunty, I couldn't stop her." My cousin looked worried herself now. Staring at her, a point of realisation slowly dawned on me. She had not, at any point, denied what the woman had said.

Mamuska sprang into action. "Jasia probably needs medical treatment. I think we should get her home to our own doctor." She was used to my developing unexpected bouts of illness and I said nothing to the contrary.

I bit my lip, staring nowhere, while they hurried about me. Did I not belong to their world? Was I someone else's little girl?

We quickly left for the railway station and I sat in stony silence as we chugged through the polluted city towards the Polish border.

I stared out the train window but saw nothing. I was looking back into my childhood, searching for clues.

At last, I could bear the suspense no longer. "I know the truth now, you needn't pretend any more," I said.

Mamuska turned to me, looking petrified.

"What are you talking about?"

"For years now you've been lying to me, haven't you?" I held my breath, everything inside me screaming for her to tell me it was a preposterous idea.

She didn't. Her eyes widened in fright and perspiration broke out on her brow. The more fearful she looked, the more afraid I became that it was true.

"You see, I know everything!" I said, turning on my coldest tone to disguise the fear burning within me. "I'm adopted, aren't I?"

"Who told you?" Mamuska replied. "I told your cousins never to mention . . ." She stopped, suddenly aware she had given herself away.

Her words were my death sentence. I lay back against the train seat, closed my eyes and felt, for a moment, as if I would faint. It was as though the sun had suddenly set on my childhood and I had stepped into a dark night that would last for eternity.

Mamuska began to talk rapidly. She tried to plead with me, to reach for me, but I refused everything. I sat like a silent corpse all the way home.

When Tatusiek opened the front door of our home, he knew at once that something was terribly wrong. There was some hurried German as he kissed Mamuska and then he turned to me with a look so tender it made me want to cry.

"Kochana, kochana." He said no more, but opened his strong arms to give me a bear hug. For a moment, I longed to run into them, but instead I held my angry head high. I turned my back on him and he, ever the gentleman, did not push.

I sat by the stove, cradling Ania and staring at the ceiling while they unpacked. No one asked me to help. A dreadful silence choked us all. Tatusiek's compassionate eyes observed me, deep in thought, and when we gathered for supper it seemed as though he had made a decision.

"Mania, we should tell Jasia who her mother is. She may want to visit her and," he hesitated, summoning up courage, "she might even want to live with her, rather than us. We owe Jasia the choice."

I listened, stunned. At another time, I would have realised that Tatusiek was trying to be fair to me and loved him for it. In that moment, though, his words meant one thing only. He and Mamuska did not want me either. My first parents had given me away and now my second parents were willing to as well. I had been rejected once. I could be rejected again.

I thought, for a moment, I was going to vomit. The whole scene began to take on an unreal quality and I watched it, detached, as if it were a movie about someone else.

"Jasia, Aunt Mila is your real mother," Tatusiek said quietly.

"No!" I broke into angry sobs and buried my face in Ania's dress. "No!" I didn't want Aunt Mila.

Tatusiek continued. "But, kochana, the story of your coming to us is a beautiful one. It is a miracle, the greatest in our lives. Listen to it, Jasia!"

His eyes had a tortured expression as they held mine. I knew I was hurting him, but I shrugged my shoulders and turned my back on them both. I drank in every word of their story, though. It was to be imprinted indelibly on my mind from that moment on.

"On a wet morning in 1951, Mamuska was kneeling on the stone floor of the attic in the apartment where we used to live. She was crying. It was the saddest day of her life. The doctors had said we could not have children."

I kept my back to them, determined to hide my interest. In my imagination, though, the whole scene still retained its movie-like quality. I pictured the tears on Mamuska's face mirroring the rain that streaked down the slanting window.

"In the Old Testament, a lady called Hannah asked God for a baby and God gave her one. Mamuska knew the story so she prayed the same prayer as Hannah. She said: 'If you would give me a child, Lord, I promise you one thing: this child would belong to you.'

"That day, so long ago, Mamuska felt certain God would answer her prayer too, so she put on her coat and scarf and went outside. As she walked through the wind and rain, she saw Aunt Mila walking towards her, pushing a pram.

"'Why do you have the baby out in this dreadful weather?' Mamuska asked.

"'I have no choice. I'm taking this child to the orphanage,' Aunt Mila said. She had just become a widow for the second time and she had to go to hospital because of a terrible illness. We think it was cancer. Her older child, a little girl, could stay with relatives, but no one could care for you, Jasia. So Mamuska offered to take you. Aunt Mila knew we would give you a home full of love and care. That very afternoon, Mamuska brought you to our house and Aunt Mila came as well to finalise everything."

Mamuska finished the story. "Do you see the miracle, Jasia? I left home with a prayer in my heart and came home with a baby in my arms. Could any story be so wonderful? God gave you to us!"

I clutched Ania and said nothing.

Mamuska was almost pleading. "Kochana, I will never forget your first hour in our home. You lay in your pram and, all of a sudden, you lifted your thin little arms to be picked up. But it was not your . . . it was not Aunt Mila you reached for. It was me. Aunt Mila saw that and so did I. When I lifted you up, you nestled against my shoulder just as though you had done so all your life. She watched you and she said, 'I believe this is God's answer for Jasia's life. Who knows what kind of life I could give her? I don't even know if I will have much of a life myself.'

"Our papers were signed within a week. There was a lot of sadness in the years after the war and things like that happened quite quickly."

Mamuska had come to the end of her story. "Kochana," she whispered to me tenderly. "We would have told you but we didn't want you to suffer. We didn't want others to tease you. We even moved house to prevent the truth from hurting you."

Tatusiek spoke again. "Perhaps it is better you know, kochana. You seemed to sense something anyway. You always cried when we read you stories about mothers being separated from babies. You always reacted when Mamuska biked with you past Aunt Mila's house. It's as though something inside you remembered.

"But, Jasia, even though many people make adoption into something ugly, this is a very wonderful story. God did a great miracle, one we have longed to share with you!" he concluded, his eyes shining.

I looked from one eager face to the other. Something in me almost wanted to respond to them, but the pain within was too great. For reasons I could not name, I wanted to hurt them. It was as though they deserved to be punished for what they had done to me.

I stood up, placed my hands on my hips and shouted: "But you didn't tell me the truth! All this time you lied to me! You lied!"

"Kochana!" Mamuska looked stricken and placed her arm protectively around my shoulders. I pried it loose.

"I'll never, ever trust you again! I'll never trust anyone!" I ran from the room into the garden and sobbed under my favourite apple tree until I thought my heart would break.

I wanted nothing more to do with them, nor with their beliefs. I would become a Communist star and find my own way in the world.

5

FORBIDDEN SONGS

"I'm leaving! This isn't my family! I'm not going to live here any more!"

The weeks following the news had become a nightmare. My parents had done their best to help me, but I had refused all comfort. One afternoon, I swept into the kitchen to make a grand announcement to Mamuska.

"I'm going! Nothing you can say will be able to stop me. So there!"

Mamuska dropped some of the coal she was loading into our fuel stove. "Where are you going? Aunt Mila's?"

"Oh, I'm not about to tell you . . ." I wanted to keep her hanging. "All I know is that I have to get away from here!"

More than anything else, I wanted her to beg me not to go, but if she had I would no doubt have insisted the more on leaving.

Mamuska certainly saw this was a no-win situation. She probably reasoned that if she did not fight me, I would have a wander and come home soon enough.

"All right, Jasia. If that's what you want," she said in a small voice, "I'll make you some lunch."

She not only made sandwiches, she went as far as wrapping them in a colourful scarf and tying the bundle to a stick. It looked just like a picture from a child's story book.

"There you are!" she said, loading it over my shoulder with a little smile. Perhaps she wanted me to recognise the theatrical nature of my antics, but I chose to misinterpret her.

"You obviously don't love me," I said. If she was not going

to take me seriously, she would be sorry. "I can see I was wrong to think you did. Goodbye! You'll never see me again!" I slammed the door and, stick over my shoulder, marched down our stone steps and out of their lives for ever.

I never looked back to see her terrified face at the window. I marched off, past Big Ears' house, telling myself that nobody wants a *za swe*.

I walked through the town and up towards the mountain route that leads to the Secret Church, a path our family had taken to climbing every year in order to celebrate Pentecost Day in the open air. It was my favourite mountain path. Beneath the bright blue sky, I looked down on the harvested fields, their golden hay cut and gathered into the missies and old men typical of our region. Primroses and daisies danced in the grass at my feet and dog-roses decorated the sloping, wooden fence beside me. Cricket song filled the air.

I stopped to rest by a stream that flowed into the Vistula river far below. A weeping willow gave me shade and I shared my sandwiches with a perky sparrow while chatting out loud about my problems. I loved willows. In my imagination, they had always looked like stooped old women in conversation and I pretended this one was listening sympathetically to the account of my tragic life.

After lunch, I put my stick back over my shoulder and climbed until the sun cast long shadows down the mountain, bathing the now tiny town in golden light. I smiled to myself, pleased to think that no one would find me up here. Then I had a better idea. I would let them discover me. My body would be mauled by wolves and bears and then they'd be dreadfully sorry. I imagined the funeral. Everybody would cry and say what a nice little girl I was and why had I died? My parents would have to explain it was because I was *za swe* and nobody loves a second-hand child any more than they do a shop-soiled garment at a sale.

Just as I was imagining the scenario, I heard a bark and panicked. Was it a wandering farm dog or a wolf? Reality dawned on me. I really might be killed in this isolated spot. I reassessed.

No, I wouldn't die up here. I would go nearer home to be sure my parents would find me. Decision made, I set off down the slope, scattering stones as I ran. The sun was a red-gold ball balancing on the jagged ridge of the darkening mountains. It would set in a few moments. I had little time to lose.

The lights of the town were twinkling when I reached it. I sighed with relief and slowed my pace. Nearer the house, I heard anxious talk in the kitchen and that pleased me. I had hoped they would worry. That meant they did, perhaps, love me after all. I resolved to test them for a few more hours, though, and lay down underneath our garden bench. I was close to sleep when suddenly another thought made me reconsider. The bench was located behind our well and my parents might not see me there, if they came looking. I might die in the blackness of the night after all. At that, I dragged the bench to my favourite apple tree. They would be sure to see it there. Besides, the spot happened to be well lit by the street light.

Sure that I would be safely found, I closed my eyes and fell into deep sleep.

Next morning, I awoke in my own bed, with Ania in my arms. I was muddy and scratched from the previous day's adventure, or I might have thought the whole thing just a nightmare. I tiptoed out to the kitchen, wondering what to expect from my parents.

"Will you have bread, Jasia?" said Mamuska calmly, as if it were any old day of the week.

I stared at her, unsure. Why hadn't she said something? I turned to Tatusiek. He hugged me and replied, "Of course Jasia will have bread, and sausage too, I think!" He winked at me. Tatusiek had a standing joke about sausages. Because we could not afford much meat, he often spread bread with garlic, claiming that if you closed your eyes you could tell yourself you were eating Poland's traditional salami. "I'll have sausage too, kochana. Sit down and we'll share it."

They kept up this behaviour throughout that day and those that followed. By acting as if everything was normal, they hoped that I would soon settle down again.

Their idea worked for a short time, but before long I began questioning again. They tried everything. They repeatedly explained themselves. They presented me with treats. They gave me outings. They even took me to Aunt Mila's house, but the visit was a disaster. Neither of us knew what to say, so we said nothing. From that day forward, we had a tacit understanding that the topic would never be mentioned between us.

In the days that followed, I retreated further and further into fantasy. I spent hours staring at the ceiling or the floor, dreaming how life might have been, until Mamuska could bear my vacant look no longer and begged me to run outside and play.

During the early weeks, I sat on the banks of the Vistula, imagining what would happen if I threw myself into its deep, cold waters. Later I took to climbing the branches of my apple tree and fantasising that the true situation was different. I was not really Aunt Mila's daughter, I was the child of a princess who had, once upon a time, fallen hopelessly in love with a commoner. Maybe I had come from another country, England perhaps. I read all I could about English life and dreamed that one day I would be a princess walking down a royal staircase in an English castle. In the end, I read so many books that I won an award for being the "most prolific reader" in our region. I was pleased, but Mamuska wasn't. She firmly instructed the librarian to restrict the number of books I withdrew.

I wandered, lost, through the next year of my life. I let my school grades plummet, now pleased when I did badly. I dropped out of Scouts, abandoning my newly won status. I lost all interest in reciting poems. I gave up drawing pictures. I stayed as far as possible from religious instruction. When people asked me what was the matter, I pouted and said only, "Nothing!" I wanted the attention, but I wanted people to feel shut out of my life. I didn't trust anyone any more. Every adult in my life had lied to me and one had even given me away.

Teachers began to ask Mamuska for answers, but she didn't know what to say. The *za swe* stigma worked two ways, causing embarrassment for both parent and child. She pacified the school by telling them we had some problems at home, but that we were working on them.

She tried hard with me, but my mind had become set. Since I was only second-hand, I interpreted anything she did accordingly.

If she cooked my favourite soup, I would refuse it out of rebellion. When concern made her more tolerant than usual, I would tell myself that, if she had truly been my mother, she would have forced me to drink my soup. After all, didn't real mothers discipline their children? If, on the other hand, she became angry and spanked me, I convinced myself that this, too, was because I was adopted. What loving mother would want to hurt her own baby? I never noticed the contradiction in my thinking. Having been rejected once, everything that happened became proof of further rejection.

Little Ania from Germany became my confidante. Even though, at eleven, I was rather old for dolls, I talked to her day and night. I often cradled her in my arms, telling her she was my little girl and I would always be her mother. If there were moments when Mamuska observed this with pain, I didn't care.

At the end of the school year, Mamuska chose the one remedy she believed in most. Religion.

She set up the idea carefully. "There's a holiday camp at Dziegielow, a little village near the border with Czechoslovakia. It's a peaceful place with woods so beautiful they have made the area a nature reserve." She never mentioned the fact that this camp was to be run by a group of Protestant deaconesses.

"What would I do there?"

"Just rest, kochana. You could relax. And," she added casually, "sometimes there will be meetings and you will listen to stories they tell." It sounded pleasant enough. I suspected nothing. With bags packed, I headed off for my summer holiday.

I spent my early hours there enjoying the woods for which Dziegielow is known. Its forest floor is covered with spongy moss in which tiny white flowers grow, unique in all the world to this part of Poland. I danced over the bright green ground with its star-like flowers and imagined I was in a fairy dell.

The next morning, however, brought a rude awakening. I had been placed in a room with a woman who was pious and proud of it, as far as I judged. She insisted I rise at five and pray for two hours before breakfast in the Dziegielow chapel. I refused.

After breakfast, the sisters held their first meeting and I saw, at last, the trick Mamuska had pulled. For months now, she knew I had been avoiding the religious instruction classes I was supposed to attend after school. They had seemed dull and strangely remote to me, as if the teacher spoke another language from another place in time. I had given up on religion.

The deaconesses at Dziegielow were different. Even though I fumed at the ruse which had brought me here, I could not help being pulled by their message.

"Each one of you knows, deep down, the ways you are going wrong in your life and you cannot change these yourself. Only God can. He died to free us from them," a sister with a gentle face said kindly.

My mind, of course, returned to the question of the weeds that lay, unsolved, within me. I knew that the way I had been behaving lately had produced more weeds than ever and my conscience certainly troubled me. Somewhere inside, I knew, too, that I was not right in being unkind to others just because of the pain I felt myself. Years later, people would debate with me whether it worries a child when she sins. Without doubt, it worried me. I was hurting my parents on a daily basis and I hated myself for it.

"You need Someone who can transform your life into what God meant it to be. You can have a new beginning with Jesus Christ and allow Him to take control of your life from this day onwards. We want to give you that opportunity today."

Here was what I had missed as a five-year-old in the Czech Sunday School. Here was my chance to take the step I had longed to take then. Here, the sisters had made the choice so clear that I needed only to stand up and move forward.

"Jasia?" A couple of Mamuska's friends approached me with what I took to be flexed biceps and a fixed smile. "Your life needs to be opened to God, doesn't it?" They looked knowingly at each other.

"Give me time, please," I replied. I was on the point of responding to the message, but I would let no one push me.

"No time like the present, Jasia," one said. "We want you to come into the other room and have a little prayer." They took my hands and propelled me, between them, to the back of the meeting hall.

The rebel in me surfaced. "No! I will make this decision if and when I want to!" I stormed.

At this stage of my life, I was in the habit of over-reacting. I charged out of the back room, through the campsite and into the street. With my head held high, I marched along the forest road, past the little white flowers and on through the green and gold fields of Dziegielow's rolling slopes. It was about fifteen kilometres to our home. My feet were blistered and my muscles ached, but I never noticed. I was too busy practising the angry speech I would deliver to Mamuska.

I never had the chance. I had just reached our front door when she, summing up the situation in an instant, took me by the ear and marched me straight out again.

Within minutes she had me on a bus and, before long, back at the camp where she apologised profusely for her wilful daughter's behaviour.

Defeated, I stayed the week. When I came home, though, I told Mamuska in no uncertain terms that while she had won this battle she had lost the war.

"That's the last time you will force religion into my life. I am going to apply for teachers' college, far from here, where you will have no influence on me any more." The college would allow me to study for the career I had always wanted. More importantly, though, being a residential school, it would give me independence from the family.

I rubbed salt into the wound. "You are not even my real mother! What right have you to march, with hobnailed boots, into my very soul? I will never let you do this again and I will never believe in your God!"

I got my way. Once resolved on my new course of action, I spent the next year getting good grades again, participating in all the Scouts' activities and starring in poetry and art. It worked. I received a scholarship for the teachers' college, packed my bags and left home.

At thirteen years of age, I was young to be entering the college and even younger to be taking on the Socialist cause. Determination compelled me, however, and I skipped up the political ladder of the young people's Socialist group. I was zealous for the cause of ZMS, the tertiary level students' group which had replaced the Stalinist Youth of earlier years. I quickly became the darling of the Party members on the college staff and went from ZMS membership to leadership. I carried the flag, led parades, gave speeches, recited Socialist poetry, drew Party posters and received privileges refused others. When, soon after I arrived at the college, Wujek Morcinek died of leukaemia, I resolved to carry the Socialist torch the more faithfully. I would be worthy of him and of the Party.

Behind my dedication to the Cause, of course, was my desire to be a success. I was on my way to a great future, one in which nobody would ever think of me as second-rate again.

To achieve my goals, I would clearly have to shut religion out of my life but after the incident at Dziegielow I had few qualms about that. Marxism had become my creed. Or so I told myself.

The trouble began the week our violin instructor died. "You will have a substitute today," a teacher announced from the doorway, just before a music lesson. "Professor Jozef Prower has agreed to take you on until a new teacher can be found. It is a very great privilege for you and I trust," she raised her voice a little, "you'll behave accordingly!"

A buzz went around the room. We needed no introduction to this man who, even as a child, had been renowned in our country for his playing.

"They say he could have been the best in Poland, if he'd

wanted to. He was instructed by the same teacher as Yehudi Menuhin," whispered one.

"He studied in Berlin, Paris and London! He's world class!" said another.

"Well, you know, he's of Jewish background and you always find artists there!" said a third.

The door opened and we waited expectantly. As a rule, visiting dignitaries swaggered into our school, flaunting their status. To our astonishment, however, this man entered with a gentle bow.

"Good morning," he said, with a sunny smile. "May I start with a little Bach?" He was so polite he gave you the feeling you were doing him a favour by listening.

Professor Prower opened his violin case and reached for the instrument, wiping it with the same care a loving parent would have given a little baby. Then he lifted it under his chin and the magic began.

We were spellbound. Never in our lives had we heard anyone play like this. As the notes cascaded, the professor's thick black eyebrows rose and fell with them and his sensitive face reflected, with passion, every mood in the music. In one moment his lips would be pursed in deep concentration, in another he would be smiling as if he were in love with the wonderful melody. Each note hung in the air of our very ordinary classroom and I closed my eyes. School dropped away and I felt I was in a great concert hall.

When it was over, we clapped and cheered, but he permitted little of that. He bowed, more like a gentleman than a performer, and held up his hand to stop us.

"No more of me," he said, "it would be my privilege to hear you play."

This man shamed us all. He was one of the greatest talents in Poland, yet he seemed genuinely immune to pride.

Before he left the school that day, he drew me aside for a moment.

"Jasia, I wonder if you would give my greetings to your parents next time you're home?" he began.

I gasped. "You know my parents?"

"Certainly. I have met them several times when visiting your area. Last Pentecost Day, I played violin at a site called the Secret Church in the mountains. Perhaps you know it?"

"I've been there," I said in flat tone. The Secret Church seemed to haunt me. "But what took you there, Professor?"

"Oh I love that place," he said with a far-away look. "The Secret Church gives wonderful testimony to those who refused to compromise their Christian faith in the face of oppression."

"I'm sorry, I thought . . . I mean, don't you belong to the Jewish faith?"

"Yes, I have Jewish blood, but I believe Jesus Christ was the Messiah," he said, adding with a twinkle, "He was a Jew too!"

"Uh huh." I did not know what else to say and left as quickly as possible.

I was bewildered. Professor Prower was probably the greatest mind ever to enter our college. How was it possible that he was a Christian?

I was frustrated too. No matter how hard I tried to get away from God, He continued to turn up in my life.

I did my best to ignore Him. I determined to be as great a success as possible. I was not content being the college's number one student of that time, I wanted to be their number one student for all time. Jasia was a name I wanted them never to forget. It seemed to me that if only I could reach that level of success I would never be rejected by anybody again.

My battle with religion was given full vent in the Party activities. In the following year, 1966, Poland was to celebrate one thousand years of Christianity and Party leaders led us into a kind of competition with the Church. If the Christians planned some special celebration, we were instructed to organise a highly tempting alternative. If that failed to attract the Christians, I made sure they were rostered for duty at the appropriate moments. In a way it was all rather infantile, a kind of "tit for tat" rivalry, but I would not admit that to myself. I was the model Socialist activist.

Czestochowa, the most important Roman Catholic site in

Poland, houses a portrait of the black Madonna which is beloved by followers across the land. Replicas of it are on view in many Polish homes and shops. This particular year, the authorities seized the painting during a church procession to Warsaw and returned it to its southern shrine. We Socialists gloated over this move until Cardinal Wyszynski responded by taking part in a procession with an enormous, empty frame. Television carried his message to millions of homes and the government realised that, morally speaking, it had lost the high ground. There was no more sensitive spot with most Polish people than their beloved portrait of the Madonna.

Again, the nation's humour told the tale. "What is the difference between the years 966 and 1966?" one joke asked. "In 966, the nation was pagan and the government was Christian. In 1966, the opposite!"

I was part of it all, bursting with bravado and self-importance, except in the presence of Professor Prower. Not only did he teach me violin, but his wife now taught me piano. Perhaps because of my parents, the two asked me to call them Uncle and Aunty, and invited me to eat quite regularly with them and their son, Emmanuel.

I found the integrity of Uncle Jozef blinding. He had turned his back on fame and fortune in the concert halls of Europe, preferring instead to help the needy in Poland. When he met alcoholics he always had time to talk, often giving the sweater or coat from his own back to warm their malnourished bodies. If I questioned this, he would insist: "I have a second sweater in my cupboard and that man had none! What would I do with two?" I myself had no time for the inebriated men who inhabited the shadows of Poland's sad cities. Alcoholism ran at an astonishingly high rate among adult males at the time and I would not have given any of them my second sweater. I would be more likely to nag my long-suffering parents for a third one, and in the latest fashion, if you please. No wonder he was popularly known, among the needy, as "the Holy One".

Whenever I visited the Prowers, my ideology sounded so empty to me that I found myself leaving my Socialism at their front door, in much the same way as I removed my snow boots.

It was a different story in my own home. I regularly preached the Socialist cause to my parents and my times with them often ended in angry debate. As a rule, my tolerant Tatusiek coped with me, repeatedly assuring me that one day I would understand. One unforgettable Saturday, however, I goaded him too far.

It started, innocently enough, in Tatusiek's garden where he was trying to cultivate a black rose. Tatusiek had successfully grown many roses in his time, but this had been his pet project and over the years he had cross-bred the flowers with painstaking patience.

"Are you disappointed, Tatusiek?" I asked that year, as his hybrid had failed to take in the way he had hoped.

"Disappointed?" He straightened his back and shook the soil from his hands. "Good things take time, my girl. It's true of flowers and it's true of people!"

"What do you mean?"

He looked at me lovingly. "Oh never mind. Just an old man's mumbling," he replied gently. "Let's get going. Today, there's a good movie in town! It's called *Forbidden Songs*."

"Will I like it?" I asked him, brushing down my school clothes. I was particularly proud to be seen in public in the uniform from my teachers' college.

"Like it? I'm not sure. But you'll find it interesting!"

"Will I agree with it?" I persisted.

He took a last look at his hybrid rose and turned his gaze toward me. "If not today, then one day you will, my girl." He kissed my forehead. "As I say, good things take time!"

Forbidden Songs portrayed the humour, courage and faith that bind Poles when they face oppression. Under Nazi occupation, the Polish underground movement in Warsaw used, among other things, music to bolster the people's flagging morale. When forbidden songs were bravely performed in public, they became just as real a weapon as a gun or a hand grenade.

Early in the film, a cheerful boy chirped, on a crowded bus:

Jesus will punish those German clowns
Who burn Polish villages and towns,
So let me sing, oh yes, let me sing,
The Germans won't understand a thing!

In the film story, a Polish woman who had been "bought" by the Nazis was sitting on the same bus with a German officer, her golden hair beautifully groomed under an expensive hat. She whispered into the German's ear, translating the song for him. He stood, cocked his rifle and the boy, in terror, jumped off the bus and ran. He was not quick enough. With a deadly thud, the soldier's bullet found its mark and the little body fell, lifeless, to the road. All eyes in the bus turned, in solidarity, to pronounce judgement on the blonde woman.

"It's a terrible thing to sell your country to please those who rule over you," Tatusiek whispered. I peeped up at him. Did he believe I had betrayed Poland by siding with the Socialist regime? The flickering cinema lit up the shadows on his furrowed brow, but he, ever the gentleman, patted my hand and said nothing more.

The film showed a Jewish waif who had crept secretly from a ghetto and I leaned forward with interest.

Tatusiek and I watched this with special attention. As it happened, a Jewish boarder had been staying in our home and bred in me a deepened concern for the suffering of her people.

I watched intently as the child on the screen sang to a haunting melody.

Just as a city dog,
I must sneak through the wall;
Gestapo search with guns
And one day I may fall.

My beloved Warsaw,
Please listen to my cries,
Look at me, my Warsaw,
There are tears in my eyes.

I gripped Tatusiek's hand as the film showed a Jewish man risking his freedom to help the little girl.

The blonde Judas whispered again to a Nazi officer and, unable to look, I closed my eyes, opening them just in time to see the Jewish man being stripped of all his possessions and placed under arrest.

Near the end of the movie, the Judas woman was given her just desserts. A music group gathered under her window and began to play a well-known folksong. Its melody was jaunty and its words amusing, but they terrified the woman in the story.

> A Polish girl walks with a German
> Hair trussed up all in a perm 'n'
> How she struts, so proud and game!
> But, lady, do you feel no shame?
>
> We'll shave that hair, that costly perm,
> And you'll be bald just like a worm . . .

They meant it too. The shaving of such women was common, during the days of resistance. The humiliated ladies did not, of course, dare venture forth until their hair had regrown. In the meantime, it was hoped, they would re-evaluate their loyalties.

As this woman was being "treated", the musicians were on sentry duty but afterwards they broke into another forbidden song and marched proudly down the street. Nobody could have missed their message. The theatre audience roared with laughter. I squirmed.

At the end of the film, though, the mood of the audience turned to anger. In 1944, the Soviet army had asked for the assistance of the Polish underground in throwing the Germans out of Warsaw. They promised that, when the moment arrived, Russian troops would pour across the Vistula to help the Poles. On the screen, that was exactly what happened and we watched as Russian tanks rolled into action, liberating Warsaw from the Nazis. Furious whispering filled the theatre.

"That was one more example of the difference between Socialist truth and real truth, my dear," Tatusiek whispered, when we later walked home.

"The real story is that the Russians broke their promise. They never crossed the Vistula river to help the Poles. They allowed Polish people to fight until they held nothing in their hands except the cobblestones from the streets. The pictures of Russian tanks were added to the movie before the government would allow it to be shown."

"But that's impossible! It was the Russians who liberated Warsaw!" I protested.

"The Poles liberated Warsaw, Jasia, and at great cost. The Germans destroyed 85 per cent of the city before they left. Hitler had given instructions that no stone was to be left standing in the city. His wish very nearly came true."

"Why would the Soviet Union, our ally, fail to help Poles?" I said, haughtily.

"Because it was in Russia's interests to have a weak, broken Warsaw. It made it easier for them to impose Socialism."

I was silent. If what he said was true, I had been sold yet another lie by the System and I, like that wretched blonde Judas, was perpetuating it as well. Being put on the defensive made me angry. When we happened to meet Aunt Mila on the road, I found it difficult to give her more than a quick hullo. She looked hurt, but I ignored it.

Once home, we sat in Tatusiek's rose garden again, looking up at the mountain slopes where the summer wind was carving a path for itself through the beech trees.

In little more than a whisper, Tatusiek leaned close and said, "There is another Russian atrocity you should know about, Jasia. But you must never talk about it, ever!"

He took a deep breath. "Have you ever heard of Katyn?"

"No." From his tone, I was not sure I wanted to.

"Katyn is the name of a Russian forest where the Soviets murdered thousands of Polish officers during the war."

"Tatusiek, you're propagating Western propaganda!" I knew the proper Socialist phrases to use for a situation like this.

"I'm speaking the truth, Jasia. At the start of the war, Russia put many Polish officers in concentration camps. One special camp was reserved for those of higher education: doctors, lawyers, judges, academics and so on. There were at least 15,000 of them. These men were not regular soldiers, they were conscripts. After the war, they would return to their fields and they would shape our country's future. It made sense for the Russians to kill them and kill them they did!

"Nobody knew it had happened until 1943, when the Germans unearthed mass graves full of Polish officers. An international team of experts placed the bloodbath at April 1940. Stalin denied any involvement, though. He tried to prove that this was a Nazi massacre perpetrated in the winter of 1941. But the dead officers were wearing summer uniforms, not winter ones. He was obviously lying."

I said nothing.

"You see, at that point in the war, Russia and Poland had become allies! It was embarrassing, to say the least, that they had slaughtered their ally's best men. Obviously Stalin had to deny it!"

"Tatusiek, you have been listening to Radio Free Europe too much. Stalin would not have done something like this!"

"Stalin?" Tatusiek stared at me for a moment. "Kochana, he did a lot worse than this to his own people! Why not to Poles?"

His face was deadly serious. "I know this is true from friends' accounts and one day, kochana, you will understand. One day the whole world will know. But, until that happens," he put his finger to his lips, "don't breathe a word about it. Terrible things have happened to people who talk about Katyn!"

"What sort of things?"

He lowered his dark eyes. "You don't want to hear, kochana."

The Socialist star in me rose to its full height.

"You can't even come up with an answer! You see that, Tatusiek? You can't prove any of this nonsense!"

Tatusiek looked hurt. I did not know it at the time, but it had taken great courage for him to mention Katyn.

"You mind how you speak!" he said warningly. "Before God, Jasia, I tell you I have spoken the truth."

"No, it is you who should mind what you say!" I said, caution thrown to the winds. "With all your talk of God and Russian atrocities, you had better watch out. I have contacts, you know. I can even report you to the police!"

I stood up and stormed inside the house. He followed, and on the only occasion I can remember lost patience with me.

"All right, go to your friends the police!" he said. "And take this with you!" He put me across his knee and gave me a resounding spanking.

I was so shocked, I did not know what to do next. I refused to speak to either him or Mamuska for the rest of the day. That night, I lay tossing, a parade going through my mind. The blonde Judas came first. The dog out of Mickiewicz's poem followed. Then came the Soviet army that failed to help Warsaw and, perhaps, slaughtered innocent men in Katyn. All seemed to march after one another in procession. Did I belong among them, I wondered. Was I failing Poland in the same kind of way?

Next morning, my parents required me to go to church and I found the sermon as disturbing as the film had been. The preacher spoke of the way Saul, in the New Testament, had persecuted Christians until he became Paul.

For just a moment, my conscience troubled me enough to waver, but not for long. There was too much to lose.

"No, God," I half-prayed in rebellion, "this is one Saul who is not going to become a Paul."

6

INNOCENCE LOST

"You are the cream of our nation's youth; Poland's hope for tomorrow!"

I had made it to the big league. I was in Krakow, attending a conference for Poland's most promising Communist students.

"Since you have been chosen for this course, you can be virtually guaranteed a place in the Party after you graduate from school!"

The Party Secretary from the ZMS headquarters in Warsaw was presiding, dressed in the prescribed Party garb for women: navy blue synthetic skirt, white blouse and red kerchief. After lengthy speeches from some of Warsaw's senior Party members, she led us in a fervent rendition of the Communist hymn and then opened up the session.

"During our time together this week, we want to hear how each of you has excelled in the propagation of the Party position. Who'll take the lead for us and speak tonight?"

My hand shot up.

"Ah, Jasia! We understand you have been highly successful in dealing with religious elements. Tell us about it."

Rarely would there be another such opportunity to win the approval of the great men of Warsaw. I outlined the strategy which had worked so well at school, and then, after a round of applause, added what I knew would be my crowning touch.

"I have met Christianity in my own home as well. My parents are therefore not always politically correct. Only recently, my father slapped me when I spoke of reporting them to the police for not showing greater patriotism."

Normally, it would have been unthinkable for me to speak ill of Tatusiek. I was, however, still bitter about the spanking. I had persuaded myself that had I been his natural child he would never have done such a thing.

Never missing an opportunity to recite, I finished my speech with a poem written by a popular revolutionary poet called Broniewski.

It doesn't matter if they crush you
It doesn't matter if they assault you
It doesn't matter if they smash your face
It doesn't matter if they knock your head against a wall
Don't worry! The victory is ours . . . !

If your heart is too heavy
Cut your breast and take it out . . .
Then your heart will be a bridge
Though completely bathed in blood . . .

After the meeting, a Party official clapped me on the back and said approvingly, "Marx taught us that all enemies of the revolution must be dealt with. You may experience persecution for your zeal, my girl, but never let it flag. Our System is the right one for Poland. We are on a crusade, and you will go far in it!"

He shook his head. "Too many of our students are what we call radishes, Jasia," he confided. "They're red on the outside but white on the inside! Only a few are beets, red to the core!"

I thanked him and tried to act the part, but inside I squirmed under his approving smile. He may have been a beetroot, but I almost certainly was not.

"By the way, Jasia," he said before leaving me, "how would you like to do further study here in Krakow? You could go to the Jagiellonian University."

Was he serious? This seat of learning, named after the famous "hairy Lithuanian", was one of the three oldest in Europe. It had housed such famous sons of Poland as

Copernicus, the man, they said, "who stopped the sun and moved the earth". To study here would be a dream come true.

"The Party always takes care of its own," he finished, writing once more in his book. "I'm sure something could be arranged for a student as dedicated as you. Never become a radish, Jasia!"

I wanted to do as he said, but that week I found it harder than ever to believe in the System. The issue came to a head when the Party Secretary took us on a tour of Krakow, the picturesque city where the conference was being held. Since childhood, I had always loved Krakow. That day, however, I discovered that, for the politically correct Communist, I did so for all the wrong reasons.

Krakow had everything I treasured. It had been the political capital of Poland from 1038 until 1596, and it was still considered Poland's cultural capital. Its streets were lined with buildings of every architectural style imaginable. Walking through them felt, to me, like turning the pages of a magical history book in which all the pictures came to life.

Our Party Secretary, however, had a sour word for every wonder of this city of kings and scholars. The Gothic arches, spires and churches were "inefficient". The regal neoclassical and Romanesque forms were "ostentatious". The curved lines and intricate stonework of the baroque buildings were "excessive". All the glories of an earlier era, according to her, paled against the perfect simplicity of dull, poorly constructed Socialist architecture.

It was a relief when her critical voice stopped for the sound I loved to hear most in Krakow. Raising our eyes high above the city's Square, we gazed at two towers, each different in shape and height. The taller one looked like a glorious crown, every point topped with a golden ball that surrounded a larger gleaming orb in the centre. Through one of the tower's narrow windows, we could see the polished end of a trumpet as the haunting "Heynal" melody began, the player finishing, as always, on the melody's broken note. Each rendition of the unfinished "Heynal" carried an implicit message: Poles would never take kindly to oppression. Indeed, Krakow's traditions embodied the very soul of Poland; its nationalism, its faith, its indomitability.

At this conference, however, I was becoming increasingly convinced that these were at odds with the ideology of the System. Could I join the Party and be an honest Pole?

Before we left the Square, we visited its centrepiece, a glorious, medieval Cloth Hall with rounded arches and an ornate, curved parapet that looked, to my mind, as though it had been embroidered in stone.

"Why do you want to waste time and money here?" Pani Marion demanded.

"We want souvenirs!" our group protested. Inside the old building vendors sold traditional arts and crafts from different regions of the country.

"That stuff is kitsch!" she scorned. "Party members should have better ways to spend their time and their hard-earned money!" With that, she stomped angrily across the grey slabs of the Square, her heavy tread sending a flurry of pigeons into the air.

"Pani Marion! I really think she should be called 'the Marionette'!" whispered one of my companions at her retreating figure. I whirled around, shocked.

He grinned. "Well, why not? She can't think for herself, can she? A marionette has its strings pulled by those above it!"

Pleased that I enjoyed his humour, he continued. "Tell me, Jasia, what's the difference between Capitalism and Communism?" Before I could answer, he quipped: "Capitalism is the exploitation of one man by another and Communism is exactly the opposite!"

It took a moment to get the joke. As its impact sank in, however, I realised how deeply this boy, without doubt a future member of the Communist Party, was already disillusioned with its teaching.

"Perhaps the Party Secretary would prefer Krakow's architecture to look like Warsaw's Palace of Culture!" he went on, with a wink.

The Palace of Culture was, in fact, no laughing matter. It

was a tall, sinister-looking building that Russia had given, with much fanfare, to Warsaw in the early fifties. Its cumbersome, rectangular shape, with a tall spire piercing Warsaw's skyline, gave it the appearance of a giant syringe. I had heard that Russia had given similar palaces to other Communist countries and it made me wonder about my companion's comment. Was there truth in it? Was the architecture of Communism to be imposed, regardless of culture or aesthetics, wherever this ideology had control in the world?

"Know who they call the luckiest man in Warsaw?" my companion continued.

"No. Who?"

"The caretaker in the Palace of Culture. He's the only one that doesn't have to look at it."

Some of the other students laughed at his joke, astounding me the more.

"Where do you get all these jokes?" I asked, astonished.

"Oh, all over the place, but mostly from conferences like this," one replied. "If you want to hear good Party jokes, listen in when tired old Party members have freed their tongues with alcohol!"

"Party members too?" I had always thought them to be holier than holy in their adherence to Marx and Lenin.

"Party members are the best source!" the boy continued. "Do you know why people dig holes around the Party headquarters in Warsaw?"

"Why?"

"They want to see how deep the roots of the members go!"

"But some of them are sincere!" I protested, thinking of the beetroot Party member.

"Oh yes, there are a few, but not many," he replied.

His humour left a bitter-sweet aftertaste. Needing time alone, I wandered away from the others and lost myself in the beauty of the Cloth Hall. Its old wooden stalls were filled with the traditional crafts that hailed from Poland's villages. I fingered carved wooden figures with characterful faces, delicately inlaid boxes, hand-worked leather belts and shoes, golden amber jewellery, tapestries, embroidered tablecloths and regional costumes. I bought a frilly blouse with colourfully embroidered flowers and hid it before we went outside to find our sulking Party Secretary.

In the sunlit Square, a group of singers stood performing, dressed in Krakowian costume. The men wore red, mortarboard-style hats and long blue coats with white pants. The women were dressed in rainbow-coloured skirts, white frilly blouses and richly brocaded vests. They laughed and sang and twirled and I revelled in the sight.

"It's as good as a fairytale, isn't it?" I said to one of the others.

"And what hope will Socialist Poland have if it builds its tomorrows on fairytales?" said a sour voice behind me. It was, of course, the Marionette and I squirmed under her steely gaze.

She showed us most parts of the city, but carefully avoided the one in which I was most interested, the Jewish quarter. Grannie Esther, the Jewish lady who was living in our home, had told me many stories about that section, but I dared not mention it to our guide. Jewish people had become the scapegoat for many of the government's ills in the late sixties. Within just a year, in 1968, we would be seeing trainloads of sorrowing Polish Jews leaving the country.

We moved on to Wawel Castle, home to the legendary King Krak, perched on a rock above the majestic Vistula river which flowed from our mountains to this area. According to the old stories, he had secured the future of Krakow by authorising the killing of a fire-breathing dragon.

When life became too hard, I still liked to indulge in my old habit of fantasy and I imagined the place as it must have been in days of yore. I could see the kings stepping out of their huge portraits, sceptres in hand, to process along the marble floors, past the walls lined with tapestries. One room had a ceiling decorated with sculptured heads and each one, to me, came alive to people the vast palace as they waited on the royal personages. Horses and cannon thundered in my ears as I took in famous battle scenes. I thought I could hear music too, as I visualised feasts at the massive, carved tables, surrounded by colourfully robed figures. I peeped into a tiny chapel where one king liked to pray and imagined his bowed head, heavy with the weight of the nation, as he knelt at its ornate altar.

After Wawel Castle, the Party Secretary called us together at the door of our tour bus. She was visibly happier than we had seen her all day.

"You've seen the Poland of the past," she announced. "Now it's time to see the Poland of the future."

We went to the outskirts of Krakow to view what the Marionette called "the pinnacle of technological achievement in Poland".

I was horrified by what followed. She showed us Nowa Huta, site of the greatest steel works in Poland, the Lenin Metallurgical Combine. The government had allocated 900 hectares of land, on the outskirts of Krakow, for Nowa Huta. They had developed a massive complex employing 40,000 workers and producing almost seven million tons of steel per year.

Every schoolchild in Poland knew of Nowa Huta. We had been taught, in the classrooms, to be proud of it and until this moment I had been. Now that I was actually on site, however, it took only one look to know I hated it. The massive ironworks were breathing fire and belching terrible clouds of black smoke. "Imagine what this pollution will do to Krakow's old buildings!" whispered one of my friends from the Cloth Hall. Tatusiek had said the same thing, but not having seen Nowa Huta for myself, I had not believed him. Now, though, it was hard to fault his logic. Krakow's ancient dragon may have been dead but surely in Nowa Huta another had risen, and it would prove more dangerous to the city than the first.

In the whispering that followed, my rebellious friends informed me: "Did you know that the government hates Krakow's residents?"

"Why?"

"Because, at the end of the war, 94 per cent of the Krakow population voted against the Communists! The Party never forgot and it never forgave!"

"But what's that got to do with Nowa Huta?" I asked, double-checking to make sure the Marionette was out of earshot.

"When they built this town, they deliberately imported a huge number of workers to dilute the strength of the opposition in this part of Poland."

Even the Marionette said the same thing, though she used different words: "Situating Nowa Huta by Krakow gives great possibilities for the elements of high intellectual culture to be mixed with the vitality of the working masses," she intoned.

"This town was built as a monument to Socialist Man. You will note the simplicity of architectural design, a welcome change after the parapets, spires, arches, gargoyles and statues that have given us aesthetic indigestion in the old city."

My friends had another quip. "You know what they say, Jasia? Communist apartment blocks are built by people who know they are never going to live in them!"

We stared at the uninspiring, identical concrete apartment buildings against the backdrop of the polluted sky. It was evident that they were constructed of poor material; the cheap paint was already starting to peel and the woodwork warping. Worse, each one stood in absolute conformity to the rules of Socialist architecture; the buildings were differentiated only by number, 1,2,3,4, and the entrances by letter, A,B,C,D . . . Not only were they identical to one another, but identical to many more that had been constructed throughout the country.

The Marionette was enthusiasm itself in Nowa Huta. "Nowhere else in Poland do we have such an excellent example of a town built to the Socialist ideal," she exalted. "You will note, for example, that there is no church to be found here. Science, not religion, is Poland's direction for the future."

"And what do the residents themselves think?" whispered my friends behind. "They are doing all they can to get a church built here. Bishop Karol Wojtyla is helping them!" Within the decade, this popular bishop would succeed and, not long after, his figure would become of beloved renown internationally as Pope John Paul II.

We strolled slowly away from Nowa Huta, passing under the shadow of a massive statue of Lenin. It was made in the heavy style distinctive to Russia under Communism. Compared to the easy grace and elegance of the statues we had seen all morning, I found it difficult to treat the Russian "art" with respect.

I left Nowa Huta more depressed than I wanted to admit. This was not my dream of Poland.

What ideology could not achieve, however, pragmatism could. The Party, probably realising how many radishes there were in its ranks, gave us a taste of a highly tempting lifestyle that week.

We slept in the most luxurious accommodation any of us had ever seen. Our building was a picture of the good life in Communist Poland, with its marble floors, red velvet curtains, fine furniture and exotic palms.

We had ham every breakfast, something I saw, in our house, at Easter and Christmas only. We had pork cutlets and fresh salads and oranges at night, all imported from abroad. We ate cakes too, but not Polish kolacz or piernik. We had chocolate delicacies from Germany.

The message was unspoken, but abundantly clear. If you join the Party, all of this will be yours. Your standard of living will be well beyond the reach of others. You will be somebody worth noticing.

Politically speaking, I'd lost my innocence, I suppose, but I tried to ignore the fact. With the prestige and power this lifestyle would bring, no one would dare speak of me as second-rate or *za swe* again.

Perhaps it was because I now knew I was living with compromise that I found my parents' integrity more convicting than ever. On my next visit home, I spent time with Tatusiek in the cellar he loved so dearly. Every detail of that little room expressed his personality. Its walls were lined with neat rows of tools, carefully labelled containers for screws, bolts and nails, and paper and pens for his design work. Carefully hidden behind these, however, was an unauthorised radio on which he could catch Western broadcasts while working.

I came at the Party issue sideways. I had not forgotten the humiliation of the spanking.

"Tatusiek," I asked, "Does the factory honour you as it should for all your hard work?"

"What do you mean, kochana?" he replied, chewing on his drafting pencil.

"Well you're . . . you're not a Party member, yet your designs keep that factory going. Are you paid as you ought to be?"

He let out a long sigh. "Kochana, if I were a Party member, Mamuska and I would not be weaving our own cloth, we'd be buying you foreign clothes. We would be in a bigger house, too, and instead of bicycles we'd have a car as nice as the one Wujek Morcinek had. I'd look like the Moskal," he laughingly brandished an imaginary cane, "and you would look like Iwonka!"

"But, Tatusiek, without your designs the factory would not have survived!" I knew this to be fact. People always bowed when they passed Tatusiek in the street. His ability was widely known and honoured.

Frequently Tatusiek came home with a furrowed brow, telling us that the factory faced bankruptcy because of poor management. Their only option was to start production of a new design, one they could manufacture with their existing equipment and resources. At night, he would spend hours in the cellar, drafting one idea after another, until at last he came up with something. From heaters to holiday homes, cutlery to furniture, Tatusiek's prototypes were patented and copied across the country.

"Kochana, kochana. Our director presents my designs to the factory as his own. That way, he climbs steadily up the Party ladder. But I don't mind . . ." Tatusiek said, drawing me close for a hug. "At least I can sleep at night with a clear conscience."

"It still isn't right!" I protested. "You should have been promoted by now!"

Tatusiek looked at me, his expression serene. His eyes never bore the tortured expression I remembered seeing in Wujek Morcinek and, if I were honest, in myself as well.

"Kochana," he continued, "Don't ask me to join the Party. I love my God and my country too much for that."

He ruffled my hair. "Have you heard the latest 'doctor and patient' joke?" he asked.

"No." This was one of the standard formats used for political humour.

"The patient says: 'Doctor, I have a double mind. I think one thing, but say another. Can you help me?' The doctor replies: 'No, I'm sorry. You'll have to go to the government doctor.' 'Why?' asks the patient. 'Because I don't treat Party members!'"

Tatusiek chuckled and reached past me to turn on his forbidden radio for the news broadcast by Radio Free Europe. It gave a depressing description of Poland's situation: longer queues, more impoverished economy, maltreatment of the Jews and massive student unrest. It spoke, too, of the uncertainty concerning Czechoslovakia and its "political spring" and the Polish and Russian tanks gathering in border areas like our own. My greatest surprise, though, came with its announcement that Gomulka was not expected to stay in power much longer. The Western commentators claimed he was getting increasingly out of touch with the Pole in the street.

As Tatusiek leaned past the jars to turn off the radio, I glimpsed something I had never noticed before. In a small jar, pushed to the back, there was a tiny metal crown.

"What's this?" I asked, pulling it down.

He turned it over in his hand and looked at me. "It's the crown from my army cap, kochana. I removed it when you were younger. We thought you might tell your teacher about it."

At that, I could hardly meet his gaze. It was not so long ago that I had threatened to report him to the police and the coincidence could not have been lost on him. Tatusiek, however, chose not to mention it.

With an expression that approached compassion, he said brightly: "Enough serious talk for one day! Come and help me prepare a surprise for Mamuska!" He moved more of his storage jars aside and reached for a huge glass winemaker. Months before, he had filled this with apples, plums, grapes, herbs and even flowers from the mountains. Today, he decided, the wine was ready for Mamuska to taste.

We removed and cleaned the glass parts of this family heirloom and Tatusiek allowed me to test one mixture. My parents drank very rarely so this was my first experience of alcohol. I loved the sweet, fruity flavour and, unaware of its potency, continued to "test" the deep, red liquid long after Tatusiek had taken Mamuska's portion upstairs.

At last, I tried to follow him, but my legs refused to carry me. I could only sit, giggling, on the dank steps, waiting for Tatusiek to help. When the two of them came looking for me, they found my cross-eyed condition highly comical.

Mamuska gave way to her giggles and I joined in. It felt good to laugh and, with life's issues proving so confusing, I found it a relief to let the alcohol take everything out of focus.

I knew I had probably made a terrible mistake in the political direction I had chosen, but it was too late to change now. In a very real sense I was wedded to the Party and, even if I had married the wrong man, there could be no divorce.

The System, as it turned out, proved a merciless spouse. At the end of term, I faced exams for which I was unprepared because of the time I had spent away from school busy with ZMS activities. In Science, my weakest subject, I floundered. I begged my teacher for a re-examination in the light of my ZMS schedule but he refused. My teacher was, I suspected, most unsympathetic to the Party position and seemed almost pleased to see the ZMS leader taken down a peg.

When I received the news, the consequences fell like dominoes in my mind's eye. This failure meant I would lose my ZMS status. It also meant the loss of my scholarship for a quarter. Panic blinded me. I imagined myself unable to stay at the college, unable to be the Party star and, worst of all, unable to teach children, my great dream.

The hollowness of my political success became clear in that moment. Socialism has no compassion for failures. It was as if I had spent my life building a house of cards and now they were all to come toppling down. I persuaded myself there was no further point in living and gave way to depression. I resolved, at the age of seventeen, to end my life.

Too scared at first to face the implications of my decision, I turned to liquor, the classic escape route chosen by Poles. It was a Friday afternoon and I bought a bottle of alcohol and a packet of candies containing vodka. Together with three giggling friends, I used a schoolgirl recipe to turn the combination into a home-made advocaat. The others joined me in drinking ourselves stupid, they for the fun of the moment, I for the fear of the future.

I spent the weekend in alcoholic oblivion and on Monday morning excused myself from classes, citing ill-health. My teachers were used to sickness since my heart condition and a chronic throat problem had claimed many of my school days.

I slipped out of school and went to the nearby Roman Catholic church where I tried to pray. I wasn't very successful, though. I was quite convinced that God would not want me. I bought two bottles of liquid sedative and returned to my room.

The directions specified one teaspoon for normal usage. I drank the entire contents of both bottles and put myself to bed. Everybody was in class and no student would be permitted to enter the boarding house for the next four hours. I could die in peace.

I sank deeply into the pillow feeling first drowsy and then quite peculiar. It was as if I was falling to a place far deeper than I had ever been before. The room started to whirl and so, in panic, did my mind. It played tricks too. All at once, I did not want to die. In those fading moments, there seemed too much to live for. "God . . .!" Why did I call His name? Why had I taken myself to church? He wouldn't want me, with all the weeds in my garden. Nobody wanted a *za swe*. Blackness encased me and I knew no more.

When I opened my eyes again, I was lying in hospital,

looking up at Mamuska's round, sweet-faced gaze. For long hours, I swung between life and death while she hovered over me like a mother bird.

"God saved your life, Jasia," Mamuska said solemnly when, at last, they knew I was going to make it.

"God? Why God?"

"He did a miracle! He made sure you did not die."

She explained. "In the moment that you . . . you drank the medicine, it just happened that one of your friends discovered she had forgotten a book and needed to return to the room."

"But that's impossible! Teachers never allow us to go back for forgotten books. It's a strict rule!"

"This time, the teacher bent the rule. Didn't I tell you God watched over you?"

She blinked back tears. "The student raised the alarm and an ambulance brought you, unconscious, here to the hospital where the doctors pumped your stomach."

Then came the greatest surprise of all.

"When did they call for you, Mamuska?" I asked.

A strange look came over her face.

"I was already at the school just after it happened, kochana."

"What?"

"I did not know why exactly, Jasia." Her eyes glistened with tears as she spoke. "When I prayed for you last Saturday, I felt something was very wrong. On Sunday it became worse, and on Monday I knew I had to come and see you. When I arrived, your teachers told me they had just put you in the ambulance."

I stared at her, trying to take in the words.

"It was just like the day . . ." she continued, tears now flowing freely down her cheeks, "just like the day God gave you to me. That time, I knew I had to leave my house and go out into the street. This time, it was the same sort of feeling."

Faith was such a straightforward matter for Mamuska. God spoke, she acted. For me, though, it was another story.

"Why, God, can I never get away from You?" I cried silently and, turning my face into my pillow, gave way to bitter tears.

During this time, the staff searched for answers. Why had the political star of their school tried to take her life? It didn't add up. The headmistress quizzed everybody concerned.

Were there problems at home? Mamuska chose not to mention the *za swe* situation. She saw no reason for it to have special relevance at this time and she was still afraid of the stigma herself.

Were there boyfriend problems? My friends told her all was well. As it happened, Aunt Ela's handsome son, Marcin, had begun visiting me frequently and I was thrilled with his friendship.

They had to wait for my recovery to find the real reason. On hearing it, my headmistress took the science teacher to task and demanded I be re-examined. In time, I regained stamina and passed the subject.

I tried to return to my usual activities but, in the weeks following the suicide attempt, found life had become painted in muted colours.

When Christmas came, I welcomed the chance to spend time in the relative shelter of our mountain town.

I spent hours walking alone, taking stale bread to deer and other animals who could not find food easily in the depth of winter. Marcin and I walked a great deal, too, and found our friendship deepening. I did all I could to avoid Aunt Mila, however. She was anxious to know what had caused the suicide attempt of her daughter but I had no idea how to talk to her and offered no more than polite niceties.

Tatusiek and Mamuska had given their all to make this Christmas merrier than ever before. It was just one month after the suicide attempt and they knew my emotional scars were far from healed. Tatusiek had slaved for hours to bake piernik and kolacz, the cakes I had loved since childhood. Mamuska had scrubbed every inch of the house, a task I was usually made to share, before I arrived. She had knitted gifts and saved her last zlotys to buy me extra books and treats. The two kept their greatest surprise, though, for Christmas Eve.

"Kochana, we wanted this to be an extra special Christmas

for you," Mamuska said when, early in the evening, there was a knock on the door. She kissed my forehead and gave me a little push. "You answer it," she said, pink with excitement.

I opened the door and found the Prower professors, together with Emmanuel, covered with freshly fallen snow. Mamuska had chosen wisely. In college, the Prowers' apartment had become a second home for me and, despite our differences regarding religion, they were people one could not help but love. There was a flurry of snow as hats, coats and boots were removed and they engulfed me in hugs.

Christmas Eve came with all the trimmings. The Nativity wafers were broken and prayers said, although with the Prowers these were much longer than usual. I watched these devout people and hoped nobody would ask me to pray the way they did. Uncle Jozef said the longest prayer of all, but I was more intrigued than bored. As he spoke, his face glowed as if he were enjoying the company of his greatest friend. I had never seen anything like it. At that moment, I was not quite sure whether Uncle Jozef was in this world or the next.

"Now, let's open our gifts," Tatusiek declared when our feast was done. I revelled in the books from my parents and the hand-knitted hats and scarves on which Mamuska had painstakingly worked, but the Prowers' gifts caught me by surprise.

Uncle Jozef had, in some conversation or other, picked up my interest in England and now gave me a book on the country, together with postcards to display in my room. He spoke English and German fluently, and had friends who sent him such treasures from both countries. I thanked them with a grateful hug and sat turning the pages in wonder. The sensitivity of this great professor, bothering to take note of the whims of a young schoolgirl, astonished me.

Close to midnight, Uncle Jozef lifted his violin and played one hauntingly beautiful carol after another. When our candles burned low, Mamuska went into the kitchen to heat borscht for everyone. Tatusiek, Aunty and Emmanuel went to help her. Perhaps all of them knew I needed time alone with Uncle Jozef.

"Now it's time for you to play for me, Jasia," Uncle Jozef said.

"But my violin is so poor, Uncle, I could never play it after you have played yours," I protested.

He looked at me thoughtfully, then he twinkled.

"Okay. Let's exchange violins! You play mine and I'll play yours."

I liked that idea and eagerly began. To my disappointment, however, my playing sounded as scratchy as always on his marvellous violin, while his was perfection itself on my cheap one.

"Kochana, it's not so much the violin that matters. It's what you do with it," the maestro said gently when we finished. "Life's a little bit like that too, Jasia. We must choose what we will do with it."

His face had a tenderness I was not used to and I could hardly meet his gaze. I had become so ashamed of my life that I felt embarrassed in the presence of this holy man. Neither he nor his God would want anything to do with a *za swe*, particularly one who had compromised as much as I.

"But Uncle Jozef," I said, blinking hard at the Christmas lights, "some lives are not made of very good material to begin with. They're second-rate. Nobody would want them."

"Kochana, once you have learned how, you can use any violin to play a masterpiece. True?" I nodded. His performance, that night, had proved it. "It is the same of a person's life as well!"

"But, Uncle Jozef, you learned from a master! The girls at school say you had the same teacher as Yehudi Menuhin!"

"That's true. But I had a second Master and He was even more important than my first. He can be your Master too, kochana, and He would make your life the masterpiece He always intended it to be."

I kept my gaze fixed on the Christmas lights, ashamed to cry in front of him. My life was certainly no masterpiece.

He seemed to understand my unspoken thoughts. Placing his arm around my shoulders, he whispered, "If He is not our Master, Jasia, our lives will never be all that we long for them!

From my own experience, I understand how, then, one can lose the desire to live. I also know how easy it is to want to end your life."

I swung round, wide-eyed. "Uncle Jozef, you came to the point of suicide too?"

"Yes, kochana. I did," he replied, his dark eyes moist at the memory. Neither of us needed to say any more. I buried my head in the safety of his shoulder and sobbed.

Was it true? Could a life as badly played as mine ever become a masterpiece?

7

THE SNOWMAN'S THAW

"I saw no point in living. That's why I tried to commit suicide. But why did you, Uncle Jozef?" I asked, next day, when a walk gave us opportunity to talk again.

His family and I had set out along the mountain route which led to the Secret Church. Emmanuel had obviously inherited his father's sensitivity to people's needs for, although he and I were good friends, he kept a respectful distance while I spoke to Uncle Jozef in private. Aunty left us alone as well. She seemed to be praying.

"My reasons were much the same as yours, kochana. I was living my life all wrong. I didn't know how to live it right. I felt too wretched to go on. So I didn't want to live at all," said Uncle Jozef.

"And you found someone to help you, Uncle Jozef?"

"There was no person who could, Jasia. It was Jesus Christ who gave me a new start, one as white as snow."

If God was on Uncle Jozef's side . . . that day, He showed it. The snow was newly fallen and its untrodden surface sparkled in the golden sunlight like a myriad diamonds. The mountain homes were hardly visible under the thick coating of white in which they were encased. It was as if God had generously ladled whipped cream over everything in sight. The purity of the scene was as near perfection as one could imagine and I was nearly blinded by it. I looked at Uncle Jozef, the man who was loved, it seemed, by everybody who knew him. His life may have been made as white as snow, but mine would never be.

"You can't imagine how bad my life has become," I said, kicking in frustration at the deep, soft snow on the path.

"I was ashamed of my life too, Jasia. It seemed utterly black when I contemplated suicide, but let me show you something." He pulled a tiny book from his pocket and handed it to me. "I've heard you are an excellent scholar, kochana. Can you read this?"

I flicked the pages as we clumped past a gurgling stream, its waters just managing to flow through the crystal ice that made tiny statues on its banks.

"There's nothing here to read!" I protested. The book had a green cover without words. Inside was a set of coloured pages black, red, white and, finally, golden. It made no sense. I handed it back.

"Oh, but it tells the best story in the world," Uncle Jozef said, returning it with a mischievous grin. "I thought you could read, my girl!"

I turned the pages of the wordless book once more, but I could make neither head nor tail of it.

"Look at the dark page, kochana. Isn't that the picture of life as you see it now?"

"Yes." There was no need to deny it.

"And why? Because sin always causes darkness in our lives. God knows that."

Sin. I hadn't used that word about my life. I wasn't sure it was necessary. I knew there were weeds, yes, but they did not seem as serious as sin. After all, I didn't smoke, I drank only rarely, I was careful about my behaviour with Marcin. Yet, in the purity of that white scene, I had to admit to compromise of a political kind. I couldn't deny lying either. I doubted if anybody connected with the Party could. It came with the job. So did hypocrisy. So did corruption. So did abuse of power. Yes, there was sin in my life. And, yes, I hated myself.

"God loves us just as we are, kochana, but He loves us too much to leave us that way," Uncle Jozef said. "That is why there are more pages in this book."

He turned to the golden one and the sunlight, bouncing off

the snow, was reflected on the page's shiny surface. "God Himself is like this page. He is absolute holiness and He made us to live in His wonderful golden presence. The tragedy is that too many of us simply endure struggle because we allow our lives to be encased in darkness."

I looked at Uncle Jozef's radiant face. Without doubt, he had found life in this presence. Everybody whose life he touched knew it.

"But if your life is like the dark page, Uncle, you can't possibly come to live in the golden presence of God!"

"That's why there are two pages between, kochana. God knew we could not help ourselves, so He did the job for us. Jesus died on the Cross, taking the weight of our sin, so that we could live in the very presence of God both now and for eternity. That's the reason for the red page. It symbolises the shed blood of Jesus."

Red meant something else to me. It stood for the Party and for the ubiquitous flag of the Soviet Union. Broniewski, the poet, had coloured his writings red with descriptions of the martyrs' blood, shed in the cause of the glorious revolution. Of late, however, I had begun to have trouble taking his poems seriously.

"And the white page?"

Uncle Jozef gestured to the wonder of the forest around us. The green branches of the trees could barely peep through their huge mounds of unspoiled white snow. "That's the way our life is seen by God. Because His Son died in our place, He now sees us as white and clean, our sin forgotten. That is why, even in His glorious holiness, He can welcome us as His children for ever."

By now, sunlight had started to reach everything in that forest with its golden touch. Emmanuel and his mother had created a comical snowman during our conversation and its smooth edges had begun to melt in the snow. I felt a bit like that snowman. The ice in my being was beginning to thaw. I glanced at the mountains above us. Up there was the Secret Church where, so long ago, I had sensed the same golden presence of God.

"And does the green cover have special meaning, too?" I asked.

"Oh yes!" Uncle Jozef said, with a smile. "Green stands for growth. In spring, kochana, the dark conifer branches around us will sprout green tips, bright with the promise of new life. In time, they will mature into strong branches on stately trees. If you begin anew with Pan Jezus, your life will blossom in the same kind of way."

Something in me froze at his words. I did not like the sound of the green page. If I grew anything in my life, it always turned out to be weeds. I could not grow anything else. I did not really want to, either. Many of my weeds were associated with the compromises necessary for me to be a successful Party member. The new growth Uncle Jozef described would mean abandoning all of that and, with it, my ambitions for the future.

I looked around for an excuse to stop the conversation and, when I saw that Emmanuel was about to go sledding, I seized my chance.

"Perhaps I should join Emmanuel now, Uncle Jozef. Would you excuse me?" I asked, lamely. He gave me a gentle smile and bowed respectfully as if signifying the conversation was done.

I knew I hadn't fooled him. He lived so close to God that I often felt he saw straight through my tactics. Like Tatusiek, though, Uncle Jozef was too much of a gentleman to say so. He and Aunty waved kindly as I headed off to enjoy the newly fallen snow.

The rest of that academic year was one in which I went mechanically through the motions. My heart was not really in the political activities any more. Yet, for the sake of graduation and career placement, I dared not do anything that would put my future at risk. All went according to plan. I graduated with academic honours and political commendation.

My headmistress sent me into the world placing, it seemed, her own mantle upon my shoulders.

"A great future awaits you. Your very first appointment is in a modern school for Party members only. You have also been guaranteed the opportunity for further study at university. My dear, the world lies at your feet!"

In 1968, however, it was a depressing world to be entering. Even with all my Party rhetoric, I could not deny that. Jewish people were now leaving the country in droves and Grannie Esther, the lady who had been living in our home, was grieving deeply. Young people had demonstrated angrily in Krakow Square, in Warsaw and elsewhere in the nation. Housewives were desperate in coping with emptying stores. A Polish idiom says that "A hungry Pole is an angry Pole". That was proved on a daily basis in 1968.

Worst of all, it was now increasingly evident that Gomulka was co-operating with Russia in its attitude to Czechoslovakia. Large numbers of Russian troops were congregating in our border region as the rabbits and deer of our leafy forests moved aside to host unwelcome armoured vehicles and military supplies.

Mamuska picked up bitter jokes in the food queues. "Gomulka and his aide returned from Moscow and unpacked their bags," she told us, one meal. "Each tried on a new suit he had bought while in the Soviet Union. 'Funny!' said Gomulka. 'It seems much too small here. But it fitted me perfectly while I was in Moscow! How is that possible?' 'Ah, but you have forgotten something,' said the aide. 'When we were in Moscow, we were on our knees!'"

Gomulka seemed to have distanced himself from the nation, unaware, somehow, of the unhappiness with which most struggled. The nation's jokes became more bitter than ever. "Many Party members have committed suicide. Do you know how?" ran one popular quip. "They're jumping into the gap between the government and the people."

Mamuska and Tatusiek hardly laughed now at these jokes. The situation was too grim. Few people were laughing that summer, Marcin included. We had become close enough to discuss marriage, much to the delight of Mamuska and Aunt Ela, but I never spoke in depth of my political position with him. I was too embarrassed. Without doubt, Poland was in the worst state we had seen it in a long time.

Amid this hardship, I was delighted when, during one
morning's shopping, I received an invitation to take a holiday.
Mamuska and I bumped into a couple of school friends, Mila
and Marysia, who were planning a vacation in Mazury, the
magnificent lakeside area I had never seen. They asked me
to join them and, to my surprise, Mamuska encouraged me
to accept. Normally we would have spent nights around
the family ledger to see if it were possible. This time, she
agreed immediately. If her eyes gleamed with rather too much
enthusiasm, I missed it and blithely packed my bags.

Within minutes of my arrival at the camp, however, I
discovered I had been tricked. Brightly coloured banners
decorated the main meeting room and each one shouted at
me with quotations, not from Marx or Lenin but from the
Bible. I had come to a Christian camp. Mamuska had pulled
off a second coup.

I gave the girls a look that I hoped they would never forget,
grabbed a breakfast roll and stormed out of the building. Last
time my mother had tricked me to a Christian camp, I had
walked all the way home. This time, I could do so again.

A breeze carried the sound of Christian songs as I marched
defiantly along the sandy track of the Mazury forest. The
light wind also turned the leaves of the beech trees and they
shimmered silver and green in its path. It cooled my face as
well and, perhaps, cleared my head a little. The situation was
not, in fact, the same as last time. I had come over six hundred
kilometres from home. There was not even a village for at
least thirty kilometres.

I decided to stay. Mazury was famous for its beauty, so
why not enjoy the place while, at the same time, making life
so miserable for Mila and Marysia that they would be sorry
they ever invited me?

In the days that followed, I sought every chance to be the
rebel, the joker and the fool.

My best opportunity presented itself when the camp administration issued a stern warning. The campsite was located
alongside a very old, Tudor-style church. Dark brown external
beams criss-crossed the white walls of the fragile building

that dated back to a time when Mazury had been occupied by Germany. We were informed that it was strictly forbidden for us to ring its ancient bell without proper supervision. One morning before dawn, therefore, I stealthily left the campsite and climbed the church tower.

At the top of the staircase, I stepped on to a wooden platform that creaked and sagged beneath me. I reached up for the rope of the church bell and pulled it with all my might. A great gong reverberated wonderfully around the area. The platform shuddered, seeming to confirm that it was too old for this activity. I ignored the warning signs and swung the bronze bell again, delighted to be doing so at a forbidden time. This proved too much for the platform. With a tired groan, it gave way to several hundred years' use and collapsed beneath me. I clung on to the rope, swinging desperately from side to side knowing that, if I let go, I would fall forty-five feet to the stone floor beneath me. The bell clanged wildly as I hung on for dear life. My adventure had become a nightmare.

The adjacent campsite quickly awakened. By the time the supervisors raced to the church, climbed the tower and risked life and limb to rescue me, my hands were rope-burned and I was nearly numb with the effort. Nonetheless, I glanced triumphantly at Marysia, Mila and the rest of the group assembled below. I had made my point.

After that, I relaxed enough to enjoy life in Mazury, participating in so far as it suited me. I delighted in the white swans at play on the crystal-blue lakes and hiked happily in the forests. I also began to appreciate the friendship of the other teenagers. They laughed a lot, played games and were, to my amazement, quite normal. That took me by surprise. I had always expected Christians of my age to be odd creatures, strange beings. They were not.

Admittedly, throughout the day I had to listen to their Bible talk, but their friendship compensated for that. There was a much warmer atmosphere here than any I had experienced at ZMS camps and slowly, like the snowman at Christmas, I could feel myself melting.

Nonetheless, I did all I could to avoid formal religious instruction. Each night, I sat for supper near the doorway so that, as soon as the preacher began, I could escape. I would wander outside to enjoy the stars in the clear, unpolluted night sky.

In time, some of the others must have observed my pattern and, to my chagrin, there came a night when I found myself sandwiched in the middle of a row of laughing, happy young people. There was nothing I could do. I was stuck. Dinner over, the group started to sing.

> O Love that will not let me go
> I rest my weary soul in You.
> I give You back the life I owe . . .

I struggled with myself. I could hear truth in the words of this song. I had frequently encountered this love that would not let me go. I thought back to the Czechoslovakian trip, the time in the Secret Church, the Dziegielow week, the suicide attempt. No matter how hard I had tried to shut God out of my life, His love had pursued me.

Could I go on running from Him? I thought of the enslaved dog in Mickiewicz's poem and the Judas woman in *Forbidden Songs*. Both of those images fitted me. Did I really prefer the Party life to a life lived with God? Did I want to be like the Marionette or like my parents? Did I prefer to live as the Moskal or as Uncle Jozef? Within me, Saul was battling Paul and I had to escape to think it through.

I left the meeting and ran down the sand track threaded between the ancient oak trees. It was a hot, balmy night and the moon was a great silver orb that threw the scene into silhouette. A sapling quivered in the breeze, its scalloped leaves backlit by the moon, and I knelt beside it. I did not know much about prayer, but I had always seen Mamuska kneeling so I supposed that was how it was done.

"God . . . God . . ." I faltered. I really didn't know what to say next. He seemed to take over.

"Why do you hate Me so?" He seemed to ask me.

"I don't know, God. I've been fighting You for too long to remember."

"And all this time, I have met your hatred with My love."

"Yes, I know." The song was right. His was the love that would not let me go.

"I'm tired of this battle," I told Him. "I don't want to fight You any more." The snowman had melted at last.

I waited in the stillness and it seemed to me that He was waiting too. There was more I needed to say.

"I am sorry, God. I know I hurt You and I hurt Your people and I hurt myself too. I know I grew a garden full of weeds. Would You please forgive me for being so naughty and terrible and may I start over, with You in control of my life?"

There, in the moonlight, I felt free for the first time in as many years as I could remember. Love had not let me go and I, at last, had come home.

I knelt in the increasing darkness, unafraid. Now that I had finally found Him, or rather, allowed Him to find me, there was so much to say.

My mind had returned, of course, to the time in Czechoslovakia when I had wanted to become God's child but not known how. As a result, I had stepped into a life of Communism.

Before I stood, therefore, one more promise seemed to spring from within me. "Pan Jezus, I want to devote my life to telling those of the next generation how to become Your children. They have the right to know."

It was time to return to the camp. I dusted the sand off my knees and wandered through the dark forest towards the lights where Mila and Marysia had waited up for me, all anticipation.

Of course I could not hide my shining secret from them. One look at my face told them the story as I laughed with pure, unfettered joy.

"But Jasia, we did feel badly that you did not know about this being a Christian camp. We are sorry!" said one apologetically.

"We just did not see any other way. We were afraid you

would go further and further into the darkness of Communism," the other added.

Darkness. Yes, I had been living in darkness, there was no doubt. I thought of Uncle Jozef's little book, with its dark page, and realised I had turned it at last. I had discovered the gold page and the light of God's presence. Suddenly, I found myself grateful to Marysia and Mila for caring enough to rescue me.

As I told the group of my lifelong battle with the weeds and my promise to tell children about Pan Jezus, they turned to the story of the Sower.

"Jasia," one of the others said excitedly, "Do you know what it says about the seed that falls into the good soil? The Bible says 'it produced a crop – a hundred, sixty or thirty times what was sown'. If you're going to work with children now, you might produce a crop that is a hundredfold!" (Matthew 13:23).

I did not forget those words. After struggling so long with the weeds, I could have desired nothing more than to spare other children the same pain.

Next day, Marysia and Mila sent a postcard to my Mamuska who had probably never been off her arthritic knees since I had left for the camp. When I saw her myself ten days later, I thought I would be embarrassed, but after one look at her tear-filled eyes I threw myself into her arms.

She, too, had a promise to speak of with me. "When the Lord gave you to us as a baby," she said through sobs, "I made Him a vow just like Hannah's from the Bible. 'I prayed for this child and the Lord has granted me what I asked of Him. So now I give (her) to the Lord . . .'" (1 Samuel 1:27,28). She kissed my cheek over and over, hardly knowing whether to laugh or cry. "At last, it has happened and we'll have a new beginning!"

My more reserved Tatusiek was next. He enfolded me in a bear hug before saying, in his shy manner, "Let me read you a verse as well." He opened his Bible at Ephesians 1:4,5,6. 'For He chose us . . . to be adopted as sons through Jesus Christ . . . to the praise of His glorious grace, which He has freely given us.' Kochana, you have now been adopted in a double sense," he concluded and looked down into my face with a warmth that I would never forget.

With the experience of years, however, he added, solemnly, "Your life as a Christian won't be easy, kochana, particularly in these tough times. But it is the best thing you have ever done and God will be faithful to you just as He has been to us."

Life was indeed tense in Poland in the summer of 1968. Shortly after my return from camp, I happened to be visiting my relatives in Czechoslovakia at the time Moscow finally ran out of patience with the liberal measures introduced by the Czech government and ordered tanks to cross the border. Rather than sending Russian tanks in first, they had Polish tanks lead the unwelcome intrusion. There was Machiavellian wisdom in the strategy. Stalin had always sought to separate satellite countries against one another in order to prevent them from uniting against him. As a result, Slavs, who were brothers by culture, now found themselves in opposition. Stalin's cunning in this, as in many things, had outlived him.

The Czech people, my cousins included, were active in resistance. With typical Slavic humour, they constantly altered the road signs and the tanks, trying to follow army-issued maps, ended up thoroughly confused. At first light of dawn, when the weary soldiers made their way into the streets of the city, Czechs met them with abusive posters and a cascade of debris. Rotten eggs, mouldy tomatoes, washing-up water and even the contents of the sewers were rained upon the intruders. I curtailed my trip and, as I hurried towards the border, received my fair share too.

The atmosphere in our border area remained tense in the time that followed. I took up my new teaching position but did not, at first, speak of the fact that I would no longer be joining the Party.

During my early weeks, I enjoyed a kind of honeymoon experience with the administration. The school principal oozed with charm, calling my teaching techniques "innovative" and urging other teachers to learn from them. I loved the children and I found it a pleasure to use the excellent facilities in this Red school, as these places were popularly called.

At the end of the first month, however, I was called upon to join the Party and when I explained that I could no longer do so, I was quickly summoned to the Party headquarters.

This was a new experience for me. Everything looked menacing, now that I was on the "other side" of the State. I walked past the line of large red flags which always graced the entrance to the ugly, soulless building. Above the door, in big letters, there was a shiny sign: Polish Workers' Party. City Committee.

I opened the heavily carved door and stepped on to a plush red carpet which ran along the marble hallway. I was surrounded by red flags and the usual green tropical palms of privilege.

A conference room to my right sported a marble bust of Lenin and, amid more flags and plants, a large slogan: "The Polish Workers' Party; the guiding light of the nation". A photo of a beaming Gomulka presided over the whole. Guiding light? None in Poland saw our tired leader as that any more. It was whispered that he would no longer have been in power except for the fact that he had co-operated with Russia regarding Czechoslovakia. By sending Polish troops, he had won for himself the upholding hand of Moscow, in the short term at least.

I reached the appointed room and found my interrogator awaiting me, seated behind an imposing-looking desk. He was rather a charmer and smiled warmly as he indicated for me to sit.

He lifted a thick file and held it up as if impressed with its weight. "We have heard you are one of the best, Pani. You have shown unusual commitment to our country and all of us are expecting great things. How are you finding your work? Is it going well?"

I was thrown by his kind approach. I had expected confrontation. "Well, I am glad to be teaching at last," I began, uncertain. "I have always loved children."

"Yes. We rarely get teachers that come with your recommendation." He smiled kindly. "How do you travel to work, Pani?"

"By train."

"Do you not have a bus pass?"

"No. I tried, but was refused." The buses ran far more often than the trains and were a much faster way to travel. I could have saved hours every day with a bus pass.

"Well, we must fix that at once." He lifted a pen and made a note, still smiling.

"But," he continued, "perhaps we should try to move you nearer the school? Wouldn't that be more convenient?"

"Yes, of course, but . . ."

"We could get you a flat in a nearby street."

"A flat?" Without the normal wait of ten to fifteen years?

"Oh yes, we have big apartments available here. You could move within the next few months."

I opened my mouth and closed it again, picturing myself sitting in a large modern flat. I would like that. Not only would it be comfortable and convenient, it would guarantee something as well. With the prestige of my own apartment, I would not be thought of as second-rate and, even though I had found new life in God, this wound was still my greatest weakness.

"It can all be arranged, Pani," my interrogator continued. "Party members are busy people! We need to look after you since you will have all the extra responsibilities of Party activities."

I knew I could not let this pass. "I'm sorry, Pan, but I won't be joining the Party."

His smile never faltered. This man was a professional.

"Well, yes, I had heard something about a little hitch in this matter but I'm sure it's nothing we can't fix."

"I have become a Christian," I continued.

My interrogator shrugged in a friendly manner. "Poland has a Christian tradition, Pani. We understand that."

"No, that's not what I mean. Going regularly to church does not make one a Christian any more than going regularly to a petrol station makes one a Polish Fiat. There's more to it than that."

His mouth twitched with humour and he raised one eyebrow, but he allowed me to talk until I had finished.

"I'll tell you what," he said at the end. "This kind of thing happens to people sometimes, but after a while they get over it. Why don't you just give yourself a little time and, later, come back here and we'll continue our little chat. Okay?"

There was no point in telling him I would not change my mind. I had no way of explaining that, having fought the truth for so long, I could never return to a lifestyle that was a hollow lie. I thanked him and stood to leave.

With perfect manners, he opened the door for me and handed me a slip of paper.

"It's your authorisation for a bus pass, Pani. As a teacher you are eligible and I can't imagine why it wasn't given to you before."

I hardly trusted my legs to carry me as I walked down the magnificent hallway. I stopped only to collect my bus pass before stepping into the heat of the summer sun. In its warmth, I felt Heaven itself was touching me.

I was going to need that touch. I feared that, once they discovered I would never change my mind, the Party would be intent on making my life hell.

8

BOTH HANDS FULL

"Pani, if you are not with us, you are against us! That makes you an enemy of the State."

The sugar coating on the pill was gone. My second interrogator was a far cry from the charmer who had questioned me first. This man was aggressive with dark, shifty eyes which, in my mind, gave him the look of a ferret.

"I am not an enemy of Poland, Pan. I just can't join the Party because I am no longer an atheist." I tried to explain further, but the ferret, true to the name I had bestowed on him, sniffed out every word he could for debate. It was impossible to complete any sentence without his clever interruptions. He could turn black into white.

When argument failed, his teeth closed on me with a more deadly bite.

"I understand that, in the past, there was some discussion about your studying at university?"

"Yes."

"Oh, it's such a pity," he said, thin lips tightening into the pretence of a smile. "We don't have any placements available for outside students in your field." I needed special permission to become an external student while holding a teaching position at the same time. Clearly I was not going to get it.

"Unless, of course, you have had some change of heart?" The ferret looked at me sideways. "Perhaps we might then find an opening . . . ?"

"No, Pan, I have not changed my mind. I am a Christian. I cannot join the Party."

"So!" He spat out the word and shut his files with a bang. "We have nothing else to discuss now. Good day, Pani. You will hear from us again later!"

In the weeks that followed, I tried to get on with my teaching, but once it became known that I would not be joining the Party my principal did an about-turn in her attitude towards me.

The innovative techniques she had praised so highly were suddenly unacceptable. She began to move against my class with a belligerence that shocked even the children.

Their pride and joy was a history nook made out of acorns, moss and stones they had unearthed from the forest floor. I had been teaching them about Tadeusz Kosciusko, one of the heroes of Polish history. After a succession of elected kings, Poland had been in such a weakened state that, at the close of the eighteenth century, it was divided between Russia, Prussia and Austria. Kosciusko had led the Poles in resistance although they were hopelessly outnumbered, and the man symbolised the courage and nationalism of every true Pole.

The children's efforts had worked well. By the end of their project they could tell me how, after Kosciusko's men were defeated in 1795, Poland disappeared off the world map until 1919. They could also tell me that Kosciusko is still celebrated in America, where he fought beside George Washington, and in Australia, whose highest mountain has been named in his honour.

While they were proud of their creativity, however, the principal was not. "Pani, this learning corner has to go!" she declared one morning, bursting unexpectedly into the classroom.

"Moss is damp and rocks are dirty!" With that, she upended our Kosciusko corner and the children watched, horrified, as the little figures they had crafted with painstaking care tumbled into the garbage.

A few days later, a second corner, in which we had set up a bowl of goldfish, went as well. The "unhygienic" fish were flushed down the drain and the glass bowl removed with an angry flourish.

After that, it was outright war. The children were furious and broken-hearted. One little girl, Renatka, brought her younger brother to me with a trembling lower lip. She was a loving little thing who knew only how to be kind and good.

"Why are these horrid things happening? Pan Jezus does not want people to hurt each other, does He?" she whispered, twiddling nervously with long black plaits, her round cheeks pale with fear.

"Pan Jezus?" I was whispering too, by now. This was not a name to be spoken out loud in any Polish school, particularly a Red one.

"Well," she continued, "Pan Jezus says to be kind to everyone. I know because my Tatusiek says that and he is a pastor!"

Sometimes I had noticed the principal particularly displeased with Renatka. If her father was a pastor, I now understood why.

Bad went to worse in the weeks that followed. My ambitions were in tatters, with both study and career advancement jeopardised. My private life was troubling me as well, since Marcin showed little interest in Christianity. Although he was still planning for our marriage, I was beginning to realise that, without the same commitment to Pan Jezus, our lives would quickly be pulled in opposite directions.

I was too new in my Christian faith to know how to handle the pressures so, amid the storm, I turned to the one person who, I was certain, would help me find peace: Jozef Prower.

He did not yet know I had become a Christian since I had not been to his town since starting my new job. His role in my conversion had been so great, however, that I could not visit him without taking some kind of symbolic gift. Before going, therefore, I went to the forest near the Secret Church and found a pine tree root that looked, to me, rather like a person praying, arms uplifted to God. I cleaned, carved and polished it for days.

"Jasia! Come in!" Uncle Jozef greeted me with his usual warmth. "This door is always open to you." His door was always open to everyone, if truth be told, such that some described his home as "the hotel". At the same time, though, he had the ability to put his busy schedule to one side and make each visitor feel he or she was the most important person in the world.

"A great deal has happened since I saw you, Uncle." I felt almost shy now that the moment had come to tell him.

"Yes, kochana. You have graduated from school with honours, I hear, and been placed in an excellent position. Congratulations, dear."

"But I have something far more important to tell you, Uncle."

"More important than your career?" He looked surprised and hope lit his swarthy face, though he waited for me to speak.

"God has turned the pages of your Wordless Book for me. Your Communist rebel has become a Christian!"

"Kochana!" He clasped me against his shoulder. "So now you are my spiritual child, my *coreczka*!" This word, in Polish, is an affectionate form of the word "daughter". Uncle Jozef was to use it of me from that day forward.

We sat together and I told him the whole story. He listened, that irrepressible smile growing broader all the time. He loved the carved root and displayed it as if it were a work of finest porcelain, on top of a dark, carved bookcase.

"But, Uncle, I need your help with so many things!" I said. I don't think I'm coping very well." I told him about Marcin and he, always gentle, suggested I give Marcin time to make his decision about Pan Jezus. I told him about the principal of the Red school and he burst into sympathetic prayer, patting my hand reassuringly.

"And there's a deeper issue on my mind," I continued. Right after I gave my life to Pan Jezus, I made Him a promise which I don't know how to keep. I think you're the only person who can help me."

He listened attentively as I explained my commitment to tell children what I had longed to hear as a little girl. I retraced my life and the wrong direction it had taken after that lesson in Czechoslovakia.

As I spoke, he wiped the thick black hair from his olive-skinned face but remained silent. His eyes were closed as often as they were open and I supposed he was praying.

"Someone has to tell these children the truth they long to hear," I concluded. "I am teaching their minds at school, but I am not reaching their hearts. I know they have deep questions, though, and they need answers. Uncle, their little lives are too precious to be wasted in the mess we adults have made of our world."

Uncle Jozef lifted his head and, to my surprise, I saw his eyes were moist.

"Jasia, let me tell you a secret. For some years, I have struggled with a great burden that I too did not know how to manage. On countless nights, I have tossed and turned because of the need I have seen in Poland's boys and girls. I too see their tears. I too hear their questions, I too know their longing, but . . ." he placed his hand to his heart with an apologetic little smile and paused for a moment. Uncle Jozef frequently had heart trouble and had been forced by his doctors to give up full-time work. He did so much for others, though, that his health was often at risk. Aunty was for ever pleading with him to slow down.

"I have begged the Lord to bring me someone else with the same vision as I, someone who could give it the full-time commitment it requires. Today, kochana, He has answered my prayer," Uncle Jozef said.

He rose to his feet. "May I show you a little task I have been working on?" He bowed in his courtly manner and opened the door for me to enter his office. It was a triangular little room, located on the corner of their old-fashioned apartment building, and housing a well-worn desk that was much too big for it. Books were stacked everywhere, together with piles of work in progress. Everything here spoke of hard work.

He handed me a file and I sat down in astonishment. It was filled with English Christian literature for children. Attached to it, there were pages of Polish in Uncle Jozef's meticulous handwriting. This gifted linguist had been translating Christian material for children. It was everything I needed for a curriculum.

I turned the pages in wonder. I had never dreamed that such literature could be found in Socialist Poland.

"But this task is dangerous for you, Uncle. The police might come . . ." Any material of this kind must have been smuggled into the country and my training in Communism left me in no doubt as to the rigours this family would have undergone.

"Don't worry, Jasia, they have been here several times already!" Aunty had returned from teaching and brought us tea. This was the only feature I disliked in the Prower household. The water in their area tasted odd and made the tea bitter. That day, though, I was too interested in her conversation to notice.

"How did you deal with them, Aunty?" I asked.

Aunty shrugged. "You know your uncle, Jasia. He loves everybody! He gave them the same kind treatment he would give any other visitor here. Tell me, Jasia, do you know anybody else in Poland who would call the SB 'kochany'?"

I laughed. The term can mean "dear friends" in Polish usage, but surely she wasn't serious about his using it with the SB? The SB was our secret police, Poland's equivalent to the KGB.

"You don't really call them that, Uncle?" I protested.

"Of course he does!" replied Aunty. "If he met the Devil himself, I think he'd have a kind word to say to him!"

"No I wouldn't," Uncle Jozef laughed. "But members of the SB are in need, just like everybody else in our sad land. Jasia can tell you that Party people are not happy people."

"He should know!" said Aunty, twinkling at me. "When I was expecting Emmanuel, Jozef and my brother were in prison. Did you know that?"

That had been in the early fifties. No one had ever told me that Uncle's faith made him victim to the Stalinist purges. What else had this man suffered? He never spoke of the hardship he had undergone.

"He still encounters the SB today, too." Aunty continued.

"Our phone is bugged, our house is sometimes raided, and he is often followed when he plays violin in churches."

"So," Uncle grinned, "it won't hurt the SB to develop a taste for Bach!"

Aunty poured the tea. "This man is incorrigible, Jasia!" she said, looking proud of him just the same.

"Besides, kochana," Uncle added, the lines on his face crinkling mischievously, "those SB men could probably explain the Wordless Book as well as I can now. And it's a good thing too. They need to know God loves them!"

Aunty threw her hands into the air in mock despair, but Uncle Jozef captured one and kissed it. Many men in Poland did this as a matter of course with all women. I only ever saw Uncle Jozef use this gesture with his wife.

Aunty went to the door. "Enjoy your tea, you two. I'm going to prepare lunch!" she said.

"But Uncle, how can you be so kind to the SB?" I demanded when our laughter had died away. I told him of the ferret, the principal and the struggle I had found with both.

"I learned a saying in prison, coreczka," he said. "When they call you for interrogation, go, 'with both hands full'!"

"With what?"

"It's easy, really. In one hand, you must carry the Word of God. That means you need to have spent time studying it so it's at the ready when needed. The other hand you place in the hand of God and that means prayer. You must give Him time beforehand, kochana. Get used to hearing His voice. Get used to sensing His nearness. Then you will face your interrogators with your hand clasped in His. I tell you the truth, once you meet them 'with both hands full', they'll never be able to frighten you again!"

Perhaps I wouldn't have believed him were it not for the light in his eyes. There was no doubting, however, that whatever this man's recipe was, it worked. Since becoming a Christian, I had not spent much time in either the Word or prayer. I had faced my tormentors empty-handed.

"Now to your work, my coreczka!" Uncle Jozef said, instinctively lowering his voice in case the apartment was bugged. "There is help on the way. A man is coming soon from the West. His name is Sam. When he arrives, I'll send you a telegram." He went on to describe a training course Sam would give in Warsaw and the development of children's work that might be possible across Poland.

We talked for hours about the need of Poland's children, discussing a hundred and one ways in which we could see that need met. He had more ideas than I had ever imagined and was deeply committed, despite the risk any one of them might bring his personal safety. I had always known Uncle Jozef to be a man of gentleness. Now I knew him to be a man of courage as well.

It was not easy to explain but, as I talked and prayed with the Prowers that day, I had the sense that God drew back a curtain and ushered me into some kind of "Rainbow Garden" where I could visualise the love of God being given to children in a life-giving way. I became increasingly excited as I realised that this was no impossible dream. It could become reality.

By the time they had fed me, prayed with me and loaded me up with copies of the work Uncle Jozef had translated, I felt ready for anything. Nothing must be allowed to stop the children's work now, I thought, as I caught the bus back towards our mountain area.

The SB called for me again. This time, though, I did my best to follow Uncle's advice and go "with both hands full". The night before my scheduled appointment, I met with Marysia, Mila and others for prayer. I was scared. I did not know what attack I would meet next day and I wondered exactly how Pan Jezus, for all His omnipotence, might have time for a simple soul like me.

That night, after we had prayed, a basket filled with Bible verses was passed around the group. Each member took one but mine, as it happened, could not have been more appropriate. It was Isaiah 41:10. "So do not fear, for I am with you; do not be dismayed, for I am your God . . . I will uphold you with my righteous right hand . . . those who oppose you will be as nothing . . ."

It was perfect for me. The thought of facing the SB had left me feeling rather like a little girl who longed for a hand to hold in the situation. Now the Lord, in His fatherly compassion, had spoken to that very need. It made more real than ever the concept of going "with both hands full".

The new SB encounter was more sinister than those before. Where the first interrogator had been warm and friendly and the second angry and heated, this man was pure ice. He froze me with a single look and spoke in a tense, high-pitched, raspy voice.

"Pani, you are a great disappointment to us. I suppose you know that?" he said, by way of greeting.

There seemed nothing appropriate to say to this. I waited.

"We invested heavily in you, Pani, thinking you could be trusted. We never guessed you would let us down."

His steel eyes were magnified through his glasses as he watched for my response. When I gave none, he moved in quickly for the kill.

"Your father is as stubborn as a mule, too. Not only has he refused to join the Party, but he is for ever lodging complaints about pollution and asking us to spend money on unnecessary measures of control. It's quite ridiculous. A little dirty air never hurt anybody yet!"

The ice-man began to clean his glasses. "Perhaps it is time to review your father's position?" he said and my stomach turned over. Dear Tatusiek. Was he to suffer more pain because of my refusal to join the Party?

"I will uphold you with my righteous right hand . . ." God had promised. "I believe it, Lord, but please, could You uphold Tatusiek too?" I silently begged, as the ice-man continued his scare tactics.

God was true to His Word. In the months that followed, Tatusiek's employers never even spoke of removing him from his post. The factory directors were adamant that they could not manage without him.

Late in autumn, I was called for my final interview. This time, I was met by a more senior official: a grey-haired, dignified man from headquarters. He heard my story once again and then gave his judgement.

"Pani, I don't agree with you, but I won't argue with you. Clearly you can't be persuaded and obviously you can't be bought." I looked up, surprised at his honest reference to the practice of bribery.

He nodded sadly. "Oh yes. I know many are in our Party for material gain. But I myself still want to believe in the System. If, perhaps, we could make a few changes, our country may yet have a bright future . . ." He broke off, as if he had said too much. It was whispered that Gomulka's forced retirement was very close now and hope had been placed in a new man to lead the Party.

"Pani, you won't be called for questioning on this issue again. I give you my word." He shook my hand but seemed, for all the hope he expressed, a sad figure as he said goodbye. He reminded me a little of myself as I had been; desperately wanting to believe in one thing, yet, deep down, sensing the folly of it.

Uncle Jozef was right, I thought, as I left him. God wanted us to love, not fear, such people.

It was, indeed, hard for even the most committed Party member to believe in the System during the closing months of 1970. Poland was worse off than it had been for more than a decade. The shelves of our drab, grey shops were emptier than ever. Fuel was expensive. With winter approaching, life had become precarious.

Poland felt itself abandoned by Gomulka. With bitter humour, the nation fought its anger at his apparent failure to stay in touch with reality.

"Stalin, Lenin and Gomulka were travelling on a train," one apocryphal story went. "They were enraged when the train came to an unexpected halt. Lenin tried rhetoric to inspire the train workers into action, but he failed. Stalin shot the driver and threatened to kill the others, but his tactics did not work either. Gomulka turned to his two companions and, drawing the train curtains closed, said, 'Let's just pretend the train is moving.'"

The crisis came to a head when, in mid-December, Gomulka raised basic food items as much as 30 per cent. The price of fuel went up too. Wages did not, however. It was the most insensitive Christmas gift imaginable for the Polish people.

Strikes and protests broke out as thousands vented their anger. The fiercest clashes occurred in the northern seaport of Gdansk, where tanks rolled and blood mixed with rain to flow freely in the streets. Nobody ever discovered the exact number killed. SB men dressed up as priests and, stumbling over the unfamiliar vocabulary, conducted the funerals themselves to prevent the Church from discovering the full picture of bloodshed. Under Communism, the Church was often described as the only true opposition party our country had. The government could not risk inciting its wrath.

The tragic situation brought many on to the political scene, among them a shipyard worker with a large moustache and great determination. His name was Lech Walesa.

Gomulka suffered a mild stroke and realised that his days of public service were over. In December 1970 he resigned. The mantle of leadership now fell on Edward Gierek, the son of a miner who, rather like my Wujek Morcinek, was therefore widely believed to understand the cause of the workers.

Gierek entered office with promises of a new start. Housing would improve. The rural sector would be better off. Food would be more readily available.

"Will you help me?" he cried, arms outstretched, in meetings all across the nation.

"We will help you!" people promised.

The exchange became a litany, he reiterating his request, they repeating their reply. As surely as "Influenza versus tuberculosis" marked Gomulka's reign, "Will you help me?" marked Gierek's. Not everybody believed Gierek could help the nation, though. Too many lies and broken promises had left cynicism in their wake.

That Christmas was, for our family, one of the bleakest on record. We ate our fish and salad by candlelight, not out of choice but from necessity because we had no electricity. The season that should have been jolly had turned sour.

In the midst of the nation's pain, I was more motivated than ever to begin the work for children. I began to cultivate the

"Rainbow Garden" as I had termed it ever since the day I had talked with Uncle Jozef.

I approached the task with confidence. After my experience as a five-year-old, I was determined not to make the same mistake with the children of this class. If any wanted to become a child of God, I would make sure he or she knew how.

To my chagrin, however, this proved much easier said than done. After a few attempts, my bubble had burst. Somehow I was going about it all wrong.

I used every technique I knew to teach the lessons professionally, treating each with the same preparation I had been taught in college and injecting as much life and colour as possible.

The children were entertained. They remembered the story. They even came to love me and I loved them in return. But it wasn't enough. They had head knowledge but not heart commitment. From their searching questions and wide-eyed honesty, I could see they were looking for a deeper relationship with God, but I did not know how to lead them to Him and I did not want to push them.

"God, I don't know where I'm going wrong, but give me an answer quickly, please!" I prayed in disappointment. Uncle Jozef's translations provided outlines for lessons, but I needed some kind of guidebook for the teacher and, as yet, he had not been given this. I simply pumped out a new story every Sunday, therefore, and the children faithfully turned up to hear it.

My school principal was less than pleased when she discovered I was teaching children about Christianity. In the year that followed, her attacks became more frequent. Knowing the SB pressure was off me now, she perhaps decided to make up for it personally.

"You're a black sheep in a Red school," Tatusiek told me. "You may not be allowed to remain in that job indefinitely." My refusal to join the Party certainly made my post unsure, but I enjoyed the children so much that I hung on until, at last, it became impossible for me to stay.

One day, I arrived early to display some artwork for my

class but, before I could enter my classroom, I heard shouts coming from inside.

"I will not tolerate your type in my school. You and that teacher of yours should be taught a lesson!"

"Stop, Pani, stop!" I heard a little boy cry. I knew that voice. It was Renatka's little brother, the pastor's son.

I threw open the door and, even after two years of life with the principal, found myself stunned. She had the young boy flat on the floor and was sitting on his back, pummelling him with her fists. Renatka stood by, wringing her hands helplessly and not knowing what to do next.

The director looked up, horrified to see I had witnessed this event. Forgetting the implications for my job, I ran across to the pair and pulled her from the child's back.

"The school authorities are going to hear about this, Pani!" I told her.

"No, Pani Jasia! Wait! Don't go! Don't tell! I like you. You are the best teacher we have here!"

I cuddled the weeping children. "The authorities have to know," I said.

"Pani, no!" she persisted. "This incident was just a little accident. It was nothing serious!" She had a slight smile on her face.

"Nothing serious?" Was this woman a sadist? Without doubt, the promise of power attracted some people to the Party, just as the pull of wealth attracted others. All the same, I found it nearly impossible to believe what I had seen and I shook all the way to the education office. Its staff, however, were much less surprised than I expected. They suggested that I change teaching posts.

"Now that she knows you know . . ." they shrugged, "she will make life intolerable for you. You'll have to leave."

"How can you speak so freely of her?" I asked, amazed.

"Hers is a well-known case!" they answered. "You're just one of a long line of people who have suffered under her."

"But can't something be done?" I pressed.

To that, they offered another shrug. "She is a senior member of the Party . . ." They left the sentence unfinished.

The education office suggested a new post which, they said, they had been considering offering me anyhow. A little mountain school, perched on one of our Alpine-like slopes, was in need of a principal. It was in need of repair, too, after years of neglect. I was excited at the possibilities. One look at it told me we could turn it into something special.

Our regional "cuckoo clock" houses were dotted over the picturesque valley around it. We could restore our school according to the same tradition, I thought, and Tatusiek, practical as well as creative, worked with me on the project plan. That summer he was studying for an engineering degree, but he took time out to help renovate. So did local parents and the children themselves. Local factories got involved too. All had become excited about the idea of a school in authentic mountain style.

After the cracked windows were repaired and the walls, desks and floors painted in bright colours, we added traditional elements. The mothers sewed curtains made out of embroidered fabric. Factories supplied the natural pine-wood furniture that is loved in the mountains. Dolls on display wore costumes from regions all over Poland. Mothers made their children matching outfits for use on official days. The end result looked rather like a traditional Polish dolls' house and the children, deeply proud of "their" school, happily gave private tours to all who came near.

I taught at this school for two years. Every day, I would walk from my bus through the lush valley and my watchful little charges would make their way down the slopes, past the gathered hay in summer or over the snowy mounds in winter. By the time I arrived at our mountain school, a dozen or more children would have joined the procession. Nearly all of them bore the same name, since this valley had throughout the generations been populated by one family, and they had become identified by location. There was "Bujok-from-the-rock", "Bujok-from-the-river", "Bujok-from-the-forest", "Bujok-by-the-bridge". They turned up eagerly for school, rain, hail or shine. I was as keen as they. None of us wanted to miss a day together.

Part of me longed to spend a lifetime in this picturesque environment, but part of me became, in time, restless. I began to see that every little Bujok, whether from the mountain heights or the valley depths, was battling needs too deep to be ignored. I was frequently witness to the abuse of alcohol, violence and outright depression in many of these homes. The children could not help but be affected.

As a teacher, I could help only so much. As a Christian, I could reach a far deeper need and it was to that, I knew, I had been called. The mountain school was wonderful, but it wasn't the Rainbow Garden.

As if on cue, it was after this realisation hit me that a telegram arrived from Uncle Jozef. In coded message, it told me that the promised training conference in Warsaw had been set.

The timing seemed right. The SB had, at least for the moment, lost all interest in me. The experience at the two schools had given me a professional foundation for kids' work. I was ready for the next step into the Rainbow Garden.

As with the last step, however, I had no idea of the trouble this one was going to bring me.

9

THE DOOR, THE WINDOW
AND THE CHIMNEY

"I can't feed dead bodies!" I was deep in conversation with
Uncle Jozef at the start of the Warsaw conference.

"Dead bodies, kochana?" He grimaced, comically.

"Well, I might just as well be doing that, Uncle! When
I try to teach Sunday School to the children, I am not
giving them the opportunity to start life over with Pan
Jezus. I'm making the very mistake that was made in my
own life!"

"But why do you call this 'feeding dead bodies'?" he asked,
with a smile on his swarthy face.

"If they had already started new life with Pan Jezus," I
said, "they would be hungry for spiritual food. But, since
they haven't, it's as if I'm force-feeding them with Biblical
principles. All I'm giving them is spiritual indigestion. That's
why I say it's like trying to feed dead bodies."

Uncle Jozef understood. "Coreczka, our visitor from the
West will help, I promise you!" He pointed out a tall, open-
faced foreigner with a bearing that told you, immediately, he
was someone to be trusted.

"His name is Samuel Doherty. He is an Irishman who directs
the Child Evangelism Fellowship for Europe. No foreigner
loves Poland more than he."

When Uncle Sam, as we termed him, began to speak, I
knew I had come to hear the right man. Uncle Jozef translated
as he posed the conference a question.

"Recently, one of our team returned from a meeting and

told us that two and a half people had found the Lord Jesus. What do you suppose he meant?"

The room buzzed for a moment. "Perhaps the half he referred to was a child?" someone suggested.

"No," Uncle Sam beamed. "The half was an adult. The other two were children! You see, my Polish friends, when a child finds the Lord, God can save a whole life. But when an adult comes to the Lord, much of his life will have been wasted already."

He backed up his point with another picture, one which, as I later discovered, was a classic in CEF's work.

"Imagine yourself standing near the top of a cliff, watching as people walked towards its edge. Suppose there were no safety fence for protection and the people simply walked on until, one after another, they fell to the rocks at the bottom. Now, what would be the most helpful course of action in such circumstances? Would it be better to concentrate on attempts to put back together those who had fallen? Or would it make more sense to build a fence at the top so that they could not get hurt in the first place?"

This question brought no discussion, of course. A sober quietness settled over the conference hall.

"Do you see now why we would rather a person find new life in Christ when he is a child? It is so much better than waiting until his life has been harmed through years of wrong living. That is why the Bible says, 'Remember your Creator in the days of your youth'" (Ecclesiastes 12:1).

My mind returned to the little Bujoks who lived in the Beskidy valley and I sketched them as I listened. A bright-eyed girl with pigtails popped out of my pen. A naughty boy with freckles followed. A sweet-faced girl with wistful eyes came next. Child followed child until twenty filled my page and I stared down at their faces. What lay ahead for them, for the little ones in the Red school and for the students in my Sunday School?

What, indeed, lay ahead for the rest of Poland's children? Did they have to grow up into a life filled with alcohol, disillusionment, compromise, corruption, crime, anger, bitterness?

Did they have to be spiritually dead? Didn't we owe them the chance to come alive in Christ? What use would it be if our Sunday Schools taught nothing more than mere Christian morality?

As if reading my mind, Uncle Sam continued: "Charles Spurgeon, the famous author from last century, said: 'Sunday schools are admirable; but what is their purpose if you do not teach the Gospel in them? You get children together and keep them quiet for an hour and a half and then send them home . . .'"

Not everybody agreed with his words. At breakfast next morning, a colleague from our Silesian region voiced his reticence.

"Kids are too young to make a decision about Pan Jezus. We must not force them by the sheer strength of our adult authority." The man seemed a little tense. His hair was long on one side and he had a habit of pulling it across his head to cover a bald spot.

"I agree that we must not force them," I replied, "but we must not deprive them either." I explained yet again how, in my early years, I had longed to give my life to God but, when no one told me how, had become lost in Communist ideology.

He pulled at his hair nervously as I described my lost years in Communism. Later I wondered why he seemed so restless. I knew it was not possible for a course like this to be held without the government's planting observers among the bona fide students. Had I, perhaps, bumped into one of their people?

"Yes, you probably met a Tobiah, my coreczka," Uncle Jozef told me over the washing-up that night.

This highly respected professor astonished me. His days at the conference were busy enough playing his "born-again violin", as many termed it, and constantly translating. Yet he was always one of the first in the kitchen. No task was too humble for him, it seemed.

"A Tobiah?" I asked.

"In the Old Testament, when Nehemiah was rebuilding the

walls of Jerusalem, men were sent to oppose him. One of them was Tobiah. We'll always have such people at our conferences, Jasia, but never mind! Maybe God will speak to them while they are observing us!"

The man's presence continued to cast a shadow across my path, but, Tobiah or no Tobiah, nothing was going to stop me giving my all at this conference. In Uncle Sam's teaching, I found the secret to watering the Rainbow Garden.

He taught us to communicate spiritual truth to children in a way quite different from any I had ever known. In essence, he advocated that we find a central theme in any spiritual lesson and apply it in two different ways. For non-Christian children, we should use it to explain their need to begin new life in Christ. For Christian ones, we should make the same theme relevant to their need for growth in Him.

Uncle Sam called for someone to try out this technique and I volunteered. Afterwards, to my delight, he suggested I come to Switzerland for additional instruction at the CEF training centre. I was enthusiasm itself. Now I could learn all I needed to avoid feeding dead bodies. There was just one hitch. The course was in English.

"Leave it with me, Sam!" For Uncle Jozef, with his perfect English, this posed no problem. "Jasia will learn the language. I'll make sure of it. Besides, she already loves England!"

How odd, but true, I thought. For so many years, I had indeed loved England. I had read books about it and covered a bedroom wall with English postcards, though I had never learned the language. Had God been at work behind the scenes all this time, knowing English would be the language that would equip me for the Rainbow Garden?

I left the conference feeling euphoric. It was only on the train home that reality hit with a vengeance.

Did I really think I was going to get permission to travel abroad? The government was afraid of defectors and understandably so. "What's the definition of a Polish trio?" ran a popular joke. "It's a Polish quartet that visited the West!" "Why are cosmonauts attached to the mother ship when they walk in space?" said another. The answer, predictably, "So they won't defect."

"Is there any hope that the government will allow me to go?" I asked the Lord. "Have I allowed my imagination to carry me away?"

By way of answer, during the weeks following the Warsaw conference, He gave me an intensive schooling in faith. I met a woman, Aunty Alice, whose faith astonished me and who was to play a strategic role in furthering the Rainbow Garden.

Aunty Alice was a Christian committed to serving Poland's Jewish people; our "Elder Brother", as she affectionately referred to them, since they are the first-born of God's people.

There could not be two Aunty Alices in this world. She combined the bearing of an aristocrat with the heart of a servant, the mind of an intellectual with the faith of a child.

Her courage left me breathless. Since Poland had broken diplomatic ties with Israel, the authorities were suspicious of anyone well-informed on the Jewish situation. They could thus have misinterpreted her labour of love as a political offence. The risks she faced dwarfed my little travel worries to their proper size.

Aunty Alice was staying in our town and, as I observed her, I saw the way she fuelled her faith. It was her habit to pray for hours, often unaware of the time passing. She knew her Bible from cover to cover and lived on its promises.

Perhaps because of the Jewish boarder who had lived in our home, I had always ached over the holocaust and its bitter fruit. As Aunty Alice described her longing for Christians to give God's love to heal the wounds of our Elder Brother, I became certain of one thing. In the future, Jewish children, "the little children of Israel" as I dubbed them, would have to be a part of the Rainbow Garden.

I became sure of something else, as well. I wanted to learn to trust God as she did. She constantly warned against allowing God to be "too small" because, she repeated often, "What is impossible with men is possible with God" (Luke 18:27).

Sandwiched between the faith of Jozef Prower and Aunty

Alice, I could not help but try to trust God in my own little test of faith.

"Ah yes, Alice is a great example to us all!" Jozef Prower agreed. He, along with his many other areas of involvement, was also committed to serving Israel and its people.

"Perhaps I can learn how to trust God for the impossible too, Uncle," I sighed, confessing to him my doubts about travel abroad.

He met my fears with a smile. "Don't worry, the Lord has already taken care of it! There's an old, bedridden lady in England who is looking for an au pair girl. You could take care of her and she, in return, is willing to give you English lessons."

"And what will the Polish government say? Will they give me a passport?"

"Tell them this is an educational opportunity when you apply!"

"But what if they refuse, Uncle Jozef?" I had not forgotten the ferret and the ice-man.

Uncle Jozef's eyes were closed in prayer and I waited till he was ready to speak. "If the Lord closes a door, kochana, He'll open a window. You'll see. Besides," he added, his eyes crinkling with a smile, "you'll go with both hands full!"

It seemed, at first, as though everything would go very easily. I was given a passport in two months and assured I could travel abroad, although there would be a further two months' delay in obtaining the train ticket. Our government's regulations were stringent. The ticket had to be paid for in Western currency by the future employer.

Travel restrictions were so resented by Poland's people that these, too, were the target of the nation's comics.

"Now there is a new law permitting people to travel abroad," ran one joke. "There is only one hitch. You must be over eighty-five and have written permission from both your parents."

Given the difficulties of travel, I was nervous when, shortly after I received my passport, I was summoned to the police station again.

"Something was incorrectly processed," said the grey-uniformed policeman, reaching for my passport through his dirty office window. I handed it to him without question. He placed it in a drawer and looked back at me, a smug expression on his face.

"Thank you, Pani. You may leave."

"Leave? What do you mean? What about my passport?" I replied.

"No passport, Pani! A new decision has been made," he sneered. "We know from a reliable source that if you left Poland you would never return. So you're not going anywhere."

"What are you talking about? Of course I'd come back! And what 'reliable sources' told you otherwise?"

He gave a conspiratorial smile. "Never you mind about that. Now go home. The decision is final."

I made my way back to Uncle Jozef's in a haze of bewilderment. Who had stopped me? Tobiah, as far as I knew, had not known of my plans to go, but there had been a morning when I had chatted enthusiastically about them with Iwonka. Could she, out of jealousy, have told her father, the Moskal? Might this be their doing?

"Whatever their motive, they're up to their usual tricks!" Uncle Jozef said, less surprised than I by the problem.

"But, my daughter, if the door is closed, we can still try the window," he smiled. He sat down to draft a letter and I observed his strategy, amazed. This man was more spiritual than anyone I knew, yet extraordinarily practical with it. It was as though he lived with one foot in Heaven and the other on Earth.

We posted an appeal to the next in the line of authority, those who held office at the regional level. The reply took only two weeks to come. It was negative.

"The window's closed, Uncle Jozef, and it won't open," I said. By now, I was frightened. I had given up the mountain school so I had no job. Were England and the Rainbow Garden just pipe-dreams?

I had the feeling God was asking me: "Are you going to trust Me? Or will you give up at a setback like this?"

I thought back to the verse God had given me when, earlier, I had faced the SB.

"So do not fear, for I am with you; do not be dismayed, for I am your God . . . I will uphold you with my righteous right hand . . . those who oppose you will be as nothing" (Isaiah 41:10).

Even with this promise, however, I can't say I was very brave. I had not yet learned to trust God for the impossible and might well have abandoned the whole idea had it not been for Uncle Jozef's daring.

"So, after the window, we try the chimney!" he told me. "Come on, coreczka, I'll tell you what to do."

In my hand, he placed the address of an office in Warsaw. I knew this to be the highest authority on such matters, but I did not realise it had an infamous reputation among the persecuted in Poland. He had sent me to what some call the Wasps' Nest. It was the very heart of the SB, a building with offices in front and, at the back, a prison for political offenders. Only after the event did I discover that some who were summoned to this place never returned.

It was an extreme step to take, perhaps, but Uncle Jozef knew this was the only "chimney" possible. No other office in Poland could reissue my passport now. "But I will pray from the moment you leave until we see you on our doorstep," he told me at our parting.

If the Party building in our local area had seemed impressive to me, this Warsaw address was palatial. There was marble everywhere, together with expensive brass lamps and the mandatory tropical plants. Displayed against this backdrop was a mass of red flags, together with countless slogans and banners. There was so much red here, I thought, it was like coming to Hell itself. I was glad Uncle Jozef was praying.

"And with whom do you have an appointment?" The receptionist was imperious. Under Communism, most workers in government places gave you the feeling they were doing a great favour by attending to you.

"I have come to see the Minister for Internal Affairs, Pani. It's about a passport matter. I don't have an appointment."

"You what?" she exploded. Two soldiers, standing to attention at the top of the marble staircase, turned to observe us.

"Pani, you don't come to this establishment according to your pleasure. You come because you are summoned. Get out of here!"

I did not move.

"Did you hear me? I said 'Out!' she repeated, her harsh tones reverberating around the highly polished marble surfaces. I cringed.

"Can you trust Me?" I knew God was asking me this question again.

"If this isn't a convenient time, I'll be happy to wait until the Minister is available," I heard myself say.

Her eyes narrowed. "Don't you understand? I told you to leave!" She bent her head to her desk.

Uncle Josef had told me this was the last chimney left. Aunty Alice had warned me not to allow my God to be too small. The Lord Himself had promised He would uphold me. I knew I could not leave.

I took a seat and began my vigil. One hour passed, then a second. At the end of the third, she picked up the phone. Discussion followed and then quiet filled the great hall again. I dared not move. I was hungry and thirsty, but, if I were to excuse myself for even a few moments, she might take it as a sign of my weakening. Five hours passed. The pani became more nervous. I was becoming nervous too. She sat. I sat.

At last, I heard my name announced over the public address system. She nodded to the stairway and I walked up the marble steps towards the soldiers at the top.

When I reached the massive wooden door, they fell into military position either side of me, as if I were a prisoner, and then, rifles in hand, escorted me inside.

"Those who oppose you will be as nothing . . ." the Bible had promised. "What is impossible with men is possible with

God," Aunty Alice had said, repeatedly. "Lord, help me trust You," I prayed under my breath.

"Sit down, Pani. This is all most irregular," my interrogator began. He was an angular-looking man with a face like a razor blade and a mind to match.

"Yes, I am sorry, but the matter is a very important one," I replied.

He silenced me with a quizzical eyebrow.

"Indeed?" was all he said. Then he opened a file and my heart sank. Did the SB have such files on all of us in Poland?

"You want to go abroad? Why?"

"I want to further my education and here in Poland that has not been possible for me."

"Yes, I know it has not been possible." He did? So he had been studying my records during my hours downstairs? No doubt, then, he knew I had refused to join the Party.

"I have the chance to learn English and I believe we young people ought to learn other languages." Uncle Jozef had warned me not to mention the training course in Switzerland.

"Indeed?" he said again. Then with the expertise of a professional he began to fire questions at me, machine-gun style. He was brilliant at his job. He made the ferret and the ice-man look like kindergarteners.

His technique was to begin questioning on one issue, leap to another, then to a third, then back to the first. He was waiting for me to make a slip-up somewhere, an inconsistency on which to catch me.

"Your father? During the war he fought for Germany?"

"We live in Silesia! At the start of the war, the Germans claimed it as part of the Third Reich. He was conscripted at gunpoint. So were at least 50 per cent of Poland's men. You know that!"

"He was not sympathetic to the Nazi cause?"

"Of course not. My Tatusiek loves Poland."

"But you receive parcels from Germany!"

How did he know that? Had the Post Office informed on our family? "Well, yes, sometimes."

"You were sent a German doll, were you not?"

He even knew about Ania!

"I liked dolls when I was a little girl. That did not make me a Nazi sympathiser!"

"Indeed!"

That word was starting to irritate me.

"You have not joined the Party, Pani."

"No, I am not an atheist, so it wouldn't be right for me to do so."

"Are you saying atheists are bad people?"

"No, I didn't say that. Only that I am not one myself."

"Ah yes," his eyebrow went up again. "You call yourself a Christian, Pani."

"That's right."

"Yet you are not a Roman Catholic?" Most of Poland's population is Roman Catholic.

"No, but I have many good Roman Catholic friends."

"Some people say that if you are not Catholic, you are not Polish. What do you think, Pani?"

"I don't agree, Pan. I am Polish and I love my country."

"But the Protestant Church came to Poland from Germany . . . just as the Nazis did." He looked hard at me.

"And your family, Pani, gets parcels from Germany! From whom? Someone your father met in the war?"

And so we went full circle. Around and around he led the questioning until I was dizzy with it all. Why did I want to go abroad? They had reason to believe I wanted to defect. Did I?

At last he came to an abrupt halt and sat, silent, for a long, intimidating moment before pronouncing his judgement.

"You're lucky, Pani."

I waited, breathless.

"This department is not normally my responsibility. The man you needed to see returns from vacation tomorrow and he is not usually open to matters of this sort. But I am willing to believe you are being honest. I will reissue your passport."

I stood to leave, breathing my thanks to him.

All at once, he was kind to me. "Prove your gratitude by coming back to Poland, Pani. I've chosen to trust you in this."

"I promise, Pan," I said. "You won't be sorry."

"Indeed?"

I managed a tiny smile. "Indeed!" I said and then, as soon as was polite, let myself out and all but stumbled down the marble staircase.

It was 11.30 p.m. when I reached the Prowers' house.

"Jasia, Jasia, you are here!" Aunty wrapped me in a great hug at their front door. "We have to tell Ziutek right away." Ziutek was her term of endearment for Uncle Jozef.

"Isn't he here?" I asked, close to collapse with hunger and fatigue.

"Oh he's here all right, but he's been on his knees since early morning, kochana. He's received no food, no phone calls and no visitors. I haven't seen him myself."

Uncle Jozef appeared, evidently weary, but with a special light in his countenance. Did Moses look like this, I wondered, when the Bible recorded his shining face after long hours spent with God? "If this is how Your saints pray, Lord," I thought, "it's no wonder I saw a miracle today."

Uncle Jozef was jubilant when he heard how things had gone. He praised God till the roof all but lifted off their timeworn building.

I was grateful to God, but less spiritual. "I'm starving!" I confessed when we finished praying.

"This little girl hasn't eaten, Anusia!" Uncle Jozef said, immediately raiding the kitchen. It did not seem to occur to him that he had not eaten either. It was only me he served. I gobbled everything they set before me as we sat around the table, laughing, crying and rejoicing at the astonishing outcome of the day. That night, I enjoyed even the tea.

My passport was returned just one week later, the policeman handing it back with barely stifled fury.

As I left the premises, I happened upon the Moskal who evidently had business awaiting him at the police station.

"We'll see whether or not you come back to Poland!" he said, his narrow-set eyes lifted haughtily.

"But of course I will. Why . . ." I stopped with sudden understanding. It had been Iwonka after all.

The Moskal swaggered past me.

"You should never have gone to Warsaw!" he said through clenched teeth, brandishing his cane.

After that, I was afraid to tell anyone where I was going. I occasionally bumped into Aunt Mila while walking, but I never mentioned my plans to her. I told myself that this was because I must take no risks, but there was a further reason. I still felt she deserved punishment and if something in me whispered that this was no way to show the love of God, I stifled it. Aunt Mila was someone I did not mention in prayer.

I did not tell Marcin I was leaving either. It had already become clear to us both that our relationship could no longer go forward. We had agreed to part.

Other friends asked why I was no longer at the school, Big Ears in particular. I fended them off as best I could, but became increasingly anxious to be safely on my way out of the country before anything else could go wrong.

Mismanagement was rife in Communist Poland, however, and when, after Christmas, the documents and Western currency had arrived for my ticket, I discovered there were no seats available on Polish trains till February.

I grumbled about the delay. It had been hard enough waiting while the passport was reprocessed, but a further time loss seemed intolerable.

Tatusiek urged patience when I met him after work with the news. "The Bible says that 'all things work together for good', kochana. God must have some purpose in it," he said as we left his factory grounds.

I looked at the dilapidated building where he had served for so many years. As long as I had been coming here, it had been a rusty place with paint peeling from its walls and panes missing from its windows. It was a depressing picture, but one replicated all over Poland where industry, like the people's morale, was still badly run-down.

"Don't you wish you could get away too, Tatusiek?" I asked as we walked through the snow-laden trees of our nearby forest. "That is such a miserable place to work."

"Oh life is never easy, kochana. But hardship is where

God enrols us in the university of life! I've always believed that!"

His moustache was white with powdered snow as he reminisced about his suffering during the final years of the war. In bitter mid-winter, the Russians had placed Tatusiek into an outdoor prison camp with no building for shelter. He and his companions had dug themselves into individual holes in the ground and drawn on the warmth of the earth itself for survival. They had lived in their holes for six months, eating worms and the bark of trees for food. Tatusiek kept his mind occupied with the tiny Bible Mamuska had given him.

"It's not suffering that matters, it's what we do with it!" he told me. "I learned a lot at the university in which God enrolled me and you must too. Stay a student all your life, kochana! Fill your mind with knowledge and your heart with wisdom!" he said, his gloved hand stroking my cheek. Then, lest the talk become too serious, he bent and gathered a handful of the glistening, sugary snow and flung it at me.

I responded with one of my own and we exchanged snowballs through the winter fairyland until, at last, we reached home.

Tatusiek stopped in our garden to put an extra layer of conifer branches on his beloved rose bushes. They needed to be kept warm during their winter hibernation, he explained, arranging the greenery protectively around them.

The previous season, although his favourite rose had not actually turned black, it had bloomed the deepest brown ever and he had been justly proud.

The brown rose was not his only achievement that year. He had also completed his degree in engineering, the fulfilment of a lifelong dream. In a way, I thought, the rose was almost a symbol of the man himself. He sought always to improve himself, in heart, mind and spirit. "Oh Tatusiek, you are such a perseverer and I am such an impatient creature!" I said, but received only teddy bear noises by way of reply.

There was something intense about Tatusiek during the final weeks before my departure. He made sure we walked frequently together in the mountains, and with a kind of urgency spoke about the serious things of life. It was as though he felt driven to instruct me in life's university.

On one walk, we stopped by the Vistula river to look at a half-frozen waterfall which had been constructed according to Tatusiek's design.

"Well, almost!" he said. "The foreman on the job stole some of the reinforcing bars to sell privately and if I hadn't stopped him would have tried to compensate by piling on extra concrete. If his plan had succeeded, this would not be standing today, of course. You must have materials in balance if you want things to last." This pattern had always worried Tatusiek. All over Poland, hospitals, hotels, bridges and other public building projects were depleted of needed materials because of the greed of the workers. That, he said, was the reason countless buildings had cracked and many bridges collapsed.

"It's a picture of our entire economy," my philosophic Tatusiek added, as we watched the white water dance through crystallised ice on the pipes. "Gierek is spending a great deal of money, but does his programme have equilibrium? He has raised wages, frozen prices, filled the shops with imported goods, improved pensions and put up a million new flats. As if these were not expensive enough, he's authorised one hundred and thirty new churches and the reconstruction of the royal palace at Warsaw. But how long can his programmes last when the economy itself is not balanced?"

With his gloved hand, he lifted my chin to meet his gaze. "Balance, my Jasia. That's how to build nations and people," he concluded. "You won't let the affluence of the West rob you of the balance in your own life. Will you?"

"I don't know what you two chat about all day! You're like a couple of kids, the pair of you!" Mamuska would say, shaking her head when we returned home from our walks.

I wasn't sure that I fully understood either. The gravity of our discussions had certainly been unusual for my reserved Tatusiek.

"Why are you telling me all these things, Tatusiek?" I said

at last. "I'm only going for a year! You act as though I'm never coming back."

He shrugged and kissed my forehead. "Oh, you never know, my Jasia. You just never know . . ." I still wondered what he meant, but had to be content with that cryptic comment.

My ticket was authorised at last and I began to prepare. Just as I finalised my packing, however, Mamuska decided that my very worn winter coat would not do for a smart city like London.

"But there's no money for a new one," she said, pencil in hand and ledger open, at a family conference.

It was Tatusiek who came up with an inspiration. Before the war, he had bought a coat with a lining of woollen tartan.

"The outside is worn through but the inside is in excellent condition! Your golden fingers could turn it into something beautiful!" he told Mamuska.

Mamuska set to work and Tatusiek outdid himself in producing a piece of rabbit-skin which they dyed brown and turned into a collar. When at last I stepped on to the train for England, I felt like a film star.

I snuggled down inside the coat as our train chugged and coughed its way across the face of Poland. Its warmth brought the comfort of my parents' love and the familiar scent of home. I was already missing them. I was becoming lonelier with each passing kilometre and felt quite terrified when, in the dead of night, we reached the East German border.

We were greeted by the blaze of floodlights and the marching of boots. Soldiers strutted on to the train, demanding passports, with their dogs on short leashes at their sides. We all but cowered with fear and humiliation as they fingered every item in our luggage, dealing swiftly with any hidden Polish crystal or other prohibited items.

I shivered at the sharp commands they gave in German, shrank from the guns on their belts and gazed up at the high towers from which more soldiers observed us. Although I was carrying nothing forbidden, I nearly held my breath till the crossing was over.

When at last the train chugged forward, I fell into a light doze and dreamed about the Nazi war films that had given me nightmares as a child. I saw Auschwitz with its horrors: the starving inmates, the little girls' dolls, the mounds of human hair and the gas chambers. At last I woke with a cry and stared into the blackness beyond the window. Suddenly loneliness and fright threatened to overwhelm me. I was twenty-two and did not want to go into this foreign world and make my way among strangers who frightened me.

"Can you trust Me?" I felt the Lord asking, yet again.

I wasn't sure I could. I blinked back hot tears and, closing my eyes, prayed for dawn to come.

In the depth of the northern winter, the sun did not rise for many hours and when it did another shock awaited me; not one of terror, but one of beauty. We were entering Holland and I stared out of the window at a scene which was, for me, the gateway to the West.

The sun began to pierce through the snowy haze of dawn, silhouetting the homes adjacent to our railway line. We rattled past high-gabled farmhouses with stately red and green windmills, all so beautifully maintained that I thought I was turning the pages of a calendar. We passed town houses too, the angles of their historic roof lines preserved far more carefully than any in our polluted cities. Everything was neat and smart and picturesque.

It was the interiors that I found hardest to believe, though. For some reason, curtains always seem to be open in Holland and, as families gathered for breakfast in their well-lit dining rooms, I could see clearly the stylish furniture and plush fabrics. Each scene was framed by plants positioned artistically in the windows, all so clean I was sure the families polished every leaf.

I cleared away the condensation my breath made on the frosty window to see it all more clearly. After a lifetime's diet of grey, dilapidated Communist architecture, the freshness and beauty of Holland left in me an ache I could not name.

Again, I felt God ask "Can you trust Me?" and, again, I could not answer. I was afraid of these foreign lands on two counts: the terror I had met in the night and the affluence I was meeting in the day.

"For the children's sake, Lord, I will go on," I told Him silently, my nose still pressed against the window pane. "But I didn't know it was going to be as difficult as this."

I would never have guessed it at the time but, as it happened, it was not the difficult things of the West that would pose the greatest danger to the Rainbow Garden. It was the easy ones.

10

THE WRONG SIDE OF THE MOUNTAIN

"And this is Goo-Goo!"

"Goo-Goo?"

"Your new employer, my dear!"

I might as well have been meeting the Queen. An aristocratic invalid sat upright in bed, her back ramrod straight and her hand stretched out beneath a lacy sleeve to shake mine.

Gathered around her pink, frilly pillows were the family members who had brought me to her, all of them attending her like courtiers.

"My dear, we are simply delighted you have come!" Goo-Goo even sounded like the Queen.

"I glad be here," I stumbled. Uncle Jozef had taught me a little English, but I was far from accurate.

Goo-Goo was not this regal lady's proper name, but it was the way everyone addressed her and the way expected of me. I listened as she delivered my introductory spiel, catching what snatches of her conversation I could. See the house . . . learn my jobs . . . be on time . . . tell the truth . . . and God bless me.

"My dear, you must be tired," she said kindly, in time, "It's a long journey from your country behind the Iron Curtain!"

I stared at her blankly. I did not remember any iron curtain on our journey. Perhaps I had been asleep when we passed it.

"Me tired now, yes," I managed, and was dismissed from the royal presence for the night.

Goo-Goo's niece showed me the home and with each room

I went more deeply into shock. It had wall-to-wall carpeting, while I was used only to mats on a linoleum floor. There was an elegant bathroom and it too was carpeted, while at home we used a tub in the middle of our kitchen. There was carpet on the stairs too, and not even Wujek Morcinek's house had that. There were two toilets, both indoors, with frilly, coloured covers that were quite unlike anything I had ever seen.

"And this is what you will give the cat each day . . ." Goo-Goo's niece said, after she had shown me round the kitchen. She opened a can and I gasped at its contents.

"You making ze joke?" I asked. We would have considered such meat a Sunday treat at home. "Zis not animal dinner!"

A funny expression came over her face.

"Jasia, I think perhaps I'd better take you around the stores tomorrow, just till you get used to things?"

We left early for the shops next morning. Goo-Goo's niece was in an elegant English suit, and I in my tartan coat.

"Oh my dear, did you ever see such a coat . . ." I heard someone murmur as I walked past a little crowd and several heads turned to look at me. I cringed, catching a glimpse of my reflection in the window of an exclusive boutique. Yes, compared to their Western clothes, my coat was heavy and gauche. More people stared and I dragged myself along behind Goo-Goo's niece, feeling like a second-hand refugee from Siberia.

Fascination at my surroundings, however, slowly restored my spirits.

"But where ze lines?" I could not help but ask Goo-Goo's niece as we went from street to street.

"The what?" she asked.

"Ze people lines?" I had not seen a single queue.

She couldn't understand me.

"Come and see the bakery, dear," she said, standing in front of a big glass door. I went to push it, then jumped back in fright. It had opened by itself. We walked through and I looked back. It was closing again.

"Good morning, ladies. What'll it be then?"

I turned around and saw the shop owner dressed in a baker's

hat and clean white overalls with a jolly red and white checked apron over the top. Behind him, there was a display of baskets lined with matching checked cloth, and a range of bread such as I had never imagined.

"Take your time, my lovelies!" the round-faced man said, dimpling.

Take our time? Shopkeepers fumed in Poland if we so much as hesitated when choosing goods.

I stared incredulously at the display of bread. I was used to one or, at best, two varieties at home. Here they sold white loaves, brown loaves, cracked wheat loaves, rye loaves and corn loaves. They came with sesame seeds, poppy seeds or crunchy wheat on top. Some were long, others oval, others twisted or plaited. I did not know what to choose and was grateful when Goo-Goo's niece placed the order.

The rest of the morning went in much the same way. So did the week that followed. "I'm living in a dreamworld!" I wrote to my parents, never mentioning the coat. "The butchers have more varieties of meat than I ever knew about and they will cut it up for you if you ask. They even smile!" I wrote every detail down. "Tatusiek, you'd love the tools here. There are no shortages. You could buy screws, nails, hammers, drills or whatever else you needed. Mamuska, you'd love the dress shops. They have wool, linen, cotton and silk like gossamer. There are floral prints, country prints, stripes, checks and swirls in colours I've never seen before. Oh and the fruit, Tatusiek! You can get oranges and bananas here and it's not even Christmas!"

In the weeks that followed, I alternated between fascination and homesickness. At times, I thought I had come to live in paradise, but at other times I longed for the familiar touch of home. One night, not long after my arrival, I awoke with the oddest sense that Mamuska was calling my name. "Lord Jesus, does she need something special tonight?" I asked and prayed for her. In the dead of night, I thought of the boy Samuel, in the Old Testament, and the way God had awakened him when needed. In the clear light of dawn, however, I decided it must have been a bout of homesickness or, perhaps, simple indigestion.

Life in Goo-Goo's kingdom was strict. Her meals had to be cooked just so. Her sheets had to be changed daily. Her timetable was to be followed with military precision. Her frilly nighties were to be clean every morning because, this ninety-year-old woman told me, with a wink, "I'm still a woman you know and men come here!"

She was equally precise in her teaching of English. I had to read, write and speak exactly as Goo-Goo did herself. Mine was to be the Queen's English as she prepared me for the English examining board of the Royal Society of Arts. It was all very exacting, but for the Rainbow Garden it was worth persisting.

In addition, behind Goo-Goo the aristocrat I soon discovered Goo-Goo the saint. This woman had spent years caring for orphans in the poverty of southern Italy and life had brought her no frills then. Hers had been a daily walk of faith in the worst of hardship. The more I listened to her, the more I understood why Uncle Josef had sent me here.

God was so important to Goo-Goo that she could not even teach me English without giving Him central place. My lessons often came from the Bible, "because, my dear, there is no part of life it does not cover!" As my knowledge of the language progressed, she added spiritual parables as well.

"A stupid man was on a boat going to America," she dictated one lesson, "but he never ate in the dining room because he was afraid he could not afford to. He lived on dry biscuits and canned goods, alone in his cabin. When the trip was over, a steward told him apologetically that the ship could not give him any refund. 'Refund?' the man said. 'Why do you even speak of a refund?' 'Because, sir, the cost of all meals was included in your ticket!' said the steward."

Goo-Goo took my paper.

"If that sounds silly, Jasia, it's supposed to be," she said, checking my spelling through her granny glasses.

If I wrote a word incorrectly, I had to write out the proper spelling one hundred times for a first offence and five hundred times for a second.

"And yet, my dear," Goo-Goo continued, "how many people, Christian or non-Christian, treat God's provision for their lives the same way as the man going to America? Are they any less silly?"

I grinned. Goo-Goo's lessons were always unforgettable and she was, without doubt, teaching me far more than English. After that dictation, I came to realise I had found more than an employer. I had a spiritual grandmother.

I was to need her, too. Not long after, a visit to a Polish family brought news that stopped my bright, new, kaleidoscope world from spinning and plunged me into darkness. The unthinkable had happened to my beloved Tatusiek. His heart, never strong since the war, had stopped just one week after I had left Poland.

Had he suspected something, I wondered, on all those snowy walks and talks when he filled my mind and heart with so much advice? Did he want to leave his daughter as prepared as possible for the future she must enter without him?

Grief engulfed me as I realised I had lost my greatest confidant. I stopped eating and sleeping and I longed to hurry home to Poland.

"Don't!" Mamuska wrote to me. "You can do nothing for him now and Tatusiek always wanted you to complete your studies!"

Her letters detailed her time of suffering, including "the night before his funeral, when I lay awake, calling you over and over, Jasia!" I checked the dates with my diary. It was the same night I had awoken, hearing my name. God had held us together, in that painful moment, through prayer.

Uncle Jozef wrote, too. He had given Mamuska Isaiah 57:1 for Tatusiek's passing and, in it, I found comfort. ". . . devout men are taken away and no one understands that the righteous are taken away to be spared from evil. Those who walk uprightly enter into peace; they find rest as they lie in death."

As Uncle Josef pointed me to the Lord, I understood, at

last, God's authorisation of my delay in leaving Poland. I had complained about the "wasted time", never guessing that the precious opportunity to be with Tatusiek had been God's gift to me. It was one more lesson in my university. As I prayed that night, I came before the Lord in sorrow, realising how much I had to learn about His sovereign hand in all circumstances.

Goo-Goo and others did their best to help me recover. They took me on outings to distract me and I tried to find courage to go on. For the sake of the Rainbow Garden, I told myself, I must not give up. Soon, support began to come from another source as well.

One afternoon, I needed to drop into an office run by a Christian organisation and, afterwards, I happened to step into the lift with a tall Scottish academic.

"You're a Christian too?" Alistair's brogue was new to me.

"I love ze God, yes!" I answered.

He smiled at my use of English. I blushed and his smile broadened.

"It's a long time since I met a lass who blushed! It's a lost art in these days of women's liberation, and that's a pity!"

At that, I blushed the more.

Alistair was in London for several months of post-graduate research. Like me, he was lonely and it was not long before we were spending much of our free time together. He showed me the sights of London and I gazed in wonder at Big Ben, the Tower of London, Buckingham Palace. It felt as though I was watching my English postcard collection come to life.

I could not afford to dress for him with store-bought clothes, so I made my own, copying the princess style offered by London's windows in the early seventies. Walking arm in arm with such a fine-looking man, I did not want to look like a refugee.

Those were heady days. I was flattered that a handsome young man with a doctorate in English literature could be interested in me, a Polish nobody. And he loved "ze God" too.

I was so delighted with this new relationship that I never stopped to ask myself if it might jeopardise the Rainbow Garden. Nor did I ask that question of a second involvement

I took on at the time: I committed myself to part-time work with Polish children.

It began with a visit to a club whose members were drawn from Polonia, the Poles who are scattered outside their own country. We ate traditional borscht, pork cutlets and kolacz.

Many of those in this club had been in England ever since the war.

"Why didn't you go home to Poland?" I asked, over coffee, after our meal.

At my question, several men glanced at one another.

"Jasia, do you know so little? Has nobody told you what happened to the freedom fighters from the war?" said an old man with an aristocratic beard.

Tatusiek had. In the days of my Communist fervour we had often argued on this point. I cringed as the men went on.

"During the war, Poland had two kinds of resistance movements; one was co-ordinated from Russia and the other from England. We fought with the latter and, afterwards, instead of thanking us, the Communist government killed or imprisoned any who came home to Poland. Even today, the risks are too great for us to return."

Yes, Tatusiek had said the same. That was the reason he had waited four years before coming home from the war.

As an avid young Communist, I'd told Tatusiek that Russia was incapable of such atrocities. Now I was sitting face to face with its victims, heroes of the war with tears in their eyes because they had not seen their relatives in Poland for thirty years.

The men set out, much as Tatusiek had done, to make sure I knew the truth before the meal was over.

"Were you never taught about the time the Russian army failed to keep its promise in liberating Warsaw?"

"Yes." Tatusiek had told me about it the day we had watched *Forbidden Songs* together.

"I was there, Jasia!" said the bearded man. "The Soviets sat on the other side of the Vistula river and they allowed Poles to be massacred! It was only a miracle that I came out alive."

The men lit cigars and poured more vodka.

"Has your generation not been told these things, Jasia?" one man asked in anger. "Has no one spoken of the massacre of Polish officers in Katyn Forest either?"

"Ssshhh!" I said, instinctively. Tatusiek had repeatedly warned me against speaking of Katyn in Poland.

They laughed bitterly. "There's no need to say 'ssshhh' here, my girl. You're not behind the Iron Curtain now. We even have a monument in England for the victims of Katyn!"

The more they spoke, the greater my shame and remorse. Why had I believed my teachers rather than my beloved Tatusiek? Now, it was too late to apologise to him.

For all my ignorance, however, I was warmly welcomed by the members of Polonia. A Polish church in London had been looking for someone who could teach their children in Polish. They had two goals. They wanted the new generation to know Pan Jezus and they were also anxious for the young ones to love Poland's culture and language. After fighting for two centuries to get their country back on the map, Polish people feel strongly about their heritage. They do not simply forget it when they move abroad.

I seized the job with both hands. In the year that followed, I spent every Sunday morning teaching and preparing Polish presentations of the Gospel message.

"I'm so glad you have this position!" Alistair said, one Sunday, when he picked me up after the class.

"You can have your heart's desire right here in Great Britain. You can teach wee Polish bairns without having to go back to Poland!"

We were sitting in the spring beauty of a London park, surrounded by crocus and daffodils. Despite the warmth of the May sunshine, I shivered. Was this job providing him with a way to prevent my working in the Rainbow Garden?

"I have to go back to Poland!" I protested. "It's the reason I came to England in the first place!"

He stroked my hand. "Things change!" he said, playfully circling my fourth finger, the one that could bear his ring.

Alistair and I had been seeing each other for over a year now. I thought I was in love, but sometimes I wasn't sure.

He seemed to be in little doubt.

"You'll make a wonderful wife, you know, Jasia," he said, with a certain light in his eyes. "You cook well, you care for your house beautifully, you sew on a low budget and you love children!"

"You're kind, but . . ." I left the sentence unfinished. Why wasn't I pleased with this compliment? I didn't quite know.

It was our habit to sit in London parks and talk until the sun went down.

"How do I love thee . . .?" Alistair recited poetry for me and I, with greater confidence in English now, responded with some lines from Mickiewicz's writings.

My beloved country, you are just like health.
Only one who's lost you, can truly sense your wealth!

I rattled on, making up my own little translation of Mickiewicz's opening lines from the most famous of his classics, *Pan Tadeusz*.

"I'm just like Pan Tadeusz," I told Alistair. "I did not fully appreciate the beauty of my country until I left it!" I tried to convince him of the wonders of Mickiewicz, but he did not look pleased.

"Well Jasia, it's nice, but you wouldn't want to give Poland or its writers an overrated position in the literary world," he said. "The writings of Shakespeare and Dickens are beyond all comparison."

It's never wise to cross a Pole about Mickiewicz. I bristled and quoted more of his work, determined to prove both his literary ability and the beauty of my homeland.

Alistair's handsome face stiffened. "I'm sure you like it, Jasia, but you can't seriously compare the culture of Poland with that of England. Think of the scholarship that has come from our part of the world!"

"So? Poland gave you Copernicus, Chopin, Marie Curie, Jozef Conrad and Sienkiewicz!" He didn't know the last name. "Sienkiewicz wrote *Quo Vadis*," I explained, pleased with my one-upmanship.

Alistair changed tack. "Jasia, think of the historic sites of England you've seen. Think of the glory of the English countryside. I can't imagine anything in Poland could compare?"

"But you haven't seen the treasures of history in Krakow! You haven't seen the beauty of the Mazury lakes and the Beskidy mountains! I love England but, to me, there's no country as beautiful as Poland."

"Aye, Jasia, but we'll not be living there!" Alistair said and silenced me with a kiss. The subject was closed.

That had become our pattern. Fundamental differences were being covered over with kisses, like Band-Aids over wounds. I was uneasy about our future together.

Sooner or later, I would have to face reality. If I married Alistair, I would have to abandon the Rainbow Garden.

The question was, in fact, becoming more complex than I wanted to admit. When I had first come to England, I had thought I would never learn to live with the affluence of Western life. Now I wasn't sure I could live without it. A subtle change had taken place within me. England had become the norm, Poland the exception. I knew now the meaning of "the Iron Curtain" and I was not sure I wanted to go back to life on the other side of it. If I stayed in England I would never stand in a queue again either. Neither would Mamuska, if I brought her here to live.

There was one further factor at work in this too. If I married Alistair and settled down to life in the West, no one in Poland would ever call me second-rate again.

"And what lies ahead for you, now that you are fluent in English?" I was asked by the examination board of the Royal Society of Arts, at the end of my fifteen months of study. I stood before three suited men and a lady for my final assessment.

"I think my future might lie in your beautiful country."

The woman, dressed in pink English twin-set and pearls, spoke with a perfect Oxford accent. "You will not mind our weather here? English weather is notorious!"

Goo-Goo had instructed me to use humour whenever

possible. "Oh, but I do find summer here very pleasant. It happened on a Wednesday afternoon last year, didn't it?" I said.

Goo-Goo's advice paid off. The men turned to the twin-set lady in surprise and the group roared with laughter. After that, we chatted at length and at the end of the exam they demanded to know who had taught me to speak English with such attention to detail.

Next day, there was a knock on the door. I opened it and found, to my astonishment, a member of the examination board waiting outside with the most enormous bunch of flowers I had ever seen. He was ushered into Goo-Goo's boudoir where, apparently, he had hoped to persuade my teacher to take on more pupils. At the sight of her age and condition, however, he thought better of it and simply complimented her on the teaching she had given. She sat up straight, all lace and frills, and purred with pride. When he left, she whooped at her success and hugged me till I was out of breath.

It was time to go, at last, to Switzerland. Alistair agreed only reluctantly to my doing so, taking every step possible to shore up our future. He introduced me to his family, placed a diamond engagement ring on my finger and showed me a house where we could live after our marriage. He tried to set a date too, but this I resisted. Something was holding me back. I had to find out what it was.

The issue became clear almost as soon as I reached Kilchzimmer, the Child Evangelism Fellowship's training centre for Europe. It was set in the Baby Alps, mountains of approximately the same height as those in my home town. From the nearest summit, we could look up into the majesty of the higher Alps, complete with rocky outcrops, mountain goats, white peaks and alpine flowers.

There, Uncle Sam posed a question to the international students gathered. "Matthew, chapter 18, verse 14, in the King James version, says 'It is not the will of your Father . . . in Heaven that one of these little ones should perish'," he said.

"Now I want to ask you to personalise this verse according to your calling. If it is for Africa, say, 'It is not the Father's will that any of Africa's little ones should perish.' Do the same if it is for Asia, or the Middle East, or Latin America, or," he glanced at me, "Poland".

His words required an honest answer of me. "It is not the Father's will that any of Poland's children should perish!" The thought was in conflict with the white wedding-dress waiting for me back in Scotland. It kept me awake at night.

Alistair's letters continued to come, but I no longer knew how to respond to them. I gave myself over to study. The course at Kilchzimmer was comprehensive and its broad range of subjects gave me everything I needed to avoid feeding dead bodies.

It held surprises too. Previously, whenever I had thought of children's work, I had considered Sunday Schools only. Kilchzimmer opened a rainbow of colourful options.

There was just one problem with them all. Everything that was suggested looked, to me, impossible for Poland.

"Home meetings are an excellent way to reach children," said one of our teachers. "We call these 'Good News Clubs'." Private gatherings of any sizeable group were forbidden in Poland.

"Public places are useful too. Since kids won't necessarily come to you, you must take God's love to the places where they gather." In Poland, the watchful eye of the authorities was always vigilant in parks and playgrounds.

"Use your community's amphitheatres or a big tent and invite children to them." Both sounded perfect, but hardly subtle. I could not imagine our ever getting permission for such gatherings in Poland.

"We've found schools a good place in which to work," said the Latin-American student. Polish schools were rigidly controlled by Party people. They would be even more difficult to work in than the other options.

"And we've reached many children on beaches," said some of the Asian representatives. Beaches? Mountains? Other holiday places? I had never even thought of ministry in such places. Our government required any religious activity to be confined to religious property.

"Camps have proved ideal for us!" Camps? You needed special permission for every camp held in Poland.

"We've found correspondence helpful for kids in remote areas," said those from Germany. My heart sank again. Letters were often checked in Poland.

Just when I was giving way to the impossibility of it all, the Lord proved to me, once again, that He is the God of the impossible. Uncle Sam, who had recently visited Poland, happened to mention that Jozef Prower had succeeded in holding camps in a house in the Beskidy mountains. They were registered as music camps, but although music was no doubt part of their activity the major focus had, of course, been on Pan Jezus.

How typical of Uncle Jozef's creativity, I thought. I could almost hear his words. "When the Lord closes a door, try the window. When the window won't open, try the chimney."

"Oh Lord, have I made You too small again?" I prayed, remembering Aunty Alice's repeated warning. Was I so sure it was impossible to work in Poland? What windows and chimneys had I not thought of?

As the weeks of study passed, the picture filled out in my mind. Perhaps a home meeting might be possible, after all. We could, perhaps, hold "birthday parties" and invite neighbourhood children so that they could hear the Gospel. Maybe a camp could be held too, as long as we were careful. Perhaps even a tent . . . ?

Just as I was brimming with ideas for the Rainbow Garden, Alistair wrote once more. I knew I had to make a decision once and for all.

Uncle Sam and his wife, who were fast becoming like parents, never judged me in my struggle. "The Lord will show you what to do," they said. "You pray and we will too."

I began to pray at dawn on the top of a nearby mountain. I loved coming here. It was very similar to Czantoria, a mountain ridge near our home which forms part of the border between Poland and Czechoslovakia.

Not long before, I had received a postcard of Czantoria from Polish Christian friends saying, "Don't forget us!"

Could I forget Poland's children in the name of romance and comfort? When things had been so tough in Poland, I had fought for my vision. Now that life had become so easy, I had almost lost it.

I gazed at the rich, green mountain slopes beneath me. The ridge of Czantoria was exactly like this. If hikers went down into one valley, they found themselves in the woods of Poland. However, if they wandered by mistake down the other side, they ended up in Czechoslovakia and were met at bayonet point by border guards.

Without doubt, I had wandered down the wrong side of the mountain.

Although I grieved, I knew it was time to break with Alistair and with my attraction to life in the West, and go back to the vision.

Once my mind was made up, there was no holding me back. I spent my final six months translating training material so that more people could catch the vision for the Rainbow Garden back in Poland.

After the translation was completed, though, I faced the problem of reproducing the material. In Poland, we had no mimeographs or photocopiers because our government was afraid of underground literature. The only option was to copy the material here and carry it back in my suitcases. It was a bulky load. The completed training material was almost two hundred pages in length and I had fifty copies to pack.

Taking mimeographed material across the border was strictly forbidden and the sentence prescribed was prison. It would be a risk.

The very thought made me terrified, but as I read and prayed in those final days, another picture frightened me more. The Old Testament prophet Jeremiah painted a vivid portrait of the need he saw in the children of his day. It was every bit as true of Poland.

"Children and infants faint in the streets of the city. They say to their mothers 'Where is bread and wine?' . . . as their lives ebb away in their mothers' arms" (Lamentations 2:11,12).

Bread and wine sounded very much like the Lord Jesus. Children whose lives might ebb away could surely be those facing spiritual death unless they found new life in Pan Jezus.

There was no question about it. I had to pack the mimeographed material. The load might look big to me, but only if I allowed my God to be too small. I had, yet again, to remember that He is the God of the impossible.

Just before I left, the Lord gave me a surprise which strengthened my determination.

During a mountain walk, I stopped by an alpine meadow that appeared to be full of bright poppies. Hidden underneath the red flowers, though, were white daisies and blue cornflowers. A sudden thought hit me. This field was, in some ways, a little like Poland.

Poland always looked red to the outside world because its people were perceived as being Communist only. If one looked further, however, white flowers could be seen there as well: Christians trying to serve God faithfully. There were blue flowers, too: Polish Jews whose faith had been under fire. There were children in each of the three groups and all of them needed the love of God.

I took a photo for posterity. "I think You have just shown me the Rainbow Garden, Lord," I whispered.

Whatever happened to me with my mimeographed material at the border, I must let nothing stop me now.

The Rainbow Garden was waiting.

11

THE SILVER WEB

Before I had left Poland, I had never heard of the Iron Curtain. On my return, I crashed headlong into it.

I had expected trouble at the border, but I had forgotten the harsh ways of Polish customs officers. When the customs officer demanded I open my bag, his intimidating manner terrified me. So did the two hours of interrogation with the man in the leather jacket. I had not expected all those questions about England and my reasons for returning to Poland.

After it was all over, I sat on the railway station for more than an hour, trying to recover. Only as my whirling thoughts settled did I recognise God's hand at work. He had used the interrogation with the leather-garbed SB officer to keep the literature safe.

I tried to thank Him, but I was still so nervous I could barely gather my thoughts. The final, threatening words of my interrogator lingered: "Now that you are back in Poland, you had better tread carefully!"

Was I going to be able to manage life behind the Iron Curtain? Had I grown soft in the West?

At last, I pulled myself together, boarded a bus and took my first look at Poland through its dirty windows. That picture, too, left me shocked.

The place looked different. The flood of goods Gierek had brought to the shops in the early seventies was coming to an end. Tatusiek had been right. Gierek's changes could not be sustained by Poland's economic structure and now, in 1975, the stores were again emptying and the queues lengthening.

Given the mood of the nation, I should not have been surprised to see more alcoholics than ever stumbling in the streets. Disillusionment had set in. The hope that people had held during Gierek's early days had crumbled into despair.

Watching the scene, I felt depressed myself. I saw, through new eyes, the dull, ill-fitting clothing, the pale, undernourished faces, the poorly stocked shop windows and the peeling walls of soulless Communist architecture. Why was my beloved country having to suffer like this?

Just as I was giving way to discouragement, I glimpsed the one sight which never fails to put a smile on my face: a child. A few rows in front of me, I waved to a little girl with bright, smiling eyes and a face shaped like a strawberry. She grinned back and soon led me in a game of peek-a-boo. "Thank You, Lord!" I said quietly. "I think You're showing me a postcard of the Rainbow Garden! Please, help me not to lose the courage to plant it!"

I climbed down from the bus and began to drag my bags home on a folding luggage trolley. My heart leaped when, from the opposite direction, I saw the round, familiar figure of Mamuska herself, carrying a litre of milk. She had no idea I was coming. It was to be a surprise. I waved, but she did not see me.

Of all people, Big Ears, now a father with a child in hand, was also walking nearby at that moment.

"Isn't that your daughter, Pani?" he said, as she was crossing the street.

"Jasia?" She dropped her milk and it spilled all over the street, but she did not stop to look at it. Instead, she dashed into the centre of the road and I, no more sensible, ran to her open arms. Holding me close, she rocked from foot to foot while the cars swerved around us. Horns beeped and drivers shouted their abuse, but we hardly heard them.

We spent the afternoon unpacking and chatting like schoolgirls as Mamuska squealed her delight at the clothes I had brought her. When at last our excitement died down, we hardly needed to voice the one thing remaining for my first day home. We left the house and walked together to the cemetery to see Tatusiek's grave. A wiry man with a cigarette was leaning against the fence as we left our cobblestone driveway.

"Who is he?" I asked Mamuska.

"I don't know, kochana. He's not a local," she shrugged.

My eyes misted over when we stood before Tatusiek's grave. "Your will be done" were the words Mamuska had chosen for his headstone. Around it, she had transplanted his beloved roses and all but the brown rose were now in full bloom. The brown rose had died with him.

I had lifted my eyes to pray when, suddenly, I noticed the smoker had followed us. He showed no interest in any of the graves but was eyeing me carefully. My heart sank. The man on the train had not been issuing empty threats after all. I was to be observed.

In the days that followed, I could not go anywhere without the smoker. As soon as I stepped through our front gate, he or one of his cronies followed me.

I longed to distribute the literature I had brought across the border, yet it was not going to be easy getting such bulky material past the smoker.

"But I must, Lord. It is the seed for the Rainbow Garden and I want to see it sown!" I told Him, sitting in the summer sunshine on our back steps. "Show me a way!" I prayed.

"You're looking at it!" He seemed to whisper to me.

Looking at it? I stared in front of me and then nearly laughed at my own stupidity. Beyond our driveway, at the very back of the garden, there was a secluded, little-used gate leading into a narrow street. Apparently, the smoker had not checked for this. He and his team only ever watched the front of the house.

After that, I was able to come and go quite frequently, carrying the training manuals out of the back gate while the smoker stood faithfully near the front one.

I delivered these, by and large, to leaders in Christian circles; those who would get maximum usage from them and pass them on to others. Soon, I hoped, we could water these seeds with personal training as well.

The attitude of the authorities, however, made that look impossible for the moment. Shortly after my return home, I was required to return my passport to the same policeman who had released it so unwillingly two years earlier. Any further travel abroad would require application all over again. While I was at the police station, they interrogated me for some hours, asking questions that were almost identical to those I had faced on the train.

Their intimidation had its desired effect. Fear and discouragement flattened me during the early weeks and I found it hard to break free from either. I was increasingly saddened, too, with the deterioration of conditions in Poland.

When, in one store, I requested a metre of elastic, the saleswomen laughed uproariously and asked whether there was anything wrong with me. They could not remember the last time elastic had been for sale.

It was the same with every pitiful shop I entered. None of the sad-looking places had been maintained. Shelves were half-empty. The few goods they had were of poor quality. The places smelled unwashed. Motivation for life was gone.

There was one glaring exception. Pewex shops sold goods of Western quality; beautiful clothes, colourful toys, expensive perfumes and fine watches. There was just one catch. All purchases had to be paid for in Western currency, not zlotys. Unlike the earlier, yellow-curtain shops of my youth, anyone was allowed to shop in Pewex stores. The outworking, though, was the same. Only Party people or those with family abroad had foreign currency.

"Why are shops in Poland like shops in America?" people joked in resentment. "In America, you can get anything with dollars and nothing with zlotys. In Poland, it's the same!"

When I could take the sorrow of the streets no more, I lifted my eyes to the Beskidy slopes that stood, comfortingly, around our mountain town. Their beauty, at least, was as I remembered. Their slopes were clothed in summer greens; the birch trees shimmering, the dark conifers tall and grand, the luminous green oak and chestnut spreading their branches protectively.

Yes, I told myself, Poland was, for me, still the most beautiful country in the world and the only one in which I longed to live and serve. The grey veil of the System, however, was like a burial shroud over the land and now it threatened to stifle me as well.

It was Uncle Jozef who put me back on my feet. As soon as I appeared, down-hearted, on the Prowers' doorstep, he opened his arms with understanding.

"Coreczka, it must be very hard . . ." was all he needed to say and the dam of tears burst within me. "Culture shock is natural when you've been abroad! So is fear! Cry it out before the Lord!" he said.

"But," I sniffed, "you never seem depressed by anything, Uncle. You're always so joyful!"

For once, I saw Uncle Jozef's brow puckered and his eyes sad. "Oh no, my daughter, I am no stranger to depression. But the Lord . . ." he lingered over the name, a little smile returning to his face, "promises that His strength is made perfect in weakness. So, you see, He understands our frailty."

Uncle Jozef closed his eyes, as if in prayer, and when he opened them, he did the best thing possible. He broke into English.

I replied, almost without realising it, my tears drying as I did so. He kept the conversation going without returning to Polish.

"Now, kochana. Let me warn you. Since you have been away so long, you can expect to be tailed for some time," he continued.

"I know. There is already someone downstairs. He followed me here."

"Well," he lowered his voice, "I can tell you how to lose him, kochana."

"You can?" When would I get used to this man's peculiar mixture of heavenly vision and down-to-earth wisdom?

"You'll have to avoid Christian work initially."

"Avoid it? But it was the Rainbow Garden that brought me back to Poland!" I protested.

"Of course, coreczka, but you must work in a regular job until your tail loses interest in you. If you begin the ministry now, the SB will be on to it immediately," he concluded, his voice still low.

"But what work shall I do?" I said.

We had been speaking English all this time. He lifted his hands, with the biggest of smiles, as if the answer were obvious.

"Teach English, kochana. You're fully qualified!"

We sat on their dark, carved furniture and he looked at the mimeographed training material. I had brought Uncle Josef several sets to distribute, knowing that he would have contact with people who would be strategic in their usage.

We discussed the Rainbow Garden at length. He told me of his music camps and, listening to him, I was encouraged. Others had already begun telling me my ideas were impossible in Communist Poland, but not Uncle Jozef. We searched together for doors, windows and chimneys which could be used for the work.

"But, coreczka, remember one thing," he said, at last. "It is not just the depression of culture shock which you will face. Nor is it only the SB."

"What do you mean?"

"There is a force at work behind both, coreczka." He reached for his much-thumbed Bible. There could be no Scriptures more thoroughly read in the whole of Poland, I thought, as he turned the pages to Ephesians, chapter 6. "You know what Paul wrote, '. . . take your stand against the devil's schemes. For our struggle is not against flesh and blood, but . . . against the spiritual forces of evil in the heavenly realms.' You're facing the spiritual battle, Jasia, and as long as you want to bring children to the Lord Jesus, Satan will oppose you."

Typically, though, his humour bubbled up again before long. "But one thing can encourage you, coreczka. If you've had all this trouble already, it's a good sign. Satan never bothers those who don't bother him. Hold on to your vision!"

A visit to the Prowers' home could fix almost any problem, I decided. Aunty served the tea I remembered so well, and

I chatted at length with the two of them. At times, though, I noticed Uncle clutching at his heart and Aunty casting anxious looks in his direction. His health seemed to have deteriorated.

"What has he been up to, Aunty? Has he been too busy?" I asked.

"Busy?" she said. "You know Ziutek! Each week he plays violin for hours, preaches, counsels, visits people in need, teaches English, follows up the construction of our new church and," she paused for breath, "translates! You ask if he's busy?" Uncle Jozef had now translated volumes of material, including a Bible for children. His next goal was the *Living Bible*.

"Please be careful of your health, Uncle," I said. "We need to have you with us for some time yet!"

His face was peaceful. "Only the Lord knows how long I have left on this earth, coreczka. That's why I love to encourage others to go on with the work God has begun in our country."

This had always been one of Uncle Jozef's strengths. He was, above all things, a great exhorter. Where some men of vision are threatened by that same quality in others, Uncle Jozef fostered it. He never wanted others to depend on him. He wanted them to be dependent only on God. He thus encouraged others, not only in the burden for children's evangelism but also in medical work, youth activity, music ministry, Jewish work, interdenominational outreach and, certainly, literature translation.

He played his violin for us and by the time I left the two of them I had a new song in my heart.

I put Uncle Jozef's idea into practice. I was given a position as an English teacher in a high school and immersed myself in the role. I opened a rudimentary language lab, based on models I had seen in England, and since it was the first in our region teachers from many schools were called upon to see it. I found the attention rather more pleasant than I cared to admit. That was, in all likelihood, a sure symptom that the old *za swe* wound was not completely healed, but I chose to ignore it.

Aunt Mila called, not long after my return, asking me to give her grand-daughter private lessons in English. To my shame, however, I turned down her request, even though I had accepted several students. Although the love of God had been poured out so fully in my life, I had not found a way for it to heal this deep source of pain. I probably wasn't looking. I told myself that the wound still hurt too much to touch.

The SB continued to keep me under observation and, at Christmas, made its first move. A teacher in our school, whom Mamuska and I called the Hippo, happened to look into our classroom one morning and saw the word "Christmas" on the blackboard. For that, he reported me to the headmaster.

The Hippo was a Party member who lived in a gracious, old, aristocratic home and was rumoured to co-operate with the SB. With typically Polish humour, Mamuska had a habit of giving such people comical names and I had inherited the trait. The Hippo had earned his because of his clumsiness in gathering information about others.

He was confidence itself as he launched into his accusations. "I saw the words 'Christ' and 'mas' on your blackboard and I know enough English to understand them!" he said importantly, in front of the principal. "You were telling your students to attend Mass at their churches and worship Christ!"

I would have laughed had the situation not been so serious. I tried to explain the true meaning of "Christmas", and showed the principal the school's textbook, which included a mandatory chapter on Christmas. My words, however, fell on deaf ears.

"We know about your religious beliefs," the Hippo sneered. "You won't be permitted to go on teaching, Pani. Just wait and see!"

In the months that followed, regional examiners were called to our school to assess the quality of the teachers.

"Your days are numbered now, Pani," he said. "With your beliefs, no examiner will find you acceptable as a teacher."

Did God set angels around my classroom? I did not know, but after the assessments there was no recommendation for my dismissal.

The Hippo was undefeated. "We can still expect a visit from the Warsaw representatives!" he told me, with a gleam in his eye. They came and, after observing the lessons, asked a host of questions.

For many nervous weeks, I awaited the outcome.

"Stop worrying!" Mamuska chided.

"But I'm so tired of the Hippo's tactics!" I protested. Under this kind of pressure, I would never have a chance to get the Rainbow Garden going.

"Of course you are, kochana, but you know what Tatusiek liked to say. This is your university of life. God wants to show you how powerful He is! You'll see!"

I was less convinced than she. Only when the results came did I realise how badly I had underestimated God's power.

Once a year, Polish schools celebrate Teacher's Day and, as a rule, hold a special dinner. That year, I was told to be certain I attended.

Iwonka, now an education official in our area, was present as well. She had a high position in the Party these days, but, of late, had become rather bitter about life and had started to drink heavily. She took a seat beside me.

The Hippo stood to make his announcements. He was himself a little drunk, but he managed his prepared speech. "Pani Jasia," he said, unevenly, "we have an announcement to make. The Warsaw authorities have commended your teaching and granted you a monetary prize."

He forced himself to smile. "They have also awarded you a scholarship for English study at Cambridge University."

I wasn't sure whether to laugh or cry. Mamuska had a saying: "There is no situation so bad that God cannot turn it to good." He had surely turned the tables in this case.

"I'm sorry I doubted you, Lord," I whispered as I walked with jelly legs to get my award.

"Congratulations!" Iwonka said, raising her glass as I returned to my seat.

"I still can't believe it!" I told her.

She shrugged. "Oh why shouldn't you get it? You have done well in your profession."

Had the alcohol softened her? I had never known Iwonka to talk this way.

"You have done well yourself," I said, trying to reciprocate. She had received a special degree from university although, it was said by some, she had spent very little time attending classes.

"Yes, but my honours came to me differently," she said, swirling vodka in the bottom of her glass.

She lifted a wisp of permed blonde hair from her forehead. "I got my degree because I was a close friend of the professor's . . ." She reached for the bottle. "We were very close, if you know what I mean!"

Corruption in Poland's academic circles was widespread. A questionable liaison between a teacher and a pupil was just one form. Students of limited academic ability often turned to what Poles called the "car key" entrance to university, when parents bribed their way with a new car. Under Communism, dubious academic degrees were, in fact, granted at every level of society. It was widely whispered that some of Warsaw's leaders had, like Iwonka, received their degrees in strangely brief periods of time and that their theses had disappeared from the university records with equal strangeness.

"I'm still amazed at the award," I said to Iwonka. "I really thought the man from Warsaw had been told to get rid of me!"

"He was, my dear, but you know what your Good Book says, 'God works all things together for good'!" said Iwonka.

My mouth dropped open in astonishment. Were the surprises, this night, never to end? Iwonka gave a cynical smile and lit a cigarette.

"You're impressed that I can quote the Bible?" She exhaled. "I didn't know you were interested."

"I'm not!" she said. "But they teach us these things!"

"Who teaches you?" I asked, still amazed.

"My father and the other Party leaders!" She spilled a little vodka on her expensive silk blouse and tried, awkwardly, to wipe it. "How do you think we can fight you Christians unless we know the Book you read?"

She drew slowly on her cigarette as the Hippo passed our table. He, now, was as drunk as she.

"How about one from me too?" he slurred. "'For God so loved the world . . .'," he recited from John 3:16.

He draped his arm over Iwonka's shoulders and the two recited together the words of Psalm 23: "The Lord is my Shepherd . . ."

I shivered as I listened to one quote after another. They knew more verses than the average Christian.

How many Party people, attending Christian meetings and spouting Scripture, had learned it from the wrong source, I wondered? God was giving me a salutary warning.

Mamuska was nearly beside herself when she heard of the award. Assuring me that Pan Jezus's university was the best school in the world, she took me shopping and found the prize money enough to buy our winter supply of potatoes and cabbage.

The Cambridge scholarship, however, turned to dust. Angry at my previous appeal to Warsaw, the local authorities were glad of this second opportunity to refuse my passport. It was almost a form of punishment. The scholarship had to be forfeited.

I was saddened, but not heartbroken. A Cambridge scholarship would have been glorious, but it would not have ushered children into the Kingdom of God. The Rainbow Garden came first.

For the time being, however, I was still unable to develop the children's work as fully as I wanted. Using the back gate, I had managed to escape the smoker and train Sunday School teachers once a month, using the material I had brought back from Switzerland. Once a year, I was also able to partake in the training of a larger group. For this "gardening" I was grateful, but it was a long way short of the dreams I carried in my heart. The smoker's persistent efforts continued to hamper further work.

I felt restricted, too, by the state of the country itself. In this year of 1976 there was a degree of nervousness in the air. Gierek was having trouble keeping Poland's restless population under control. Humour, always a barometer of our political climate, told the story.

"Why does Gierek sit in the front row at the theatre?" asked a popular joke. "So that, at least once in his life, he can say he has everybody behind him!" was the answer.

In June, Gierek finally increased food prices by up to 60 per cent and the country all but erupted. Workers went on strike in the north coast seaports, including Gdansk. Others, near Warsaw, tore up railway line on the track that runs between Moscow and Paris. Further south, they struck at Party headquarters with rioting and arson. The government retaliated. Workers were arrested, imprisoned and even killed, in some cases. Thousands were made to take "the path of health": running between lines of the milicja who held batons and beat the workers as they passed. The nation was outraged. Gierek withdrew the price rises, but the situation remained taut and the atmosphere heavily oppressive. The government placed more ideological pressure than ever on the younger generation.

This was obviously not the time for me to go full-time into the Rainbow Garden, but, as well as the training already established, I made the most of the legal options that were available. I taught Sunday School and that year I committed myself for a summer Christian camp as well. Since these were conducted on religious property, the SB could not fault me for my involvement.

The day before the camp was to begin, we received a message from Uncle Jozef. Could he visit the following day, he asked, to speak about a matter of life and death importance? He planned to come early next morning.

That night, to my surprise, I had a terrible dream. Someone was pursuing me with a gun and I was battling to get away from it until, in the end, the gun was raised, a bullet seared my brain and I fell dead. I gave a cry and sat up in bed, clutching my head. Mamuska, red-faced and puffing, came running.

"What happened?"

"They killed me!" I said with a rueful grin. I explained the silly dream and she sat rocking me as if I were a child.

"Perhaps it is not so silly?" she said, her soft, dimpled cheek against my forehead. "Do you think God is warning us of something?"

"But what?" I asked.

"Well, there was great pain in your dream. Sometimes God can use that kind of thing to alert us to someone else who might be in great pain."

I recalled the night in England when the Lord had woken me to pray for Mamuska.

"Well let's pray, just in case," I said to her.

We knelt together for prayer and prayed, in general terms, before returning to sleep. Next day, we rose early to prepare for Uncle Jozef's visit. He was never late.

Mid-morning came, however, and there was no sign of him. I waited until lunchtime to call.

Aunty answered.

"Uncle isn't here yet, Aunty," I began.

"He's gone, Jasia . . ." She sounded distracted, as if searching for words.

"Gone? He's already on the bus?"

"Gone! Gone!" Her voice broke at that. "He's with the Lord. It was his heart. It happened in the night . . ."

"No!" I told the Lord when I put down the phone, dazed. "No! He can't be dead! Poland cannot yet do without him! Neither can I!" I felt I had lost my second father.

I stayed on my knees in shocked silence until, at last, the Lord seemed to nudge me back on my feet. "Remember the children," I felt Him urge. "Go and fulfil the vision you shared together."

I looked at the clock. There were just a couple of hours before a group of children would gather for their camp. I had to go to them.

That camp was in Mazury, the lakes district where I had given my own life to the Lord. In the weeks following, I saw a tiny section of the Rainbow Garden flourish in this north-eastern corner of the country. As little ones gave their lives to Pan Jezus, I knew we were seeing answers to the faithful intercession for children that had marked Uncle Jozef's life. I was glad, for that reason, to be there, busy in the work he loved, but I grieved to miss his funeral.

Hundreds had attended, Mamuska told me later, and the skies had opened with a massive downpour as if in sympathy.

This "Apostle of Love" as he was called, was paid fitting tribute. During the service a story was told that better than any, perhaps, summed up the story of his life.

A young child, who lived in the apartment beneath the Prowers', was sent off to Sunday School by his parents. The teacher was giving a lesson on God's character and, as she spoke, the child was quick to put up his hand.

"I know this Pan," he volunteered, confidently.

The teacher nodded her approval and went on with the lesson. She described Pan Jezus's love, gentleness, humility, honesty and so on. The child's hand popped up throughout the lesson as he told her how very well he knew this Pan.

Delighted, she asked her student to wait behind after class.

"It is wonderful that you know Pan Jezus," she said. "But how did you come to know Him so well?"

"Oh I've know him for ages," the boy replied. "He lives upstairs and he plays the violin!"

It was Pan Jozef, not Pan Jezus, that the child knew. He had seen the Master in the servant, though, and the mistake was understandable to all who mourned, that day, for Jozef Prower.

His death left a void that was, for me, impossible to fill. I never found out the matter of life and death to which he had referred on the phone. All I knew was that I must hold on to the vision alone, for the time being. I could continue the limited gardening I had begun, and I could help Aunty Alice a little in her ministry to Jewish people, but, by and large, I was still very restricted by the smoker. I could only pray for the time when God would give the green light for full-time work.

For two years, the Lord gave me a lesson in waiting. The country approached crisis point. Shops emptied more fully than ever, queues grew again, divorces increased, the birthrate fell and the heavy hand of the government tried to quell the increasing unrest. In April 1978, Lech Walesa was one of those, in Gdansk, who founded the Baltic Committee for Free and Independent Trade Unions, the beginning of the movement which would later develop into Solidarity.

The nervousness of the politicians became the greater when, in October, our Cardinal Wojtyla from Krakow was declared Pope John Paul II. In that moment of pride, Poles forgot economic hardship and political turmoil and squared their shoulders with new hope and dignity. All spoke proudly of the Pope's many accomplishments; his ability to speak five languages, his creativity in writing drama and poetry, his love for nature, his sportsmanship and his academic scholarship. At the same time, Poles loved the compassion, faith and humour they saw in the face of this man. The governments of the Eastern bloc shuddered, however, to see a Pole in the Vatican.

The nation was in such crisis that the SB must have decided I wasn't important enough a problem to worry about any more. They lost interest in me and I found Uncle Jozef's advice had paid off. I was free, at last, to work more fully in the Rainbow Garden.

I should have been delighted that this longed-for moment had come. To my shame, however, I suddenly found I lacked the courage.

How had it happened? How had I allowed myself to lose the very impetus that had brought me back, brimming with enthusiasm, from Switzerland? Perhaps the continual presence of the smoker and the constant attacks by the Hippo had undermined me more deeply than I realised. Perhaps, too, my teaching job brought financial security I did not want to release and it gave me longed-for status as well. It felt good when people lifted their hats to me in the street and that old wound, the feeling that I was second-rate, was not sufficiently healed for me to resist the temptation. Perhaps, more fundamentally, there was the sense of loneliness regarding the Rainbow Garden. Most Christians I knew still thought my ideas for reaching children were too radical for our country. They wanted the work confined to Sunday Schools and, with Uncle

Josef dead, I had found no one who would even consider the doors, windows and chimneys.

Aunty Alice was the exception. As always, she reassured me that I must not worry if my vision was too big. "Just be sure your God is not too small! Remember, with God all things are possible!" I heard her words, but I did not make a move.

The Lord Himself confronted me on my reluctance.

During a school camp near Gdansk, on the northern coast, I attended a programme of national dance for children, staged in a huge outdoor amphitheatre. The men performed in embroidered trousers and coats and the women in floral skirts and colourful bodices. While they watched the show, I watched the children, observing the multitude of young faces gathered under the green-roofed canopy of trees.

"You could hold a children's gathering of this size for Me, one day," the Lord seemed to whisper as I took in the scene.

"In Communist Poland, Lord? Are You serious?"

"Trust Me. You will, one day, if you are obedient . . ."

I still could not bring myself to step more fully into the Rainbow Garden, however. I was rather like the flies of my childhood poem, "the Silver Web", who allowed themselves to be caught while boasting of their cleverness in eluding spiders. I, too, had allowed myself to be trapped, though I was not courageous enough to admit it.

In the end, the Lord used illness to force the issue. I collapsed with intolerable pain and was sent to hospital.

Doctors suspected a gall bladder condition but the initial tests revealed nothing. "Your condition is probably psycho-somatic, Pani," my doctor said with a knowing wink at a colleague. "After all, you are single! Just take a rest."

I lay "resting" in hospital for two months until, when I could bear the pain no more, I began reading medical books for an explanation. Everything continued to point to a gall bladder problem, but the doctor insisted that he could do no more to help me.

While I used those weeks to search for my own diagnosis, God used them to search my heart. At last I could see the silver web for myself. If I came out of this hospital alive, I resolved, I would not lose another minute, I would give my all to the Rainbow Garden.

One morning, my doctor called me for a consultation and, as we spoke, his daughter happened to drop in.

"Pani Professor!" she said, looking at me in surprise. She was one of my students. "Tatusiek, I had no idea you were treating my teacher!"

The doctor turned to me, astonished.

"Nor had I!" he said.

"Well, look after her well. We all love her!" the girl said cheerily, before heading out of the door.

Silence followed her departure.

"If I had only known, Pani," he said, "I would have authorised a second test for your gall bladder."

"A second test?"

"Sometimes gall bladder conditions fail to show up on the first one. There is another test that is often more thorough but," he shrugged, "it's more expensive. If I had only known you taught my daughter then of course . . ."

I understood him. I was not a Party member. I had not offered him any bribe. There had been no reason to waste such an expensive procedure on me. That was often the case in Poland's sad hospitals.

"I'm authorising the test today," he said, adding, as a kind of reprimand, "but you should have told me you taught my daughter!"

The test results confirmed severe problems with the gall bladder. After the operation, the surgeon came to my bedside. "I don't know why the diagnosis was left so long, Pani, but we found a terrible mess in there. You had one foot in the grave by the time you were brought to us."

As I recovered at home, I realised God had given me a second chance at life. "Forgive me, Lord," I begged. "I will go full-time into the children's work now, whatever happens to me!"

My sense of conviction was further confirmed as I watched television from my sickbed. Pope John Paul II was visiting his native land and the emotion in our country could have been cut with a knife.

One unforgettable moment, for me, came during a gathering in Warsaw.

After the Pope had spoken, a voice in the crowd suddenly broke out in a forbidden hymn asking God for Poland's freedom after its generations of suffering.

"Mamuska, listen!" I cried. As a rule, I only ever heard this song when she sang it, in a whisper, in our busy kitchen.

A second voice joined the first. Ten followed. Then a hundred were singing. Soon it was a thousand.

Mamuska joined in too, not caring who might hear her outside the window.

On television, the whole crowd was now singing. It was as though the decades of Communism dropped away in that moment and people reached out to embrace one another and weep together as their great cry went up to Heaven.

Pope John Paul II tried to address the crowd but, choked with emotion, he finally put his head into his hands and wept. Mamuska's beautiful voice continued beside me as I wept too.

Afterwards, the crowd burst spontaneously into Poland's national anthem. "Poland is still Polish as long as we are alive . . ." The song was written by freedom fighters during the years when Poland had been removed from the world map.

The Pope urged his countrymen to find courage in God now, as well. Although he spoke of many things that day, one struck me with special force: he urged Poles to take care of the spiritual life of the nation's children.

God was using this to spur me on.

I had been called to evangelise children and I had been caught in a silver web spun out of fear, loneliness and the need for success.

It was time to kill the spider and get back to work.

12

THE FOIL HOUSE

"I told you Pan Jezus has a sense of humour!" Mamuska was giggling, but praising God at the same time. Her combination of humour and faith had always been unique.

Perhaps the Lord Himself smiled too. Right after He freed me from the silver web, it so happened that my next assignment was to garden at the summer week held annually at Dziegielow, the very place at which I had created such a disturbance in my stormy childhood years.

There was a second reason Mamuska twinkled as well. Out of a constant stream of kids who found Pan Jezus that week, the very first had been a little girl named Ela. Her mother was none other than Marysia, the one who, as a teenager, had invited me to the camp where I myself found new life in Christ.

Why this of all places? Why this of all little girls? I did not want to read too much into it, but the two seemed extraordinary co-incidences. Perhaps God was showing me the pain of my own childhood when I had tried to live without Him? Perhaps He wanted to ratify my decision to help other children avoid that pain?

I began to travel as much as possible and saw many more children respond with the same enthusiasm as Ela and the others at Dziegielow.

In time, I was invited to the Great Green Carpet area which sweeps across the centre of the country. Its terrain is quite different from our mountain region in the south. Huge expanses of flat fields stretch as far as the eye can see. The earth here is fertile and the crops, in late spring, are such a lush green and bright gold they nearly blind the eye with their brilliance.

I showed the children a giant jigsaw puzzle from CEF called "The Man who was different". "If you would have your life different," I told them, "you must turn to the Man who was different. He died for your sin and He alone can give you a new start."

The completed picture showed Christ with arms out-stretched in welcome to all comers. The children gathered were, by and large, between the ages of six and twelve, but they quickly grasped the point.

Afterwards, a quiet hush settled over the group for a time of prayer. Then a lady said something to a little girl with round, brilliant blue eyes and a face like a doll.

It happened to be Mother's Day and all the children had brought flowers. For some reason, though, instead of taking her posy to her mother, "the Doll" brought it to me. I was just whispering that she should take it to her own mummy when, down the aisle, there was a stampede of little feet and all the other children followed suit.

When I tried again to redirect the children, the mothers laughingly brushed aside my protests. I ended up covered in bouquets of golden daffodils, red tulips and purple iris. I was covered in children, too; they were around my neck, sitting on my lap and snuggling against my shoulders.

"Aunty," said the Doll, "we would like you to move here and work in our church."

"Yes, Aunty!" "Would you?" "We want you to stay!" Little voices chorused their support. Why were they suggesting this? I did not quite understand. I had spoken to many groups of children in recent months and, while they had responded to the love of God, none had suggested I work full-time in their church.

"We have needed a children's worker for a long time," said one father. "Would you consider it, Pani?"

"But I couldn't, I'm sorry," I began. "I am working in the south of the country. I have many commitments there . . ."

The children persisted, brushing aside all my objections until I felt strangely nonplussed. It was quite impossible to say yes to them. Yet, for some reason, it was equally impossible to say no.

"I tell you what. How would you like me to take you on a summer camp?" I said, by way of compromise. As soon as the words were out, I could have bitten my tongue. How was I going to hold an illegal Christian camp? It could be dangerous and, moreover, I had no place, no money and no time.

"Yes, yes!" "When, Aunty?" "Where?" They clamoured about me.

"Perhaps in the mountains where I live? I'll let you know!" I heard myself say, still wishing I could have withdrawn my impetuous suggestion.

The children continued to chat with excitement as we walked out of the church.

"You shouldn't disturb this pani!" a stern-faced, well-dressed lady told them. "You mustn't ask her to come and work here when she's needed elsewhere." She smiled at me, but it was a brittle smile. Why did it look almost like a warning?

An older lady was much kinder. "You have become Mamuska to the boys and girls of our church, today," she whispered in a hoarse voice, coming close. "And something has happened to me too, Pani."

She spoke into my ear, a frail, bent woman. "I've been attending church for over eighty years. All that time I thought that turning up at this building was enough to make me a Christian. But now, I realise it wasn't. I was only a church-goer. Never till today did I understand what it was to have a personal relationship with Pan Jezus. This 'child' wants to thank you!"

She kissed me and hobbled away, leaving the children to crowd around for goodbye hugs.

I was encouraged by her words, but as I took the bus home the doubts about the camp returned. "What on earth made me promise a camp?" I asked the Lord. "Was it You? Or was it me?"

As if He did not know, I reminded Him of all the difficulties I would face. "If this really is Your idea, Lord, I need a sign, and quickly!" I finished.

At that, a friendly mountain woman boarded the bus and sat beside me. We chatted and, before the journey was over, I wondered if the Lord had sent me an angel. The woman was a Christian who had a large home in the Beskidy mountains. She would be delighted to offer it, free, for a Christian camp.

"Okay, Lord! I believe You! I will go ahead with the camp!" I said shamefacedly, as I continued my way home.

Shortly after, the church pastor phoned with further news. It concerned the old woman who had told me she had given her life to Pan Jezus. "It was just in time," said the pastor, his voice trembling. "She died yesterday."

I put down the phone, the seriousness of life and death overwhelming me. Admittedly, this woman was very old, but it remained true that one could never really know how needed a message may be in someone's life. It might be more important than I could ever guess to take the camp. I devoted the following weeks to preparation for it.

Summer was in full bloom when the children arrived, bubbling with excitement. Most had never been beyond their wide, flat plains before and everything was a discovery.

They gazed in wonder at the lines of green running across the Beskidy slopes, the dark conifers mingling with the brilliant new growth of birch and lime trees and the whole scene delicately framed with pink dog-roses.

Golden sunshine toasted us all that holiday, and with it came the sense that God Himself was bathing us in the warmth of His love. We swam in the upper reaches of the Vistula river and spoke of Pan Jezus, the Living Water. We sat on an ancient wooden fence which quickly collapsed under us, and said that none can sit on the fence regarding Pan Jezus. We lay on our backs amid mountain wild flowers and looked up at the bright sunshine created by the Light of Life. We stood in silent awe under the green canopy of the Secret Church and bowed our heads before the One for whom it was built.

I could not tell which of these children was already a Christian so I structured the lessons with the double application which Uncle Sam had taught: inviting children to come to Pan Jezus if they had not done so already and offering spiritual food for any who had.

To push them would have been a mistake. I waited for them to come to me if they wished to give their lives to Pan Jezus. The first to do so was a curly-haired girl called Maritka, the sister of the Doll. Although still of primary age, she was so intelligent that I had dubbed her "the Philosopher".

"Aunty, wake up!" she said, tugging at my sleeve at one o'clock one morning. "I have to talk to you. It's urgent!"

"What's the matter?" She looked so serious that I was worried.

"I want to give my life to Pan Jezus!"

"Well, kochana, but . . ." I said sleepily. "Pan Jezus wouldn't mind waiting till morning!" I ventured.

"No, Aunty, I can't sleep!" She pulled me out of bed and, awake at last, I went with her to the dining room.

"I have so much sin in my life that I want to ask Pan Jezus to forgive it now and let me start new life in Him." There were tears in her eyes.

Does a child understand the issue of sin? At Kilchzimmer, Uncle Sam had said that, often, children agonise over it, even to the point of sleeplessness. That had been true of my own childhood battle with the weeds. Now I was seeing the same truth at work in our little Philosopher.

"I couldn't let it go another night, Aunty! I want to make a new start with Pan Jezus."

With her head on my shoulder, she prayed until, peaceful at last, she went back to bed.

I planned to sleep in next morning, but at six I found myself woken a second time.

This time it was Moniczka, the little Doll. She slept in a separate room from Maritka so she had no idea of her sister's midnight visit.

"Aunty. Wake up! I really need to talk to you!"

"You too?" I rubbed the sleep from my eyes.

"Yes, Aunty, and it must be now!" It was like a replay of the midnight episode.

She sat facing me, legs swinging either side of my lap, and she tugged at my hair as she spoke.

"Aunty, I get bad-tempered and I sometimes don't tell the truth and I am unkind some days and . . ." She had such a long list of sins that we could have sat there all day.

"Pan Jezus knows all about them," I told her. "The important thing is that you want to start anew."

"So now may I accept Pan Jezus as my Saviour?" she said, blue eyes looking straight into mine.

After she had scampered away, I stayed a moment, looking out of the window as the first rays of dawn painted the tips of the mountain slopes in pink and gold.

"Is there any joy as great as this?" the Lord seemed to ask me. "Are you sorry you gave up your teaching job?"

"No, Lord," I whispered back. Without doubt, He had called me to work in the Garden. Was He also calling me to leave the south of Poland and work full-time with these little ones?

More whispered chats followed. Grazynka, a black-haired, blue-eyed girl, came to pray. Renatka, an olive-skinned girl with brown plaits, did too. I sat with Ewa, a little one with a face like an angel, and her brother Marius, whom we nicknamed Falkonetti because he was as untamed as the bird. Reniusz, a round-faced boy with freckles, came too, requesting that he give his life to Christ the day after "because it's my birthday tomorrow and I want to remember this decision my whole life long". Tomek, the organist's son, said nothing openly, but his brown eyes spoke volumes. Each was different. Each had his or her own personality. Each, though, was certain of the need to be adopted by God.

As well as lessons outdoors, I gave them formal teaching indoors too. They faced the same childhood struggle I had known, torn between the dogs and the wolves, already under pressure to become as beets or, at least, radishes. In our atheistic regime, they would meet opposition to their faith. "Give them solid food, don't just entertain!" Uncle Sam had warned us. Now that most, if not all of them, had given their lives to the Lord, I could see that they came at that food with the appetite of a hungry man. I was not just feeding dead bodies.

They listened eagerly to stories of faith, among them that of the child in the New Testament who brought the Lord his lunch of loaves and fishes in order to feed five thousand people.

If I was giving the theory, the Lord Himself gave them practical application of our lessons. From the start, both the children and their parents had known money was tight, and as we went on our supplies started to run out. We needed to ask Him for loaves and fishes enough to feed us too.

"Let's ask Pan Jezus for tomorrow's food!" I told the children one night as we gathered, in pyjamas and slippers, for evening prayers. Next morning, we found eggs and fresh bread rolls waiting on our doorstep. The children were excited. "He answered today's prayer, Aunty. What shall we pray for tomorrow?"

The food kept coming. Next time, it was fruit. Another time, it was a huge piece of meat. Once, we were given the left-overs from a wedding feast and dined like kings on venison, chicken and beef. When that food ran out, the sisters at Dziegielow handed us a gift of cash and with it we bought more. Never once did the Lord of the loaves and fishes allow us to go hungry.

Not only did the children pray for food, they asked God for His protection, too. Since ours was an unregistered camp, any public activity could put us at risk; walking in the mountains, swimming in the river or simple sightseeing. The children prayed and God answered. Neither SB nor milicja spotted us.

By the end of camp, they had become little prayer warriors and, during our final outing, I found myself challenged by their faith.

Together, we took a chairlift up to Czantoria, the tallest mountain in our region. The ride carried us through the forest branches over a carpet of ferns and wild raspberries. The children revelled in it, their little voices echoing in song, up and down the mountain, as they praised the Creator in whom they had found new life.

At the top, I suddenly realised the obvious. Behind us lay Czechoslovakia. In front of us was Poland. This was the very scene I had been sent in Switzerland, when trying to decide whether I would marry Alistair or come home to the Rainbow Garden. How grateful I was that the Lord had returned me to the right side of the mountain.

In front of us, the gold and green fields of Poland stretched as far as the eye could see. The gleaming Vistula river ran from its nearby source to Krakow, on to Warsaw until, at Gdansk, it flowed into the sea. If only the message of salvation could flow in similar fashion to children throughout the entire land, I thought.

From their comments, our little campers could almost have been thinking the same way.

"You know what, Aunty?" they said, crunching into the crisp skin of barbecued sausages. "Next year, we'll have another camp and we'll have twice as many children."

"And the year after that, twice as many again!" another said confidently.

"So when are you coming to live with us?" Falkonetti concluded. I did not know quite how to answer him. Czantoria seemed to be turning into a place of confrontation for me.

"I still don't see how I could!" I began. "For one thing, I don't have anywhere to live."

"So we'll pray and Pan Jezus will find you a place." The others had crowded around to hear the conversation.

"And I don't have anyone to look after my Mamuska. Her health is not strong! She needs me to help her around the house," I continued.

"We'll ask Pan Jezus to find her a special friend!"

I knew I had fallen in love with these children, but I could see no way I could make the situation work. "I'm afraid it still looks impossible," I sighed.

"Aunty, it is you who taught us that 'what is impossible with men is possible with God'," they replied, confidently. I had no answer to that.

When we parted, they promised that they would pray regularly for me. They meant it. No adult supervised them, but after the camp they met faithfully in little prayer huddles, asking Pan Jezus about my two questions.

On my return, I found the first answer waiting. Mamuska told me joyfully about Ewa, a new friend. Ewa's faith was one of few words, but untold acts of loving, selfless care for others. She came from the mountains and, used to felling trees and harvesting crops, had already proved of wonderful support whenever Mamuska needed help. In the short time I had been away, she had broken up a delivery of coal, cut wood and knitted warm socks for Mamuska's arthritic feet. Moreover, Ewa, like Mamuska, was a widow and the two understood one another.

God had answered my first question and He dealt with the second almost as quickly. The pastor of the church rang to tell me that an apartment had been made available for my use. It would need renovation, but, he said with a smile in his voice, the children wanted me to know they would help.

During the days and nights that followed, my mind was constantly tossing over the decision. One night I had a dream from which I awoke in fright. I was trying to help a boy and a girl who were battling for their lives, caught in a patch of quicksand. "Help us!" they shouted. I grabbed a branch and extended it to them, but they continued to sink. "Help us!" they shouted again. "Don't leave us. We need you!"

I sat up in bed, perspiring. The situation was directly parallel to that of the camp children. They were begging me for help. How could I even contemplate ignoring their cry?

"Was that just an expression of my fear or was it of You?" I asked the Lord afterwards.

The answer, I believed, came almost immediately. My Bible reading brought me to Isaiah 6:8: "Then I heard the voice of the Lord saying, 'Whom shall I send? And who will go for us?' And I said, 'Here am I. Send me!'"

I could fight God no more. I accepted the position.

The more I prayed about the move, the more I could understand why God was leading me there. In this central, fertile region of Poland, it is common to see greenhouses or as we Poles call them "foil houses", in which delicate seedlings are cultivated before transplanting. In a way, devoting myself to this group of children would be like working in a foil house from which, later, I would be able to take ideas for wider work in the Rainbow Garden.

In my final weeks before moving, however, friends saw the situation differently. "You're crazy, Jasia!" they told me. "It's such an unstable time in Poland. You'll be in trouble!" "How will you support yourself?" "You won't have any formal employment registration. The government will investigate you." "Stick to Sunday School teaching only. You'll never get away with your other ideas for children's work! This is a Communist country!"

Instead of deterring me, their comments spurred me on. I was certain, even as Uncle Jozef had been, that the Rainbow Garden could be planted in Poland. Clearly, though, it had to be tried before others would be convinced.

One friend who did not laugh at the idea was a young Englishman who visited Poland that year.

He had come to speak to students and I had happily accepted when a Polish friend brought him to our home to ask if I would interpret for him. Communism taught young people that Christianity had nothing to offer intellectuals and, I believed, this kind of students' work was greatly needed.

The young man's name was David. He was a college instructor in mathematics and, as it happened, a Christian of Jewish origin.

He told me he was planning to visit Auschwitz the day after we met and I was taken by surprise, therefore, when he reappeared on my doorstep the following afternoon.

"You're not going to Auschwitz?" I asked, in surprise.

"Oh, I've already been, but there was still a little time left this afternoon and I missed you . . . uh, that is . . ." he gave a gentle shrug, "I missed being here in your home. It has such a welcoming atmosphere."

I glanced at him, astonished. We had only just met. How could he possibly miss me?

"But I won't come in if I'm disturbing you?" he added, politely.

"No, no, you're welcome, of course!" Still confused, I opened the door, though my heart was beating in rather an odd way.

We spent a few hours chatting and I definitely found him likeable. David had ginger hair, matching beard, sensitive blue eyes and a warm, relaxed smile. By the time he left, I felt quite at home with him.

The next day, we went together to the campsite and I escorted him to the house in which accommodation had been arranged.

"We've been expecting you," the hostess said kindly, leading us up a pine-wood staircase. David and I spoke in English and when we reached the top of the staircase, she took me aside.

"Forgive me," she said in Polish. "We prepared the room for Pan David only. I hadn't realised he was bringing his wife."

I blushed, always my weakness, and David's blue eyes caught it.

"What did she say?" he asked.

"Nothing!"

"Tell me!" he said, with a persuasive grin.

"She thought, at first, we were married," I mumbled, awkwardly.

"Did she?" He smiled and his eyes held mine with an expression that took my breath away.

As I translated for David, I came to like him more and more. He had a firm faith, a good intellect and a deep desire for worship. He sang for the students in a gentle, pleasant voice and had a love for the Lord which was nearly tangible.

In the afternoons, he had no lectures scheduled and the two of us slipped easily into the habit of using them for walks in the mountains. David enjoyed nature and he loved Poland, to my surprise. We walked past the wooden mountain cottages and talked about the richness of Polish culture and the greyness of the System. We sat under pine trees discussing Polish history and the way the country had, for generations, been between the hammer and the anvil of Russia and Germany. We looked across country from the tops of mountains and I spoke of my vision, of the children, of the longing to see Poland's new generations brought to Christ. It was very easy to talk to David.

It was easy to pray and read the Word with him too. David opened the Psalms for me in a way I had not seen before, showing me the music written by "my namesake", as he called the Psalmist. "Our lives need to be like music too, lived in perfect harmony with the Lord," he said, often breaking into quiet song as we sat on the mountain slopes together.

In time, it seemed we found it increasingly harder to part. When the evening lecture was over, we would meander towards my bus stop and, although neither of us spoke of it, always managed to arrive a little late. There was an hour's wait between buses, so we would walk and talk again, only to miss the next one too as a rule. Most nights, I caught the last bus available.

Was I falling in love, I asked myself as I bumped my way home in the dark? I wasn't sure. The experience with Alistair had been too painful for me to risk the same kind of problem again.

David picked this up. One afternoon, he and I were walking under shimmering birch trees, the sun turning their delicate leaves and making them look as if they were nervous, I thought.

"Nervous?" he asked, as I shared my thoughts aloud. "What makes you say that?"

"Oh I don't know. Birch trees are my favourite, but somehow they always remind me of frightened young brides." The words were out before I could stop them. I could have kicked myself for my clumsiness.

David bent to pluck a daisy and, lingering over it a moment, kissed the flower gently before handing it to me. "Does something make you afraid to be a bride, Jasia?" he said, his expression tender. I twisted the white flower in the golden sunlight and looked down into the patchwork fields of the valley. He gave me time to answer.

"I think I want to tell you," I said at last.

We sat together and I told him all about Alistair and the agony of the final decision. I spoke of Marcin as well. Wujek Morcinek used to say that you tell the whole of your life story to one person only. In David, I found that person. I was so much at ease with him that, in the end, it was easy to confess the reason for my fear.

"I have been called to work with Polish children and I know I couldn't contemplate a relationship in which I would be asked to leave my country. My call is here," I said.

I read him Isaiah 61:1,2, two verses which had convinced me I was on track.

"These words were spoken of the Messiah, but aren't they true of us too when we take His love to others? 'The Spirit of the Sovereign Lord is on me, because the Lord has anointed me to preach good news to the poor. He has sent me to bind up the broken-hearted . . .' Many of Poland's children are poor and broken-hearted. They need Him and I could never leave them."

His ginger beard brushed my cheek. "I promise, Jasia, I would never ask you to leave Poland. Besides, I love it too." He took a deep breath of the mountain air as we gazed over the fields of green and gold. "I can breathe much better here than in England."

"Breathe?" Most foreigners made no secret of the fact that they found our regime stifling.

"Yes, breathe, spiritually speaking, because there is so much more hunger for God in Poland than in England. The System has left your people empty in more senses than one. I would like to work here and help meet that need among Poland's students."

We talked about the state of the nation. During that very August of 1980, massive shipyard strikes had broken out in Gdansk, unlike any the country had known before. Community support had been so great that food and clothing had been passed over the fences to the strikers as they slept on the premises. The unrest had spread to other factories across the country, including the giant steelworks at Nowa Huta, the "monument to Socialist Man" near Krakow.

David was so well versed in Polish affairs that he even offered a political joke.

"Do you know who has the greatest car in Poland?" he asked, grinning. "Gierek! His steering wheel is in Moscow, his driving seat is in Warsaw and his brakes are in Gdansk."

Everywhere, people were sensing that the brakes in Gdansk were truly slowing the vehicle of Poland. Change was in the air. We knew it, and the rest of the world did too. The moustache and voice of Lech Walesa had quickly become familiar in households all over the globe as he urged Polish workers to stand in solidarity with one another. At the end of the month, just before David was to leave, Walesa announced the establishment of an independent trade union. Gierek had a heart attack several days later and was forced into retirement.

"But I don't believe any political change, alone, can meet Poland's deepest need," David said. "Only the Lord can do that."

He prayed quietly for Poland and, afterwards, I looked into his blue eyes with gratitude. I was beginning to realise that we had a depth of unity I had never experienced in any other relationship. "I thought I loved Marcin and I thought I loved Alistair too," I told him in the end. "But now that I have met you, I wonder if I truly loved either."

His gentle hand ran through my hair and he looked at me with the expression I found so eloquent.

"I loved you from the first day I met you," he said. "That's why I had to come back to your home on the second afternoon. I've never felt this way about any other girl."

When the time came for his departure, the two of us could look honestly into the future.

"Separation is always a good test," he said. "We English say, 'Out of sight, out of mind' if a relationship is not to last. You and I will see if that is the case with us, although," he reached out to hold me close, "I can tell you now there is no chance of that happening on my part!"

He placed an envelope into my hand and, despite my protestations, insisted I keep it. "It's a little money for the

Rainbow Garden," he said. "When you begin work in your Foil House, it will help you set up your apartment and it will, I hope, do something else as well."

He looked at me in silence for a few seconds and, just for a moment, I thought I glimpsed tears in his eyes.

"Poland is at an unprecedented point in its history. We can't predict what will happen next. Nor do we know what the SB will do if they discover your work with the children. You could find yourself in the lions' den, my Jasia. I would like the things you buy with this money to remind you that my prayers will be with you, whatever you face."

When he left, I found myself aglow with love and it seemed impossible for it not to touch all whose paths crossed mine. David and I had spoken of my adoption and the *za swe* syndrome and, after he had gone, I knew there was one long-overdue change I needed to make. For the first time ever, I felt I could offer love to the person whom I had avoided all my life, Aunt Mila.

Before I left for the Foil House, I saw her in the town and went out of my way to speak to her. She was incredulous. To my shame, I had always crossed the street in the past and pretended I had not seen her.

"Jasia! How are you? How is your work?" she began tentatively, but soon a host of questions tumbled out on both sides.

We spoke at length on the street together and, when we parted, I knew a substantial first step had been made in the healing process. In the future, I thought happily, we could develop a relationship that would help both of us deal with the past.

I had a deeper peace than I had known for a long time when, at last, I left for the Foil House.

My arrival there was unforgettable. As soon as the children knew I had come, they began to appear at my doorstep and, true to their promise, did all in their power to furnish "our second home", as they called my apartment.

They made a whimsical picture. A knock at the door revealed a boy balancing a chair much too large for him, brought from his grandmother's attic. Another knock came from an excited group, struggling with different parts of a wardrobe. A third knock brought a young girl carrying a lamp "with just one piece missing, Aunty". The stream of children went on and on. When they saw I did not have a dining table, they searched until they found a second-hand one, extendable "because then you'll be able to have us all to dinner". A shy little poppet arrived with a fragile hall-stand, "just big enough for Bible verses so all your visitors can take one". They were full of ideas. Watching them come and go, I could only love them the more.

We painted the place in bright colours and, as with my room in Silesia, filled it with books and pictures of children. David's money bought everything else I needed: a bed, cutlery, crockery, saucepans, fabric for curtains and a mat for the floor. His presence was all about me.

This gave me great comfort when, soon after my arrival, I discovered I was to have an opponent in the Foil House.

One morning, the pastor welcomed me to the church office with pink roses and good news. The church committee had voted on my stay and the majority were in support of it. He beamed with delight and so did a lady who had come to do some occasional book-keeping for him.

When the pastor left, however, her smile went with him.

"The pastor said the majority were in support of your position, Pani. The vote was not unanimous!" she began, ominously. I remembered this lady now. She was the one who had spoken so tersely at the end of the Mother's Day service. There was a cultured air to her bearing, but, beneath her expensive coiffure, she wore a sour expression that seemed to indicate she had found life a bitter disappointment.

"I did not agree with the idea," she scowled. Her haughty eyes held mine in a glare until the pastor returned, whereupon her winning smile reappeared once more.

"Lord, this woman is a chameleon!" I thought. It seemed she could change shape or colour according to the situation.

"Believe me, if I were you I would leave . . ." she said

intimidatingly, when the pastor was safely out of earshot again. "If you stay, you will be sorry!"

My legs quivered as I left the office. I tried to tell myself this woman was not to be taken seriously yet I knew she held an authoritative position in the community. She probably had the power to get what she wanted.

"But You told me to come here, Lord!" I whispered as I climbed the stone steps back to my apartment. "How can I leave? I have only just begun!"

13

INVISIBLE HATS

"This was no accident, Pani!"

An electrician had been called when the power in my apartment failed.

"What do you mean?" I said, stunned.

"Your electricity did not fail. It was deliberately cut!" he answered. "Someone seems to be out to make your life miserable!"

I listened to him, my mind whirling. Was this the first of the Chameleon's tricks?

"I know why she is against you," Ala, our brown-eyed organist, later told me. She lived downstairs and offered me tea in her kitchen. Little Tomek brought me a piece of cake, his dark eyes concerned.

"The pastor is not married and that old lady has set her heart on seeing her god-daughter become his bride. You're a threat!"

"Me? Why?"

"You're not married either!"

"But that's ridiculous. I'm not interested in the pastor. I am already involved with somebody else!" I protested.

I told Ala about David, although normally I spoke little about our relationship with others. In those months, David was very active distributing Christian literature and I could have jeopardised the project if I had engendered too much interest in him.

"I think that old lady is a bit eccentric!" I concluded as I stood to leave.

"She is!" said Ala tapping her forehead knowingly. "Hers is a psychotic case. But don't let her get you down, Jasia. If she wants to get rid of you, she'll have to do so over my dead body!"

"Be strong and courageous. Do not be afraid or terrified because of them . . ." Mamuska quoted in a letter. "For the Lord your God goes with you; He will never leave you nor forsake you" (Deuteronomy 31:6).

It was not only I who needed such verses. The children needed them too as they began meeting opposition to their faith at school. Olive-skinned Renatka had become a Christian at camp and loved the songs we had sung in the mountains. One of them, a Jewish Christian song I had learned from Aunty Alice, was her favourite. When her school held a competition for international music, she proudly performed it and won the contest. Afterwards, she was invited on to the stage to explain its meaning.

"It's Jewish and it talks about Pan Jezus as my Saviour and Rock," she declared confidently.

A ripple of disapproval ran through the staff, though nobody said anything overtly. On her way home, however, Renatka was waylaid by a group of older boys opposed to such Christian zeal. She ended up in hospital, bruised, feverish and so badly beaten that her two front teeth were missing.

"I am so sorry that you have suffered like this," I said, at her bedside.

"Don't be sorry, Aunty. Pan Jezus suffered far more than I did so I don't mind," she lisped through the gap where her teeth had been.

"But you've lost your two front teeth, kochana!" I said, stroking her dark hair.

She patted my hand. I was not sure who was comforting whom in this visit. "Aunty, when I was little, I lost my baby teeth and I wasn't afraid. So why should I be afraid now that I have lost some grown-up teeth?"

The more the children grew in faith, the angrier the Chameleon became. She was constantly on the lookout for an opportunity to attack and, when the requirement for coupons was widened in our country's beleaguered economy, she saw her chance.

"You have no coupons and you won't get any, Pani," she said with a little smile. "How do you plan to live? By faith?"

She had a valid point. Although my appointment had the internal agreement of the church committee, it did not have formal government sanction. No salary was possible for my position, but since the Chameleon was the one person who could have helped me obtain regular coupons, the parents had counted on her giving me support.

When she refused, I too wondered how I would survive. I could teach a few hours of English, privately, each week, but that brought only a few zlotys and no coupons.

Without coupons, I was not eligible for coal, sugar, flour, meat, cheese, rice, oats or butter.

There were two basics, however, which were never rationed, eggs and potatoes. They, together with flour Ala gave me, enabled me to make the potato pancakes which are the traditional fare of our mountains. These became my staple.

In addition, our shops managed to stock supplies of food items produced in the local area. There were two specialities at the time. They made a Polish version of Worcestershire sauce which, if added to water, gave me something like soup. They also manufactured jelly crystals and these I used for the children's visits. In those days of rationing, children were permitted just one bar of chocolate per month and anything sweet was a treat.

I thus settled into a nightly routine of soup or pancakes. It was not the best-balanced diet, but it enabled me to keep the Rainbow Garden going and that was all I cared about.

The more I saw of the Chameleon's opposition to the work, the more convinced I was that the children needed to learn independence in their Christian walk. If she won, I could be pulled out of the Foil House any day.

Every Saturday, the children and I met not only for our Good News Club, but afterwards for informal outings as well. The woodland of a nearby park was a favourite venue. In the shortening days of autumn, we would sit on a carpet of fallen leaves, scattering nuts for the squirrels to store away for winter.

One afternoon, we sat together watching a squirrel scamper up the trunk of an oak tree and leap skilfully from branch to branch across the golden roof of the park. More squirrels began to approach us for nuts and a shower of leaves, in rust, orange and red, fell with their busy movement.

God's creation could, I believed, always point back to truth about the Creator.

"They have learned to fend for themselves!" I told the children. "God wants us to do that too. Life may bring winter for you some time and you may need to manage for yourselves if ever that happens."

"What do you mean?" Tomek asked, quickly. Being Ala's son, he had a full picture of the problems I had with the Chameleon. The others crowded closer.

"Well, right now I can help you find spiritual food as we study about the Lord together, but you may not always have an Aunty to teach you. You may need to feed on your own one day."

"But how would we manage without you?" Falkonetti protested. He had, true to his name, been chasing animals all over the park, but concern now quietened him.

"The Word of God is enough!" I replied. "You all have a Bible at home, don't you?"

"Yes, but it's on the shelf!" someone protested.

"Then you need to get it off the shelf!" I answered. "It must become your daily food. God has put in it everything you'll need, no matter how hard a winter you may face."

Although I would never let on to them, I had a further reason for suggesting this. I knew that some of these little ones faced problems at home and I prayed that, once they understood God's Word in sufficient depth, they could pass it on to their families as well.

"But we've never used the Bible like that in our house!" some persisted.

"Then I have a story for you!" I said and recounted

Goo-Goo's parable of the man going to America. "If you leave your Bible on the shelf, you'll miss out on all the wonderful food it contains, just as the man missed out on the ship's smorgasbord!"

They became motivated. Together, we scanned every book of the Bible so that no part of it would be a mystery to them. We studied background historical material for use at school when they met mockery for their faith. They memorised God's Word and, in time, could confidently search it for themselves in order to find answers to their questions. Their faith deepened and their knowledge grew.

It was not mere head knowledge either. It brought behavioural changes. The most evident was in Falkonetti.

One meeting, I noticed he was doing no fighting or kicking or shouting. He sat, listening, like a lamb.

"Are you sick today?" I asked, surprised.

"No," he replied.

"But you're not yourself!" I persisted.

"That's because I'm different now!" he said, disarmingly.

"Why?"

"Last week, Aunty, when you talked about Pan Jezus's promises, there was a rainbow outside the window. I know that rainbows are pictures of God's promises so I decided to make Him a promise too. I am His child now and I'm not the same boy any more." As I listened to him, I smiled inwardly. The Rainbow Garden was indeed a good name for this work. Never again did we have a problem with Falkonetti's behaviour.

David was elated at each indication of growth in the Rainbow Garden. He was sure now that our future lay together. So was I. He had never really needed to ask whether we would marry. Neither of us could imagine life without the other.

"I have found a way I can move here legally," he told me, one visit, his blue eyes shining eagerly under his ginger hair. "I have been given approval to teach English at a university and, as soon as I have learned Polish, I can teach Mathematics there as well. Our future is coming together, Jasia!"

It seemed, indeed, that God had given us matching roles.

My work would be with children, and his with young people.

Our mutual sense of calling included another facet too. We were both certain that Jewish people would be included among those we served and, that trip, we visited an old Jewish man in Warsaw. He was one of only a few thousand Jews who had stayed in Poland after the exodus in 1968.

"Adonai Roi", David sang an age-old Jewish song, his ginger hair tucked under the traditional *kippah*, which he loved. He kept his voice quiet for the old man's safety.

The yellow glow of candlelight picked up the light of their eyes as the two sang traditional songs. When they had finished, David sang a newer Jewish song written by friends who called themselves Messianic Jews. This old man did not believe Christ to be the Messiah, but David's gentle spirit touched him and he listened as David sang of God's peace: "Hevenu Shalom Alechem". He also allowed David to read the description of the Suffering Servant in Isaiah, chapter 53. "He was despised and rejected by men, a man of sorrows, acquainted with grief." As the old man listened, tears trickled down his cheeks and he and David bent together in prayer. I watched the scene and wished, with a pang, that Uncle Jozef, another Messianic Jew, were still alive. How greatly he and David would have loved one another.

At the close of the evening, the old man called the other members of his family to meet us. His daughter and her husband brought three toddlers into the candlelit room and I hugged each of these little ones in turn. Most Jewish children had been taken to Israel now, and I always prayed for the chance to meet any who remained. David enjoyed them too. He picked up the baby and, holding him close, looked at me with an expression that was understood by everyone in the room.

"'Sons are a heritage from the Lord,'" David said, quoting Psalm 127 with a twinkle. "'Blessed is the man whose quiver is *full* of them!'" Everybody smiled and I didn't know where to look. He and I planned to have at least ten children, but in that moment I found it hard to meet his loving, amused gaze.

"Amen!" roared the old man, laughing. "May you have many children and may they be blessed by the Lord. *Mazel tov!*"

"Sometimes I think that happiness like this could come only in a dream," I told David later. "It doesn't seem possible it's happening to me!"

We had left the Jewish family and were strolling in Warsaw's Old City, one of my favourite places in Poland. Although this area was fully demolished by Hitler, the Polish people painstakingly re-created its renaissance and baroque architecture according to old Italian paintings of the square. "The city that would not die", as it was called, thus came back to life in all its traditional pastels: peach, cream, beige, dusty pink, powder blue. Statues were resculptured and set in the niches where their look-alikes had stood for centuries. Frescoes reappeared on the artistic façades. Artistic signs were rehung.

We climbed into a horse-drawn carriage and took a ride past the buildings, their historic lines silhouetted against the night sky. Moonlight highlighted the gold in the frescoes and the brass of the polished signs and doorknobs. David loved such places as much as I did. Somehow, God seemed to have given us both the same spirit.

"What we have found is no dream, Jasia," he said in his confident way. "All my life, I prayed for you, without knowing your name, nor the country from which you would come. Now, at last, I have found you and," he stopped to lift my face into the moonlight, "I'll never let you go. This love comes only once in a lifetime."

When David kissed me, it was unlike anything I had experienced before. Some men took for themselves in such moments, but David wanted only, ever, to give. As his arms surrounded me, I looked up into his caring face and felt as though I had stepped into a film with a fairytale ending. There was something so royal about this man that I could almost have been marrying a prince.

Long after he left, David's presence always lingered with me and his letters, too, helped keep him close. In them, he often quoted from the Psalms and I, inspired by his insights, began to draw great comfort from them in my own reading.

David, like Uncle Jozef, was convinced that the more the work grew, the more Satan would attack it.

Psalm 18 was a favourite. "In my distress, I called to the Lord; I cried to my God for help . . . He rescued me from my powerful enemy, from my foes, who were too strong for me" (verses 6 and 17). Reading both the Psalms and his letters, I sensed a kind of double support. It was as though I was living in the fellowship of two Davids: mine and the Psalmist.

The Rainbow Garden continued to grow in the months that followed. The kids remained enthusiasm itself and allowed nothing to keep them from the club or lessons. Even when they were ill, they found a way to turn up. Their love for Pan Jezus deepened, moreover, and soon they were planting the seeds of the Garden in their own homes.

Maritka and Moniczka, the Philosopher and the Doll who had woken me at camp, were so changed that their father was astounded. In time, he asked them questions.

"So we explained how we found Pan Jezus as our Saviour," said the Doll. Her great blue eyes seemed to fill at least half of her face, as they peeped through delicate wisps of hair on her forehead.

"But, Aunty, we don't know if we said it properly, so we want you to talk to him and make sure."

I met her father for the requested talk, but found myself redundant.

"I had to change when I saw what happened to my daughters," he told me. "They were living the truth and I wanted it for myself."

Another little boy became so changed that his parents took him to a doctor for a check-up.

"What did you think was the matter?" I asked.

"He was difficult before, but now he is so easy to live with that we didn't recognise him," they grinned. "We like the change, though. We're not complaining!"

A third father told me he had come out of alcoholism when he saw his children's changed lives. They had introduced him to the Lord as well.

Soon the parents came to me with a new request. As well

as meetings for children, could we hold meetings which they could attend too?

The Garden was growing, but the more it spread, the more the Chameleon dropped hints. Without registration papers, she repeatedly commented, didn't I expect to be regarded with suspicion by the authorities?

One morning, there was a knock, early, at my door.

"Who is it?" I called.

"Milicja! Open the door!" said a man's voice.

"Milicja? But why . . .?" My heart pounded.

"We want to ask you a few questions, Pani."

"Of course," I said. What else do you say to police? "But I'm dirty. I've just been crushing coal." A few of the parents had shared their rations of coal with me and I looked like a chimney sweep after working with it.

"Can I clean myself up?" I asked. I had filled the bath to do a wash, though clearly there was no time for that now.

"We'll wait." The answer was civil, but barely so.

I took a deep breath and looked quickly around the room. I had just a few moments to hide anything they should not see. But what? My mind went blank and I ran around the flat like a chicken without its head.

The most dangerous item was a Polish translation of an English article concerning Jewish people. It was sitting in the typewriter on my desk and could not have been more obvious. Had I been thinking clearly, I would have hidden the paper away. As it was, I left it there and, going into the bathroom, threw into the water a few items that needed washing. Fear had rendered me senseless. I opened the door.

"Come in," I said, smoothing my dress with blackened hands. In the flurry, I had forgotten about washing them too.

Three uniformed men immediately began to search the place.

They made straight for the desk and I suddenly saw the forbidden Jewish work in the typewriter. Whatever had I been thinking of, leaving it there?

"He rescued me from my powerful enemy . . ." the Psalmist had said. I hung on to that verse now as I realised my stupidity. "I'm sorry, Lord. Only a miracle will save the day now," I prayed.

These men were well trained. They began to pull down the books from my shelves, shaking or thumbing through each one to see if any papers were secreted inside. After checking, they dumped the books in a careless pile on my desk until there was such a mountain of volumes that the typewriter was completely buried beneath them.

I watched in amazement. They were so busy searching for the hidden that they had missed the obvious. None of the men had even looked at the paper in the typewriter, but all of them assiduously checked every page of the books on the shelf.

"Well, Pani, nothing seems to have been hidden here," said the leader when the shelves were quite empty. "We can return the books now."

"Oh, no thank you!" I said quickly. "I keep those books in special order, each in its own category. I'll return them later."

"As you like, Pani," the leader shrugged and directed his men towards the rest of the flat. The bathroom was the last place they searched.

I went with them into the room and watched as they poked through the washing in the bath.

Only then did I notice that amid the soaking clothes I had placed my best top-coat and a pair of leather shoes. I stared at them in disbelief. I did not remember putting them there.

"Interesting washing, Pani," one of the men said, pulling out a shoe. He checked it, suspecting it might contain hidden material. With such a strange assortment of items in the water, I could not blame him. I could only suppose that panic had driven me to place this ridiculous "washing" in the bath.

At last they left and I sat quivering on the floor, trying to piece it all together. Finally, after a good, long cry, the whole scenario made sense.

Yes, emotion had made me irrational when I realised the milicja were at the door. If I had thought clearly, I would, without doubt, have pulled the Jewish papers from the typewriter and hidden them in the "safety" of the books.

Had I done that, however, I would have played right into their hands and probably be undergoing questioning at the police station right now. God had spared me from my own wisdom and replaced it with His.

"He rescued me from my powerful enemy . . ." The words had proved true, I realised gratefully. Who, though, had sent my visitors? Was this the kind of thing the Chameleon had meant when she said I would be sorry if I stayed?

If so, it would not have been difficult for her to motivate their interest in me. She would have needed only to mention my lack of formal documents and the authorities, already nervous at this sensitive time in our country's history, would have wanted to investigate.

The government was becoming increasingly disturbed by the process of *odnowa*, the renewal of Socialism which was under way, and the SB was on full alert. Poland was heading along an unchartered course and the Party was desperate to ensure it retained control.

Its nervousness had grown with each passing month. October had seen Walesa swear the oath of Kosciusko, the Polish hero who led the resistance against Poland's aggressors at the end of the eighteenth century: "I will never abandon my country. I will serve it till the day I die." In November, a huge crowd in Warsaw gathered for a service to honour the men who were massacred in Katyn Forest. In December, the government had been forced to allow the erection of a monument, in Gdansk, commemorating those martyred in the 1970 riots.

All over the nation, there was a new tune on everybody's lips, a Solidarity song with a moving melody. "So that Poland may be Poland!" said the words, echoing the heartcry of Polish people down through the centuries.

Times remained hard, though, and many whispered that the government deliberately witheld supplies of goods from the shops in order to force a confrontation with Solidarity. I did my best to fool Mamuska that my diet and health were not suffering, but her bright eyes missed nothing. "You look half-starved," she stated, on my next visit home.

Together with her friend, Ewa, she had prepared special food for my arrival.

"I'm sorry the meat is not better, though," Mamuska said with a mischievous wink, "but the sausages got married again this week."

"They what?" I asked.

"Got married, kochana!" she shrugged. "The butcher always offers me new varieties of sausages for which I must pay higher prices but, when we eat them, we find they're just the same as last month's. Only the name has been changed. So, you see, they get married!"

Mamuska giggled and Ewa's strong features crinkled with laughter too. "Oh politics!" she said, putting a weary hand through her grey hair. "What are we to think? Ever since Solidarity's come about, I've seen the Moskal in the street telling everybody how he never wanted to be a Communist at all and that now he's glad he can live by his true convictions. Iwonka's saying the same thing. So is your Hippo! Do you suppose they just change hats with the weather?"

She served a special desert I had not seen before. "We call it crisis cake, Jasia! Everybody's making it now!" she explained, blue eyes twinkling. "The recipe is easy. You first steal two eggs and then add whatever you have in the house!" I giggled. Jokes about eggs were common, these days, when they were in such short supply. Crisis cake was no joke, however. It was a well-named product of the times. As a rule, Polish cakes require rich ingredients, but crisis cake had been simplified to utilise whatever ingredients Polish shoppers could find in the stores.

The country and the economy continued to teeter in those difficult months of 1981. Some placed hope in another Polish politician, our new prime minister, General Jaruzelski, seen almost always in dark glasses, sitting very straight in his seat of power. However, there was increasing unrest in the Party as hard-line Communists became nervous at the concessions being won by Solidarity. Their worry was not only national, but personal too. If Solidarity, now ten million strong, brought too many changes, their quality of life would suffer. Money and privileges were already being taken from some. Corruption was being exposed in others.

It was at this time that tragedy struck at the heart of Poland's people. We watched, horrified, at the assassination attempt made on the Pope. People wept and tongues wagged. "Moscow's behind it," they said, in whispers loud enough for many to hear. "The Russians are nervous about the changes in Poland. They are afraid the rest of Europe may follow and they think our Karol Wojtyla is too powerful."

Only a little time passed before Poles were to grieve a second time when Cardinal Wyszynski, the leader of the Roman Catholic Church, who had been loved and heeded for decades, died of cancer. The nation mourned.

People said that, of the three Ws, Wyszynski, Walesa and Wojtyla, Walesa was the only one to whom they could now turn.

He was coming under increasing fire from the Communist Party. Although Walesa stressed that Solidarity did not want to overthrow the government, many Party members felt threatened by the fact that Solidarity could now claim all but a few of the workers. "Solidarity is not just a trade union," some said, "it is the nation itself." Such talk frightened the government.

Was this uneasy alliance between the Communist Party and Solidarity going to end in disaster? No one knew.

Even with storm clouds gathering, however, God gave extraordinary growth in the little Foil House. Politics may have been struggling to deal with the empty shops, but His love was reaching empty hearts.

During those months, the Rainbow Garden grew in four directions.

It grew in number. Many of the children brought others to the Lord, and in the camp we held that year we saw their little prophecy come true. The number who came away was double that of the first camp.

It grew in breadth. I was now often asked to take the Gospel to children in other areas. I visited major cities in the Great Green Carpet area, as well as Mazury's sapphire-blue lakes.

It grew in interest. Not only was more territory now being gardened, but the Lord provided more gardeners as well. When I travelled, I found increasing numbers of people interested in being trained for children's evangelism. Two of them, Dasia and Lidzia, made it a point to visit the Foil House and became increasingly busy gardening themselves.

It grew in support. Under Solidarity, passports had been made more readily available to Poles and I was invited to Western Europe for a holiday. I could not help but speak there of the Garden, and those listening became excited about it. One man who knew the long months I had waited for a passport decided to give one Austrian schilling for every day of the time. He wanted it to be used in the Foil House. A little boy presented me with a bag of Disney toys, "one for every child in your special club", bought with the savings from his pocket money. I couldn't have guessed it at the time, but these two gifts were the first indication of international help which would later be given to the Rainbow Garden.

Two weeks before Christmas, I went home for a weekend with Mamuska. On the way, I noticed a kind of restlessness in the air, and wondered why. There were more soldiers than usual in the streets and people were talking in anxious tones.

When Mamuska opened the door for me, she looked terrified.

"What is it, Mamuska?" I asked. "You look scared to death!"

"I am," she said in a whisper. "Get inside, quickly!"

"But why?" I asked, as she pulled the door shut behind me.

"Haven't you heard? The country's at war!"

"How can we be at war? Who is the enemy?" I said, pulling off my boots.

"We're not at war with anybody . . . we are at war with ourselves . . . oh, I don't know!" she said, red-faced as ever, but not, for once, making much sense to me. "They're talking about it on the radio."

I turned it on to hear for myself. General Jaruzelski had made a speech that was broadcast throughout that day. As I listened, I understood at last.

The general announced that the country was on the verge of an abyss and at the point of national catastrophe. Therefore, he said, he had needed to place the country under martial law.

No wonder Mamuska had said we were at war. This term, in Polish, is the same as our country's word for war and the irony could have been lost on no one. In a sense, the country was at war with itself, the government against the people.

That night, I felt as though World War Three had indeed begun. Headlights played on the walls of my bedroom as tanks rolled through our town until dawn. For hours, too, we could hear the crunching of the soldiers' boots as they marched along the snow-covered streets.

Mamuska sat at my window, her face white with terror. "It's exactly like the last war, Jasia!" she whispered, terrified. She looked as though she expected to see Hitler rounding the corner of our street.

Terror filled my mind as well, though for different reasons. With the country under martial law there would be much greater restriction on travel and far heavier control over documentation.

The more I thought, the worse the picture became. The Rainbow Garden would immediately be under threat. With sudden realisation, I turned to Mamuska.

"I have no legal way of getting back to the children!"

"Oh kochana. You're surely not thinking of going. Look out there into the street!"

More tanks rumbled by, as if to prove her point.

"It's too dangerous for you to go on with that work now. Stay home and get a teaching job!" Mamuska said, wide-eyed.

"God called me to it, Mamuska. I can't just give up because of this. If anything, the children will need me more than ever! I think it's best that I leave in a few hours, before the soldiers have time to get all their controls in place."

"But," big tears welled up in her eyes, "when will I see you back here again?"

I could answer her only with a hug and a prayer. I knew just one thing. We could not let the Rainbow Garden die.

I got back to the Foil House within twenty-four hours. Although I was supposed to have documents for travel, I feigned sleep on the train, asking the Lord for His cover. He answered. The soldiers did not wake me.

As the machinery of martial law established its vice-like grip in Poland, the situation did feel more and more like war. People had the sense that we were again living under occupation.

Within a few hours, tanks and soldiers had filled the streets of every major city. Thousands were arrested that first night and day. Concentration camps housed some. Prison held others. There was talk of suicides, though no one knew how voluntarily these deaths came about. A curfew was established. Strikes were forbidden. Travel abroad was banned. The press was placed squarely under the government's clenched fist. Telephone lines failed, by and large, and those still in operation were bugged. Internal travel was heavily curtailed; petrol stations were closed and public transport required special documents for travel.

All of this took place under a new Military Council for National Salvation, consisting of fifteen generals, an admiral and four colonels. It was set up in a hurry, though, and apparently none of its members noticed that the committee's initials, WRON, were very close to the Polish word for black crow, *wrona*. The aggressive crow is one of the least-loved birds in Poland.

The comics picked up the irony. Poland no longer used the eagle as its symbol, people said, angry and resentful. It had been replaced by a black crow in glasses and military cap.

The children knocked at my door just hours after I returned.

"Aunty! We were afraid they had arrested you when we could not find you at home!" they said, concerned.

They and their parents, not knowing I had gone to Mamuska's for the weekend, had searched for me the night martial law was declared.

"My daddy went to the police station asking for you, but

he couldn't find you. He was sure you would be on the list!" said one.

"But I wasn't here, kochana. I was with my Mamuska. Perhaps Pan Jezus kept me safe by having me there." I replied.

"All the same, Aunty, mightn't they come back for you?" Grazynka asked.

"Well if they think I am away right now, they might not come back for a little while and perhaps in that time the worst of the storm will have blown over!" I told them.

"But they'll see you walking in the street!" The Angel, Falkonetti's sister, was close to tears.

"Yes, they might . . ."

There was a moment of silent thought until, suddenly, Falkonetti piped up: "So we need to pray that God will give Aunty an invisible hat like Jasiu!"

He put a smile on all our faces. Polish folklore has a story of a boy who, when wearing a special hat, can go anywhere without being seen. "He is Jasiu, you are Jasia! So you can have an invisible hat too! We'll ask Pan Jezus to give you one." Falkonetti spoke with complete trust. He was definitely not the same child he had been twelve months before.

"But what about our meetings?" I asked the children. Our Good News Club had never been legal, since it was held in my private residence rather than on church property. Now, though, meetings would be far more difficult. Under martial law, no more than six people could be gathered in any place without permission.

"Don't tell us we have to stop!" "We need to be together." "We're scared by all those soldiers in the street!" They were all protesting at once.

We made a plan. They would arrive and depart, at set intervals, in groups of twos and threes. Our singing would have to be kept very quiet.

After they had left, I sank weakly to my knees. Quite how we would cope under martial law, I wasn't sure. Across from my window, I looked into a factory that was supposed to be making household items. We had now discovered that, in reality, it had been making extra munitions for the army. The imposition of martial law was going to be very thorough.

"Lord, can the Rainbow Garden continue?" I asked and found myself smiling as I prayed Falkonetti's prayer. If it were to go ahead, it seemed we would all need invisible hats.

14

THE EAGLE, THE CROW
AND THE RAVENS

"But Aunty, how will you stay alive?"

The children were becoming worried as, in 1982, the black night of martial law entered its second month.

In February, the government had raised prices between 300 and 500 per cent. It was needed by our mismanaged economy, but there would have been outright revolt had martial law not muzzled the nation.

The country had no option but to cope. "What's the difference between martial law and war?" asked the cynics. The telling answer: "In war, both sides have the right to shoot."

"You don't have coupons and you have hardly any income, Aunty. What will you do?" the little ones asked.

I too wondered but, as I prayed, I recalled a story Uncle Jozef had once told me.

During medieval times in Poland, a peasant called Pan Dobry lived in a cottage with a thatched roof and an earthen floor. When he and his family could not pay their rent, the landlord threatened to evict them. They knelt for prayer, sang a hymn and then slept in peace, sure that God would help. Next morning, a raven perched on their wooden window ledge, carrying in its beak a golden ring that bore the crest of Poland's king. Why had it come? Throughout the hard winter, the Dobry family had fed this bird, and he had become a kind of pet. When the king visited their region and dropped his ring, the raven had picked it up and brought it to the family it knew best. Next day, Pan Dobry brought the ring to the king who gave him a fine reward. With it, he could not only pay the rent, but purchase a home of his own. This was a happily-ever-after story.

"There will always be a raven, Jasia," Uncle Jozef had concluded, quoting as well Paul's verse: "My God will meet all your needs . . ." (Philippians 4:19).

One weekend, I had invited Marylka and Grazynka, two girls who lived far from the church, to stay in my apartment. On the Saturday morning, though, I had a mere ten zlotys and that was not enough to buy more than two bottles of milk. How was I to feed my little visitors throughout the weekend?

"Lord, please, I need a raven today," I prayed, while cleaning the apartment. The door bell rang soon after.

"Hullo Aunty! I couldn't wait so I came early." Grazynka skipped in happily. "Can I help you prepare?"

"Well, you could buy milk." I gave Grazynka my precious ten zlotys and she scampered off, suspecting nothing. I went to my knees.

Moments later, there was another knock at my door. It was the postman.

"Telegram for you, Pani. It's a money telegram, today."

"A what?" I had never heard of a money telegram.

"You just sign here, Pani, and the cash is yours."

The raven had come.

I watched in amazement as he handed me one thousand zlotys.

When Grazynka returned, I gave her a full shopping list and asked her to return to the store. There was enough for everything needed and plenty to spare.

The money was an anonymous gift. I never discovered who was behind it, but it was, unmistakably, another lesson in the university. Clearly God wanted to teach me how to trust Him.

I needed to learn that lesson well as the economic situation worsened in Poland. Even the basics were now hard to get. Because they would not "feed the Crow", Western governments imposed sanctions and refused Jaruzelski's government loans. At the same time, in protest, Polish workers were on a go-slow campaign that reduced local production by 60 per cent.

More ravens followed, however. Support began coming for Poland from friends in Western Europe. One day, a worker from the Child Evangelism Fellowship arrived with a car-load of much-needed children's clothes.

I was glad to see her, but I was a little embarrassed. That particular weekend, I had not even sufficient for my usual potato pancakes and had planned to eat bread for my meals. How could I possibly offer this to a foreigner? It is an important part of Polish tradition that guests be served the best.

I did not know how to solve the problem, but I put it aside for the moment as the joy of her gift overwhelmed me. Grazynka's family was in great need and their home was hardest to reach by public transport. Why didn't we go there, right away, I suggested with excitement, while we could use my visitor's car to bear the load?

We left immediately. When Grazynka's mother saw the clothes, she was speechless. Like me, though, she felt a little ashamed.

"I have nothing to offer in return!" she said.

It is also Polish tradition that one return a favour with a favour. I tried to reassure her, but she was adamant that something must be given.

"Wait!" she cried, suddenly. "I have an idea . . ." She disappeared for a moment, and returned with a live chicken in her hands.

"Let me at least give you this!" she said, eyes alight.

We thanked her and she left to behead and defeather the squawking creature. I thanked God. With this bird, I would now be able to feed my friend supper, after all.

I was silent as we drove along the sandy track that connected this remote home with the main road. We were surrounded by birch trees and the final rays of the sun filtered gently through their layered branches above us. This was the place where Grazynka's mother liked to pray, since their tiny house afforded her no quiet corner. "The trees know all my secrets," she had told me once. "I have watered them with my tears."

I knew of few families with need as great as theirs and I thanked God that we could, for once, bring a little sunshine into their sad lives. I thanked Him once more, too, for the miracle of the bird on the back seat.

"Some vegetables to serve with it would have been nice, Lord, but I don't want to be greedy . . ." I mused, still looking out of the window at the dancing shadows of the birch trees.

"What's that up ahead?" my friend asked suddenly.

"Where?"

"In front of us. Look!"

Where the track met the main route, we could see something lying on the road. She stopped and I got out to check. Then I began to laugh out loud.

"It's a cabbage!" I shouted and jumped back into the car with it. Now I could serve chicken and vegetables

"Lord, You are incredible!" I said, looking up at the pink and orange Heavens stretching over the darkening fields. They were strewn with wisps of rose-coloured cloud as if to honour the Creator who cared so faithfully for His people.

"There is just one little thing," I whispered to Him, though later I wondered at my boldness. "That cabbage is wonderful, but it's tiny. If I had two, and borrowed potatoes from Ala, I could make a chicken and vegetable dish that would stretch far enough to feed my guest for the whole of her stay."

A few kilometres later, just as we were stopping for petrol, we found a second cabbage lying on the ground.

I grabbed it, giggling, and the garage attendant gave us the explanation. Apparently a vegetable truck had passed along this road and stopped for petrol. Without knowing it, we had tailed this vehicle and our gleanings had come from its massive load.

That was the story, humanly speaking. For me, though, there was something else going on. God had heard my prayer and met my need, albeit in humorous fashion. It was a lesson for life. If I were obedient to His call and served faithfully in the Rainbow Garden, He would provide, no matter how great the odds.

Our Good News Club continued, although meetings often took on a more sombre note during those dark times. The kids whispered their fears.

"Aunty, I hate it when the tanks roll through the streets at night."

"The Crow is hateful! I can't sleep at night when I think about how nasty the soldiers are!"

"It feels as if Poland has turned into a scene from the war films they show at school."

"I know it's easy to feel angry," I told them, "but how does God instruct us to deal with hatred?" I sent them into little groups to look for answers. They now knew their way around the Bible well enough to search for verses themselves.

The responses came back quickly. "Bless those who persecute you; bless and do not curse . . . Do not repay anyone evil for evil . . . as far as it depends on you, live at peace with everyone. Do not take revenge . . . If your enemy is hungry, feed him; if he is thirsty, give him something to drink . . . Do not be overcome by evil, but overcome evil with good," offered one group, quoting from Romans 12:14–21.

"Make sure that nobody pays back wrong for wrong, but always try to be kind to each other and to everyone else," brought another, from 1 Thessalonians 5:15.

"Love your enemies and pray for those who persecute you," came a third from Matthew 5:44.

"But, Aunty, how do we do it? How can we love people who are cruel to us?" they asked, little faces anxious.

"Years ago, I was nasty to people myself . . ." I said, explaining how I had once worked against Christians and how difficult I found it to cope with love in people like Uncle Jozef. "God's love in him helped melt the cold, hard snowman I had become until, at last, this 'Saul' became 'Paul'," I told them.

"So, you see, if we offer the sunshine of God's love, we will melt hatred whenever we meet it. That's why Pan Jezus says to love our enemies."

It did not take them long to come up with ideas. "Aunty,

shall I take the soldiers something to eat?" "I could offer them a piece of chocolate!" "And I could take some piernik!"

Once started along this line, they related the same truth to the Chameleon.

"Shall I take her flowers on Women's Day?" one asked. "And I could give her my latest drawing!" said another.

The more I got to know these children, the more I loved them and was, without doubt, convicted by their example. I realised that I needed to do something about the Chameleon myself. Although I could not afford a gift for her, I set to work, using calligraphy, to make her a greeting card. I can't say I found it easy. I had to ask the Lord to do a work in my own heart before I could work. I could not, however, teach the children one thing and live another.

The children carried out their little plans faithfully, offering tokens of love both to the soldiers and to the Chameleon. I could only wonder at their creativity. With such evidence of God's love in action, I thought, the Rainbow Garden could not help but grow, no matter what dark times gripped Poland.

God continued to answer their prayers, too, for my "invisible hat". To our amazement, no soldier stopped me in the street. They seemed, moreover, to be making fewer outright arrests in these days. Perhaps they felt their grip had by now been firmly established and they did not want to antagonise the population further.

Why, though, had the Chameleon not used this time to ensure I was arrested? I often asked myself this question. Was it because she had less influence with these army units, sent from Warsaw, than with the local authorities? Or was it because they were interested in Solidarity people only and they knew my focus was spiritual not political? I never knew the final reason. I knew only that God kept me safe.

One night, however, I brought trouble on myself. I was visiting a friend who was struggling with cancer and I could not get home before curfew.

"Lord, I really need an invisible hat this time," I prayed, as I saw a group of soldiers across the road.

"Stop Pani! Show us your papers!" they shouted, and,

despite my desperation, I hid a smile. They were dressed in Polish uniforms but spoke with a heavy Russian accent. There was no doubt that the hand of Moscow was strongly upon the imposition of martial law in our country.

"We've seen you, Pani! Stop!" the soldiers shouted again. There were three of them. The military and the police always patrolled in threes. The jokers said there was good reason for this. It allowed the group to have one who could read, another who could write and a third to keep an eye on the intellectuals.

I ran to the nearby park where the children and I so often fed squirrels. Stupidly, I tried to hide behind an acacia tree, but months of pancakes and potatoes had left me wider than the trunk and it was of no help at all.

"We're warning you!" They raised their rifles to add muscle to their threat.

"Lord! Help me!" I cried desperately. In that moment, I clung to another verse from David the Psalmist. "He who dwells in the shelter of the Most High will rest in the shadow of the Almighty" (Psalm 91:1).

The soldiers ran. I prayed. Then the Lord astonished me.

For no reason at all, the lights of the park suddenly went out. I had never seen that happen before. This park, being central to the town, was always fully lit.

The soldiers could no longer see me in the dark. I seized the moment and ran home, certain that the Lord had, once again, protected the Rainbow Garden.

The children and I continued to need His protective hand during the summer months that year. We had planned another camp, but did not, of course, have permission to hold it. Neither the kids nor their parents were daunted by this, however. The number of those attending was again double that of the previous year, true to the children's earlier prophecy. We ended up with so many that we were going to need extra help and I spoke to two of the gardeners I had met earlier. One of them, Dasia, was planning her own camp in the Beskidy mountains. The other, Lidzia, was free to help me.

"You have such crazy ideas, Jasia! Camps! Clubs! I've never heard of anything but Sunday School teaching for children! But," she grinned, "I like this craziness and I think it's going to prove quite contagious!"

"Contagious? Then just be sure you catch the bug!" I told her. The phrase was to become a standing joke.

Mamuska was staying in Ewa's home, high in the Beskidy mountains, and the two of them invited us to hold the camp there, surrounded by the beauty of the larch and pine trees. Ewa, with her giving spirit, made her house available to the group free.

We spent afternoons at camp in the shade of giant conifers, listening to the bell-like sound of birds in the woods above us, and talking of the deep things that worried the children.

"Aunty, there are things I don't understand . . ." a Roman Catholic girl began, one day. "Why do Catholics and Protestants fight each other in Poland when Pan Jezus says we must love each other?"

"Yes!" added a curly-haired boy with a large dimple. "I get into trouble when people hear you are Protestant, Aunty. They tell me the Protestants come from Germany, just like Hitler, and they call you a Nazi!"

"And I get into trouble when I tell people my friends are Catholics!" said someone else. "The adults say I'm only supposed to be friends with Protestants. But that's not what the Bible teaches."

Reniusz, also a deep thinker, spoke up. "Well, the truth is that the Protestant groups fight one another as well!"

"Why, Aunty? Why?"

They crowded around, waiting for answers. I looked at their eager, intelligent little faces. They were all there. Grazynka, Falkonetti and the Angel, Renatka with her missing teeth, the Philosopher and the Doll, Marylka and so many others. They had all been hurt by this issue since, in the Good News Club and camps, we had never placed any restriction of a denominational kind. Everybody had been welcome.

I was silent for a moment. Denominationalism was certainly

stronger in Poland than many countries. I wondered, sometimes, whether Communists had encouraged it knowing that, if we Poles fought one another within the Church, it would weaken our stand in the nation. I did not say this to the children, though. I answered them with a poem which Uncle Jozef, himself very interdenominational in stance, had included in one of his books for children's work.

> "Love!" says the Saviour of the world,
> And who dares resist His commands?
> It is He who died for our sins,
> Now, "Love!" from His cross, He demands.
>
> "Love!" And don't ask whom you should love,
> Christ makes no exceptions at all.
> You must love your neighbour as yourself,
> Just read it! That's the Gospel's call . . .
>
> And who is your neighbour? Any
> Who, like you, their cross gladly bear,
> Who weep or laugh, as you have need,
> And crown of thorns willingly wear.

At the end of the discussion, the children came up with an idea. Instead of meeting in my flat only, they would turn the cellar of the same building into a kids' club. It would give neutral ground, rather than a denominational church environment, in which they could share the love of God. We decided to start work as soon as we got back to the Foil House.

As with the earlier camps, the loving shadow of the Almighty kept us safe throughout our holiday. His love, indeed, seemed to touch everything. The Bible studies centred on it. The beauty of creation declared it. Mamuska radiated it, becoming everybody's favourite granny. She sang to little ones on her knee or laboured long hours turning our simple food supply into an artistic masterpiece. Ewa's was a labour of love as she strove, night and day, to shoulder the greatest physical load. Lidzia, with a constant smile in her eyes and a great affection for the children, sang, counselled and toiled to deepen each one's relationship with God.

Just as I was basking in the joy of the camp, news came to the mountains that put a knife-wound in my heart. Aunt Mila was dead. Her heart had given way while she had been queuing for bread.

I had to walk alone to talk it over before the Lord. I took the forest route, past little ferns and fallen acorns, weeping quietly. "Our healing had only just begun!" I whispered, ashamed. Through tears, I laid it all at His feet; the sense of her rejection, the grief at the shared times that now would be no longer possible, the guilt that I had not done more to breach the gap. I sat on a rock beside falling water and begged God's forgiveness and His comfort. After a few hours, I was able to return to the camp. There was a pain in my heart during the days that followed, but I could continue with the children.

Before our vacation was over, the Lord brought us an extra dimension to the Garden and perhaps a glimpse into the future. Dasia arrived in our valley with her camp in tow, and guided by the sound of our children's singing made her way up the mountain to visit us.

One of the boys Dasia brought made a deep impression on us all. He was obviously highly intelligent, with brown questioning eyes and a kind, caring face. His name was Bartosz. We had invited a foreign guest to speak of God's love that day and Bartosz seemed to listen with special interest. Had God touched him?

"I'd like to see a young man of that calibre become a children's worker one day!" I mused to Mamuska, after the group had left.

Lidzia was nearby. "I would like to do more of this kind of children's work myself!" she said, adding with a grin, "I think I have caught the bug after all!"

"Then make sure you infect others!" I told her. "Poland has millions of boys and girls and every one of them needs God's love."

After our return to the Foil House, the children gave their

all to the renovation of the cellar. There was no carpet in the stores, but they found a damaged piece nobody wanted. There was no curtain fabric in the shops either, but Ala supplied us with some of her own. We gathered a motley collection of old chairs and painted them all glossy white, with paint bought from our Austrian schillings. We painted the walls a light green and made the place look a little like a fernery. With the remaining schillings, the children bought a tape recorder and a ping-pong table, "because our friends will love coming to a place like this". As the cellar began to take shape, the kids became more excited. They were sure it was the ideal venue to offer the love of God to their peers.

The Chameleon did not share their enthusiasm. "You've brought nothing here but trouble, Pani. How long do you think you can get away with this work?" she exploded, one day. "Other people teach Sunday School and leave it at that. But you do all these extra things! Why don't you give them up?"

"We have to seek children in all kinds of different ways! Many never come to church," I began tentatively, but she cut me dead.

"I am telling you to give it up, Pani! Sooner or later you will anyway. I'll see to it!" A funny expression came into her eyes and I shivered.

In the face of her threatening, could I trust the shelter of the Most High? Before long, the Lord allowed me a further test in this university class. I was walking home to my flat, just before curfew one night, when I had the oddest feeling that, somehow, I was being warned of great danger. I could not explain it, humanly speaking, but the more I prayed, the more certain I felt.

When I neared my front gate, I came to a stop as if glued to the ground.

Was I imagining things? I waited. From behind the fence, I heard a slight noise. Was someone there?

I stood still, heart pounding so hard I was sure it would be heard on the other side of my gate. Ten minutes passed, then twenty, then thirty.

At last a man walked out, looked furtively up and down

the street and ran off. As the street lamp caught his face, I recognised him. He was a man I saw occasionally with the Chameleon. Only as he left, though, did I notice that he was carrying a heavy wooden baton, the kind seen often in those frightening days. He had obviously been waiting to attack me but, once curfew had passed, must have concluded I was not coming home.

David was, of course, desperately concerned when he heard about the situation. During his next visit, we stayed with friends in Sopot, near Gdansk, on Poland's north coast. We talked for hours as we walked its pier.

"Things will be so much better once we're married," he said comfortingly. "We'll set the date next time we are together. First, though, I have an important trip I must make."

"Where to?" I asked, looking out on the ocean and dreading the thought of his being on the other side of it.

"Lebanon," he said quietly.

"But isn't that dangerous?" I said, concerned. This was 1982, a year when Israeli and PLO forces were engaged in serious conflict.

"Don't worry, I'll be safe," David said reassuringly, but a little shiver, for some reason, ran down my spine. Nonetheless, I understood his need to go. He wanted to be part of a peace-keeping team that would help heal the wounds of this tragic time.

We talked and prayed about our future together as the sun went down. It was as though the Lord took a great paint-brush and, using the sky as His canvas, merged long strokes of purple, pink and silver across it. David knew of my love for sunsets and held me close as we watched the drama of God's handiwork.

At last, he kissed me goodbye as the sun, a brilliant orange orb above the horizon, seemed to lower itself into the ocean. In a moment, it had disappeared.

David's departure felt a little like that to me. Suddenly, the warmth of his presence was gone and I felt a kind of chill every time I thought of his journey to the Lebanon.

Poland continued to boil with unrest. August 1st brought

the anniversary of the Warsaw Uprising, the tragic moment in World War Two when the Russians had failed to cross the Vistula to help the beleaguered Poles. In Warsaw, people gathered to honour the dead and place flowers in their memory. The milicja removed the flowers but more kept coming. It reminded me a little of the unbowed attitude in the movie *Forbidden Songs*. The Polish spirit is not easily crushed.

When I returned to the Foil House, I found the SB again waiting for me. An intelligent young man paid me a visit in which he quoted Mickiewicz and asked me out for coffee and concerts. He almost seemed to be playing the suitor, but he recorded every word I said.

I decided that those who would later listen to his tapes might as well hear the Gospel. When, therefore, he accused me of taking no part in odnowa, the renewal of our country, I seized my opportunity.

"I certainly am participating in odnowa, but in a different way than you," I said. "I believe true odnowa comes from within a person. If Poles were changed on the inside, our country would be changed too. But only God can change a person on the inside, not rules or laws. Did you know the Bible itself talks about odnowa?"

"The Bible?" He had thought of odnowa in a political context only.

"Psalm 80 is called 'A prayer for odnowa'," I told him. "'Restore us, O God, make your face shine upon us, that we may be saved.'

"And 2 Corinthians, chapter 5, verse 17, says, 'If anyone is in Christ, he is a new creation; the old has gone, the new has come!' You'll never find odnowa because you don't believe in God. Only He can give it!"

As he took the tape away, I prayed that its contents would speak to those who would replay them. As before, though, I sank exhausted to the floor. How many more of these visits was I to endure?

I turned to Aunty Alice for help. "Just don't let them in the house," she, a veteran in such matters, told me. "Ask if they have a permit before you open the door. They are not legally permitted on the premises unless they can produce one and, as a rule, you'll find they can't."

I tried it. The SB visited twice more and both times, thanks to Aunty Alice's counsel, never came inside. Frustrated, they changed tactics.

They sent me a student of English. She was a tall, Amazon type who did very little study but asked so many questions that I wondered if she were SB. In those days, increasing numbers were co-operating with the authorities.

"When a person wakes up in the morning," said one of the current jokes, "he should look into the mirror and say, 'Be careful. One of us is SB!'"

After a couple of lessons, I was certain of my suspicions and I confronted her. She admitted the truth and left. Next lesson, however, she returned to my door, bearing a huge basket of eggs and begging me to go on teaching her. She explained that she had been promised a trip abroad if she got the necessary information from me. I felt sorry for her, but there was, of course, no way we could continue lessons. She was heartbroken. Now her trip would be forfeited.

Such rewards marked the lives of those who co-operated with the System. At that time when most Poles were struggling, the Moskal and Iwonka were also receiving privileges. So was the Hippo. Mamuska had told me that all three had, since martial law, reverted to Communism.

Times remained heavy but the Rainbow Garden, if anything, grew the more through this dark chapter of Poland's history.

The Foil House kids were never without their Wordless Books and frequently explained the love of God as they saw their school friends struggling to cope with the pressure of those difficult days. I needed to make the Wordless Books out of cloth now, since their paper versions had already been worn out.

They always required me to be home after school, too, in case they needed to bring others to my door. I was supposed to mend broken hearts, sick hamsters, torn shirts and aching teeth as my children brought a stream of little friends to visit, "so that you can love them, Aunty, and lead them to Pan Jezus".

These little lights shone at the community level as well. Grazynka was observed by a young man whose home was a kind of mecca for alcohol and gambling. His fascination with her faith led him to Dziegielow from which he returned a new man. He led his family to the Lord too, and together they presented Him, instead of cards and vodka, to all comers.

The children even looked for ways to lighten my load. A number of the older ones now taught Sunday School and assisted in the Good News Club. I saw double blessing in this. They would be equipped if ever the Chameleon succeeded in removing me from the Foil House.

Their greatest focus for service, though, was the cellar. They had pinned their hopes and dreams on this, believing it to be the ideal place from which they could spread the love of God to a greater breadth of friends in the community. They laboured faithfully and rejoiced when, at last, it was ready.

Forty-eight hours after its grand opening, however, we were told there had been a terrible accident. Water pipes had burst, and the entire cellar flooded. Investigation showed that the damage had been deliberately inflicted.

In shock and disbelief, the children worked to remove the water, but the place never recovered. It was too damp a location to be dried out properly after such major flooding.

Could the Chameleon really go as far as this, I wondered, watching the children sitting with their heads in their hands? They had poured heart and soul into this project. Was there to be opposition to every new development in the Rainbow Garden?

I was still reeling from this news when, not long after, a knock at the door brought the postman once more, with a telegram.

"It's an overseas one, Pani. Please sign for it."

"Overseas? Could it concern David?" My heart lurched. Surely nothing could be wrong . . .

I took it and closed the door, tearing the envelope open in

sudden dread. It was a very long message from two of David's friends.

"We are deeply sorry to inform you of terrible news," it began and I sat down, dry-mouthed with fear.

"David came to this part of our troubled world as a messenger for peace. Tragically, he has given his own life for this cause. He was caught in crossfire while serving his mission. We were with him in the hospital before his death and he wept as he spoke of you. 'What will happen to my Jasia?' he said, over and over. It is impossible to express his depth of grief at the future you two can no longer share. We pray that God will give you His strength to bear the pain of your terrible loss. David was a great gift to us all."

I stumbled to my bed, clutching the telegram. For hours, I lay motionless as my mind whirled, trying to take in the message. David was gone. With his death I had lost my best friend, my spiritual confidant, my partner in the vision and the love of my life.

The next day, I could not get up. My body and mind seemed paralysed. I discovered, now, why people talked about their hearts being broken. Mine felt as though it had been torn apart and its great, open wound would never heal.

I thought life could have no more blows to offer, but I was wrong.

A few weeks later, a second telegram, this time from Warsaw, was brought to my door.

It stated that the authorities had received a complaint from the church I attended and a request that I be removed. As it had been lodged by the secretary of the committee, the post now filled by the Chameleon, they said it clearly reflected the choice of the church as a whole.

The telegram stated, categorically, that the children's ministry had to stop.

15

TILLING THE SOIL

"God?" I sobbed, angrily. "What are You doing? First David! Now the Rainbow Garden! Everything I loved and committed myself to is dead!"

I was lying on my bed at home, grieving and ill. My final weeks at the Foil House had passed in a whirl of sorrow and pain. The kids, together with their parents, had travelled to Warsaw to request that my dismissal be revoked, but to no avail. The Chameleon had won. As if to rub salt into the wound, she had seen to it that my last weeks were without heating of any kind. I had contracted pneumonia.

"Why is God allowing this, Mamuska?" I asked from my sickbed. "Have I done something wrong? Is He punishing me for some kind of sin?"

Mamuska was firm. She was angry with the Chameleon, but not with God.

"Trust Him, Jasia," she said, repeating her lifelong theme. "There is nothing in life so bad that God can't turn it to good!"

I didn't want firmness. I wanted sympathy.

"You're wrong, Mamuska! No good can come out of this!" I protested.

She opened her Bible. "Do you remember what Joseph said to his brothers after they sold him into slavery? He told them, 'You intended to harm me, but God intended it for good, to accomplish what is now being done: the saving of many lives.'" She read the account from Genesis 50:20.

"You'll be able to say the same one day, kochana. Satan has

been against the children's work, but God will bring good out of the situation. You too will see the saving of many lives!"

Mamuska did her best to care for me. Although our local pharmacies had little on their shelves, she tried all the traditional Silesian remedies she knew. She wrapped my feet in cabbage leaves to reduce the fever. She placed hot sauerkraut over my lungs to cure my congestion. Ewa brought her the fat of rabbits and foxes which she placed over my neck to heal my throat.

Nothing worked. For weeks, I lay struggling, seeing little beyond our icy garden. I could hardly think about the future without David. Nor could I envisage a future without the children. Some days, I gazed as the snow pelted sideways across my window, driven this way and that in a wild dance by the wind. On other days, I watched huge snowflakes fluttering gracefully to earth, stacking themselves on the nearby woodpile and making tiny hats on the fence posts. At quieter times, when all was still, I stared at the ghost-like trees, looking, to my mind, every bit as dead as the Rainbow Garden. I had hoped my time in the Foil House would lead to a bigger work with children. Now, though, it looked as though every effort had been thoroughly crushed.

When I looked further afield, at the broader picture in Poland, the view seemed no brighter. That October of 1982, the government continued in its oppressive stance by passing a new law to ban Solidarity and a sense of heaviness hung over us all.

That same month had seen huge numbers of sorrowing Poles flock to the Vatican for what ought to have been a happy day. The Pope was to canonise a Polish martyr, Father Maximilian Kolbe, who had been interned at Auschwitz and had given his life for a fellow prisoner. Some of those attending had been dressed in Auschwitz uniforms with a flag of an eagle bearing a crown of thorns and a cross. The delegation had wept and so had the nation to see Poland, after so many years, still carrying too great a weight of suffering.

Martyrdom lay just around the corner for another Pole as well. Father Jerzy Popieluszko had already gained the attention of the government for the popular masses he led. He spoke out openly against the pain being inflicted by the nation's leaders, though he urged his flock to echo the words of Christ in praying, "Father, forgive them, for they do not know what they are doing" (Luke 23:34).

Everywhere I looked, life seemed to be as bleak as I felt, so that when spring followed that sad winter, it took me by surprise. Long ago, Wujek Morcinek had spoken of meeting the suffering of Dachau with "honey from the flowers" and the renewal of the "white summer wind". I, however, seemed to have permitted mid-winter to grip my soul. I hardly heard the rivers start to run or the birds celebrate with their piping. I barely noticed the snowdrops and daffodils pop their merry heads out of the muddy ground and quite forgot that the same Creator had the power to shine His golden warmth into my life and that of the Rainbow Garden as well.

God had not forgotten me, however. When the deaconesses at Dziegielow heard about my illness they brought Western antibiotics strong enough to overcome the pneumonia. With renewed strength, my outlook began to change. I realised God was, indeed, trying to breathe new life into me once more.

"But, Lord, please, breathe it into the Rainbow Garden as well!" I begged. As dead as the Rainbow Garden looked to me, I could not give up on the call God had placed on my life.

He answered my prayer with a visit, one Wednesday night, to the home of a doctor and his wife, Henry and Alina Wieja. As we spoke together, I began to see the future in a new light and, for the first time, I understood what God had been doing in the past.

This couple longed to see the Gospel taken to a broad cross-section of Poland's community: married couples, women, students, prisoners and, to my joy, children. They wanted to see God's love spread through preaching, teaching, literature and the media. In their fellowship I felt I had come home. The unity in vision for Poland was deeper than I had experienced with any of my countrymen since Uncle Jozef's death.

When they asked whether I would be interested in leading the children's work, I did not need to think twice. Mamuska was right. My time in the Foil House had not ended by accident but by design. The Rainbow Garden was not going to die, it was going to expand. As her Bible verse had said, this new step could, indeed, result in the saving of many lives.

I had to bow in shame before the Lord that night. "Forgive me, Lord. I have so much to learn about Your ways. Do keep me enrolled in Your university!" I told Him. The next day, as I read my Bible, I wrote the date against 2 Corinthians 1:4–6. "Praise be to the God of all comfort, who comforts us in all our troubles . . ."

Wednesday evenings with the Wiejas became a regular thing after that. They gathered a group of people with different callings in order to see the various parts of the vision fulfilled. We were to need one another's fellowship, moreover, as, humanly speaking, what we were attempting looked almost impossible. In recent months, the government had continued to rule the country with a heavy hand. Lech Walesa had been freed, but many Solidarity leaders were still in jail. Martial law had now been lifted, but there was little difference to show for it. Without those long evenings of prayer, it would have been easy to lose heart.

In time, though, the first step in fulfilling our vision became clear. We began with the summer programme of evangelism which the sisters at Dziegielow had always held so faithfully, the week of outreach which had played so important a part in my rebellious childhood. The Wednesday group decided to build a larger outreach on this foundation. We invited Stan Mooneyham to preach, erected a huge marquee and saw thousands come from all over the country. The resultant crusade amazed us. Scores of people began life anew with Jesus Christ.

I was excited, but not completely satisfied. A huge number of adults had gathered to hear the Gospel in the tent, but too few children had been able to hear it in the relatively small space available for them. In time, I believed, there had to be a second marquee beside the first, one filled with children's worship and laughter.

Always impatient, I wanted to see this happen right away.

"But I'm just one person, Lord. It would take many children's workers to hold such a huge crusade. How do I go about it?"

It was, again, Aunty Alice through whom He gave the answer. She held a camp for any interested in caring for Jewish people and, with my desire to find the blue flowers of the Rainbow Garden, I attended.

Aunty Alice's vision was huge. She would, like me, need to see large numbers of people involved to complete the task.

First and foremost, she longed to see our Elder Brother receive God's plan of salvation, both individually and as a nation. In response, Aunty Alice wanted to see us motivate many Christians to obey God's command in Isaiah 40:1. "Comfort my people, says your God." She had specific ideas. Old, lonely Jewish people should be looked after. Jewish graves, damaged through the excesses of anti-Semitism, should be given care. Jewish museums should be respected and supported.

And Jewish children? Yes, she explained, people would be needed to work with them too, but not yet. After the exodus of 1968, there were very few in the country who openly practised their faith. I had occasionally met Jewish children at school or with David, but they had often been instructed by their parents to keep their heritage hidden. For the moment, then, I resolved to learn all I could from Aunty Alice so that later, when the time was right, I would be ready to offer God's love to the little children of Israel.

Aunty Alice had a further goal for the Elder Brother as well. Many people believed that, one day, there would be a mass exodus of Russian Jews to Israel and that they would travel overland via Poland. Aunty Alice wanted to build a farm to house them en route.

So how did Aunty Alice, one individual, expect to see so many goals fulfilled? Her answer was wonderfully simple, but life-changing for me. She believed in the principle of multiplication.

What if four of us, within a month, each brought one other person into the work, she asked. There would, of course, be eight. What if the same happened the following month? There would be sixteen. After six months, there would be 256 people involved. After twelve months, 16,384. Aunty Alice believed in the God of great things.

I had come to this camp expecting to learn more of the blue flowers in the Rainbow Garden. In her multiplication principle, however, I learned what I needed to care for all three colours.

After the camp, I set to work immediately. To allay government suspicion I began teaching again, but I spent every spare moment travelling to nearby villages and towns, and then on to the Great Green Carpet and beyond. In each place, I spoke of the need to evangelise Poland's children, urging people to get involved. I visited many individuals as well, speaking one to one about the vision, and inviting them to the Training Institute.

I had two goals now for the Rainbow Garden. The first, the setting up of the Children's Tent at Dziegielow, would need a group of fifty gardeners. The second, the spreading of the Rainbow Garden throughout Poland, would need an army of them.

I thus spent long months sowing seeds and tilling the soil of the Garden. Wise old King Solomon, perhaps a more patient individual than I, once wrote that there is a "time to plant and a time to harvest" (Ecclesiastes 3:2, *Living Bible*). I was eager to see the harvest, but in the meantime I felt God, the Master Gardener, urging me to invest as much time and travel as possible in sowing.

Just as this planting was taking root, however, Mamuska, to everyone's surprise, suddenly collapsed with a massive stroke.

"There'll be no miracles in this case!" the doctor told me. "You'll never see her speak or walk again. She will die within a week."

I disagreed. So did Ewa, who had now become our resident angel. She gave every moment she could to helping restore life to Mamuska's paralysed body. Together, we set about cooking, shopping, washing and carrying our chocolate-eyed "baby" until we could see movement and speech starting to return.

Although we saw progress, the weeks that followed were heavy. It was a long, slow path back to health for Mamuska. She became discouraged.

"Kochana, my illness will spoil your work!" she said, with big tears rolling down her pale cheeks. "Put me in an old people's home. You'll never be able to do your task while you have to care for me."

For once, it was my turn to give her own advice back to her. "There is nothing in life so bad that God can't turn it to good!" I told her. She recognised the words and gave a wan little smile.

"You're learning your university lesson after all," she said, struggling with slurred speech.

God did, indeed, turn the situation for good. Prior to this, I had been required to teach full-time, but now my hours were cut in half. The government permitted part-time work if one had a relative who was an invalid. Ewa, moreover, had become one of the family now, and shared many of the nursing responsibilities with me. As Mamuska improved, I thus found that instead of less opportunity to work in the Garden, I had more. God was showing us again that, just when we thought things were at their worst, He had His best in store.

I continued with the multiplication principle in preparation for the future growth in the Garden. It was not dramatic work. Tilling the soil never is. The outworking of a vision, people say, is 5 per cent inspiration and 95 per cent perspiration. I continued to talk with as many individuals and groups as I could, however.

Some had questions, of course. When, in October 1984, Father Jerzy Popieluszko was brutally murdered, the country mourned and potential gardeners were the more disheartened. "Maybe we could do this work if the Communist System left our country, but . . ."

"But," I always replied, "we cannot wait for the System to collapse. We have to start now!" When they heard that God had already proved this work possible in the Foil House, they became excited about it and, slowly but surely, I saw the Master Gardener drawing many more people into the work.

It was not only Polish people that He motivated, moreover. At this time, He sent us several ravens from outside the country. Two ladies, introducing themselves as Pauline and Peggy, visited Poland from the organisation Christian Mission to the Communist World, founded by Richard Wurmbrand. P and P, as I termed them, asked many questions about our work and looked for practical ways to help. Their mission sent a tape recorder capable of duplicating a large number of blank cassettes which allowed us to multiply our teaching messages, a projector for film strips, visual aids and books for children. Every gift was thoughtfully chosen to make it far easier to develop the children's work. A church in Shrewsbury, England, adopted me as well, backing the work with prayer, support and encouragement. Uncle Sam helped too. He made sure I received a typewriter on which to prepare lessons and training material. CEF also brought visual aids and other help for lessons.

God sent another raven too, though one of quite a different kind. He did not bring help for the Garden itself. He brought help for me.

Ever since David's death and the return home, I had found it harder to combat my lifelong battle with the *za swe* syndrome. Perhaps the loss of his love left the old wound open. Perhaps the hurt from the Chameleon, even though I knew her psychotic tendencies, had disturbed the old wound. Perhaps, as well, it had become painful when well-meaning people asked why I wasn't married. There had been a few relationships since David, but none of any consequence.

Whatever the reason, I had found myself tired of this long-standing struggle and begged the Lord to free me from it.

The way He answered caught me by surprise. One evening, I was translating for a foreign speaker when the message became painfully relevant. The visitor was Bruce Thompson. He was from the group Youth With a Mission.

Bruce talked about the walls we construct in our lives and the way that, sometimes, these can be out of alignment.

He said most people who came to him for help had been

rejected at some point in their experience. A rejection syndrome then developed in their lives. They came to see themselves as second-class compared to other people and, as a result, their walls became crooked.

Rejection. The word hit me with deadly accuracy. For so many years, I had told myself I was only *za swe*, a second-class person. Why else would I have been given away as a baby? Why else would my mother have rejected me?

"Some personalities become brick-bound and the person within is no more than a prisoner behind the walls of his heart," Bruce said. "As each of our negative responses becomes habitual, another brick is added to the wall."

These bricks, he added, were not constructed according to the perfect plumb-line God gave His people in Amos 7:7,8. They were more like old buildings with a dangerous lean.

He proposed a brick-by-brick study and, at this point, produced a visual aid on which I had to write the Polish translation.

My face reddened with each brick he named. Self-pity. Self-hatred. Inferiority. I could identify with every one.

"Insecurity is a direct result of the messages of rejection we receive in childhood." It was all so clear as he spoke. "If people accept rejection repeatedly, they begin to think they are rejectable. Hope falters and discouragement sets in. Following a human plumb-line of rejection is a great handicap and, if allowed, could rob us even of life itself." Yes, I had been at that point when I had attempted suicide as a teenager.

I kept writing the words into the bricks, but found it increasingly difficult to do so. When Bruce went on to speak about the way rejection can make a person rebellious, I identified the more. Pride, stubbornness, bitterness, competitiveness. Each brick formed part of the crooked wall in my life.

"Bruce, it's me that you've been talking about all night!" I said, when at last the evening finished. "Can you help me get rid of this rejection syndrome?"

He listened sympathetically as I poured out my story. "It is Jesus Christ alone who can set you free," he said when I was done.

"But I have been a Christian for quite some time!" I said. "How is it possible that I still have this problem?"

"When a person becomes a Christian, it does not necessarily mean his wall is restored. Now you need to ask the Lord to reconstruct your walls according to *His* plumb-line," he replied.

It took me a few hours. Together with Bruce, I worked through all the areas in which the rejection syndrome had affected my life. I began to think of the attention-getting mechanisms which had marked my life: tricks to get the attention of others when I had felt second-rate. How many AGMs, as I nicknamed them, had I manifested? The poetry-reciting. The art. The Communist involvement. The academic ambition. My list went on and on.

So did the list of those against whom I felt bitter. Not only were there names from my childhood, but from the present too. I had always used humour to deal with those who had brought hurt, but deep down, I knew I had resented them. In prayer, I asked God to help me forgive the Chameleon, the Moskal, Tobiah, Iwonka, the Hippo.

The hardest question of all came at the end of the evening. "Do you think, now, you can forgive your natural mother, Jasia?" Bruce asked quietly.

I hesitated. He reminded me of the illness she had faced when she gave me away and the hopelessness of life as she must have seen it.

"Could you say, 'Mummy, I forgive you'? Could you speak the words out loud?" he said.

"Mummy?" I had never called her anything but Aunt Mila. "Perhaps I could think of her as 'mother' . . . Would that do?" I ventured.

"But could you manage 'Mummy'?" he persisted gently.

We prayed and, at last, I could. In that moment, something was released within me and I felt truly light-hearted for the first time in years.

After that, everything seemed suddenly easy. It was no problem to identify the patterns that had resulted from the fear that I was second-rate.

"If we confess our sins, He is faithful and just to forgive our sins and to cleanse us from all unrighteousness," Bruce quoted from the King James version of 1 John 1:9.

There was no doubt that these patterns, however understandable they now seemed, were sin. I needed to break with them.

"If you meet those patterns any more, you'll know how to deal with them in prayer," Bruce said, quoting John 8:36. "If the Son sets you free, you will be free indeed."

This man was, indeed, a raven and his help was God's gift to heal years of pain. I was a different person after that night. At the same time, though, he pointed me so fully to Christ that he left me in no doubt it was the Lord Himself who freed me, not Bruce Thompson.*

Life changed after that night. I could now think of Tobiah, Iwonka and the Chameleon with compassion, not fear. When others joked about my being single, I could joke back. I could see my adoption as the great miracle it truly was. God had lifted me out of one home and into the care of Tatusiek and Mamuska because He had a perfect plan for me. Instead of feeling like a second-rate human being, I felt like a much-prized daughter of the King of kings. It was as Tatusiek had said so long ago. I had been adopted by God in a double sense.

I found, very quickly, that I wanted to take this message to children everywhere. In my childhood, rejection had come through adoption. For other children, the causes were different. Some developed a rejection syndrome because of authoritarian parents whose standards they could never meet. Some experienced rejection because their parents were too busy, even in Christian work, to be available for them. Some underwent rejection when parents separated or divorced. Some felt it when alcoholic parents lived beyond their reach in a semi-permanent stupor. Some experienced it because of race or physical handicap. As I thought of the

---

* Bruce Thompson's book, *The Walls of my Heart*, can be obtained from Crown Ministries International, c/o Dale Buehring, 9 Winstone Lane, Bella Vista, AR 72714, USA.

breadth of children's needs, I found myself grateful that I had experienced it too. Now I could evangelise children with a greater understanding of their need.

It was in 1986 that, at last, we were ready to launch the next stage in the Rainbow Garden, the Children's Tent at Dziegielow. I had prayed and searched for fifty gardeners. The Lord, in His gracious manner, had given seventy.

The Children's Tent was quickly filled to capacity with little boys and girls, bright-eyed in their discovery of God's love. Up to four hundred attended each day and the seventy gardeners were amazed at the interest and seriousness of these little ones.

I stood at the side of the tent, thanking God as I looked at their upturned young faces. So many years before, at the amphitheatre near Gdansk, I had struggled to believe it possible for anything this size to be held in Communist Poland. Now it was reality. Again, the Lord had shown me that my God had been too small and, again, proved Himself to be the God of the impossible.

As the week progressed, moreover, we began to see that real changes were taking place inside the Children's Tent. The teaching given was not feeding dead bodies. It was bringing new life in Christ.

One three year-old was among the most restless children I had ever encountered. He had ants in his pants, disrupting each meeting even more than Falkonetti had during my early months at the Foil House. After a few days of the crusade, however, his mother came to talk with us.

"I am not the religious type and never came to these Dziegielow things. But my son has changed my life."

"Your son?" As far as we knew, this boy never listened to a word spoken. Clearly, the Lord works in mysterious ways when it comes to children with ants in their pants.

"He's only three years old, but, as he showed me his Wordless Book, the mystery of religion disappeared for me and I understood the love of God. Today, I came to the crusade so that I could start new life in Pan Jezus myself," the mother explained. The situation was just as the Lord had led in the Foil House. First the children were finding Christ and then, through observing the little ones' changed lives, the parents were discovering Him too.

Similar stories continued all week as we saw Pan Jezus at work in a host of other little lives.

The children came from areas all over Poland, as well as a few from neighbouring Czechoslovakia.

One afternoon a little boy called Piotrus came to me after the meeting. We spoke half in Czech and half in Polish as he gave his life to Pan Jezus.

"Do you understand who He is?" I asked. I wanted to be sure these children knew what they were doing.

"Today I do," he replied, wiping blond hair from his serious blue eyes.

"Do you know why Pan Jezus died for us?"

"Today I do."

"Do you want Him to become your Saviour?"

"Today, yes."

"Today?" Every reply brought this word. I could not understand why until Piotrus explained that he had never heard of Pan Jezus until this week. The word "Christian" was new to him. So was "God".

One of our keenest gardeners, Malgosia, gave him a Czech Bible and some stickers bearing the words "Jesus and me".

"I'll put them on the door of my room," he told her, "and then everyone who comes to our house will know that Jesus and I live together!"

He became thoughtful for a moment.

"I don't suppose He'll be able to hear me at school, though, will He?"

"Why not?" asked Malgosia.

"Because, at school, they have told us there is no God. He probably won't be able to hear me through the school walls."

Malgosia explained that walls did not shut Pan Jezus out of any situation and Piotrus, much reassured, went happily back to Czechoslovakia. We later heard he continued very committed to his new Friend.

Child after child responded to the message. Some were so serious it was hard not to smile.

Malgosia introduced me to a bright-eyed girl whose curly hair and winning, confident manner reminded me of Shirley Temple. This little one had found the Lord Jesus through Malgosia's teaching and now her first concern was for others to know Him too.

When Malgosia introduced her to me, she was determined to find out where I stood. "Is Aunty Jasia a Christian?" she asked Malgosia in a very loud whisper.

"Yes," Malgosia smiled.

Shirley Temple examined me closely. "But has she really made Pan Jezus her personal Saviour and Lord?"

"She really has!" Malgosia answered.

The little one was taking no chances. Looking me straight in the eye, she said, "So you know that He died for you so you could be forgiven your sins and go to Heaven?"

"Yes! He forgave me too! I was such a naughty girl you can't imagine!" I replied.

Shirley examined me sideways until, at last, she gave me the nod of approval. "Well, that's all right then!" she said, and scampered off to the Children's Tent. I had to laugh and yet could not fail to be encouraged by the depth of Shirley Temple's understanding.

Perhaps my greatest joy of all that week, however, came with a visit from my now grown-up Foil House kids. To my delight, I realised that the term Foil House had become a misnomer. All the seedlings had been successfully transplanted into the harsh weather of life in Poland and their growth was evident. Although some were now at university, all had a commitment to come together regularly and had remained "family" to one another in the love of God. With the Chameleon recently dead, moreover, they now had the freedom to work with the new generation such that, they informed me, I could consider myself a spiritual grandmother.

As they hugged me and told me their news, I thought back to the hopelessness I had felt when I left them. How wrong I had been to think the Rainbow Garden had come to an end. I had been working alone in the Foil House, the first stage of the Garden. Now, we had seventy new gardeners serving in the tent, most of whom were able to enrol in the Training Institute which would begin afterwards. As well, there were many more who would visit us for lectures on a part-time basis.

Enthusiasm was gripping us all as the week of children's evangelism came to an end. Like a cold shower, however, a voice from the past placed a chill over my excitement.

"Remember me, Jasia?" It was Tobiah, the balding student who had questioned children's evangelism so many years before in Warsaw. I supposed that the authorities now wanted accounts of this children's work and he was the obvious one to ask. He lived in our region and feigned interest in the Garden.

"Who are the foreigners that come here?" "What support do they give you?" "What Polish students look like future leaders in children's work?" Tobiah asked a hundred casual questions. Each point he raised was exactly like the kind of questioning I had met in the SB man at the Foil House, or the ice-man and the ferret prior to that. There was a recognisable pattern that all of these people followed.

"Well, Jasia," he said at the end, "such large numbers look like a breakthrough for this work in our country, but," he still pulled nervously at the hair which covered his bald spot, "you don't know how long all of this fervour for children will last."

"If it is of God, it will last!" I told him.

"You can't be sure of the depth of commitment in these kids, nor that of your new contingent of children's workers, especially," he gave me a funny look, "if they encounter opposition."

"Opposition? What do you mean?"

"Oh, you know what I mean! Not everybody approves of this sort of work," he said, adding cryptically: "You never know what might happen, Jasia. We'll wait and see what the future holds."

It sounded very like a veiled threat.

16

HOW DOES YOUR GARDEN GROW?

"Dinka's barking! Is it the police?"

Our first Training Institute had begun at last and fifty-seven students had come to Dziegielow for instruction.

Dinka was a yappy little dog who belonged to Lidzia and had, for some reason, a particular dislike for men in uniform.

A glance out of the window showed that Dinka had alerted us for good reason. Police were on their way.

"You know what to do!" I said and the students quickly left the chapel. Earlier, I had warned the students to disappear for a casual stroll in the woods under these circumstances.

Foreign teachers had come to train the students and we asked them to lock themselves inside their rooms and under no circumstances to open the door.

When the police reached the chapel, they surveyed the almost empty scene in frustration.

"Do you have formal permission to meet here?" they demanded.

"We are on church property. We don't need it."

"But you have unregistered foreigners with you!" That was true. We could hardly have registered foreign teachers for the purpose of training children's evangelists.

For a moment, I wondered how they knew about the teachers. Then I remembered. Tobiah had dropped in a few days earlier.

"All right. Since we cannot prove foreigners are teaching here, we will take a look at your facilities," the police continued.

We had not thought of this. Our facilities were clean but very minimal. All fifty-seven students had cheerfully managed with just two toilets and one shower. While everybody had remained quite healthy, the police could, nonetheless, use this as a pretext to stop the Training Institute.

"We will lodge our reports in the morning! The health department will close this camp. You won't be able to continue, Pani!" they said, looking smug, and left. This was a favourite tactic of the government. Rather than any blatant attack on religious activity, they preferred the indirect approach. "Catching a frog with another's hand," we called it, since this way they achieved their goal but kept their own hands clean.

We regathered the group to pray and, afterwards, one of our gardeners suddenly brightened.

"I have a friend working in that department! This is one frog they won't catch!" The matter resolved itself as soon as she made contact. God had, once more, protected the Rainbow Garden.

The Training Institute lasted four weeks. We would have preferred a three-month course, much like that I had attended in Kilchzimmer, but there was, of course, no way we could get governmental permission for that. Instead, Uncle Sam split the Kilchzimmer course into four parts and the enrollees committed their holiday periods, over the next four years, to attending them. This was a huge undertaking and I was elated to see so many students accept it. With numbers like these, we could truly begin to see the Rainbow Garden grow.

The students came from a variety of sources and backgrounds. Ela, the daughter of Marysia, was there. Lidzia was too, with her snappy little dog. Dasia had enrolled and brought Bartosz, the young boy who, we now learned, had indeed met Pan Jezus at the mountain camp and whom she since discipled. Malgosia had joined us. So had Maritka and Marylka, two of the older kids from the Foil House. Olgierd, a gifted student who dreamed of studying law, had come because, he said, children's needs are "of greatest importance". Zbyszek and Nela, two biology graduates from Krakow, now directed their talents to a different kind of planting, that of the

Rainbow Garden. Many of those who came, in fact, were students or graduates of high professional calibre in medicine, engineering, economics, music and education.

Their approach to their work reflected their professionalism. Exams were held throughout the course and, if the students received a grade lower than 95 per cent in any subject, they insisted on sitting it again. "We have to study hard to qualify for the jobs we hold in the world, so how much more should we study for the work of God!"

When I saw the seriousness of their commitment, I looked ruefully at the one set of notes I had left from my train journey back from Kilchzimmer to Poland. If only I could have photocopied or mimeographed them, I could have put a set into the hands of every student. Since that was not possible, this dedicated group sat copying notes by hand for hour after hour.

At the end of the course, we gave them an afternoon of recreation in the beautiful woods. To my surprise, however, they failed to show up at the appointed time. I had just begun to worry when Olgierd appeared through the chestnut trees shouting: "It works! It works!"

"What works? Why are you late?" I asked.

"The training works!" he said. "In the woods, we met some kids from a children's camp, so we held a meeting with them!"

"What with?" I asked. This group astounded me. They had been given a well-earned afternoon of recreation but even that they used to garden.

"The Wordless Book!" chorused the group who, by now, had joined him. One after another explained, in amazement, how children had responded by giving their lives to Pan Jezus. They were not feeding dead bodies, they were offering new life in Christ, and many joyfully echoed Olgierd's words about the training: "It works!"

The children at the camp asked them to go back the following afternoon, but that visit proved to be a different story. The teachers responsible for the camp threatened to call the police unless they left the children alone.

"But we can't abandon these kids. They've just become Christians!" the students protested.

The next day, after a morning of prayer, Olgierd quietly took Wordless Books to the little campers and returned with the names and addresses of all who had given their lives to the Lord. Long after the course, the gardeners were still writing faithfully to each one.

The rest of the vacation period saw the Rainbow Garden germinate in ways that were entirely unstructured. The students, no longer content with an afternoon for children in the woods, began to travel elsewhere in Poland to share the Good News. They would set up a tent somewhere, begin playing with the children of the local area and, in time, tell them of Jesus's saving love. They called these weeks "half-camps" because, although they gave the kids a week of activities, they did not take them away from home to do so. I did not organise these activities. They were totally spontaneous.

Malgosia, the one who had brought Shirley Temple to the Lord, went a step further. After the weeks at the Training Institute, she vowed to open a Good News Club in her home.

"You're not afraid?" I asked. Of all those in training, Malgosia was perhaps the shyest, and in that sense the least likely to take such a difficult step. If she were reported for holding this unregistered club, she could be in trouble.

"Well, I did not really think I could do it," she told me, "but it's no good telling the Lord I can't, because He just reminds me that He can! He gave me Deuteronomy chapter 20, verses 3 and 4: 'Do not be faint-hearted or afraid; do not be terrified or give way to panic before them, for the Lord your God is the one who goes with you to fight for you . . . to give you victory.'"

She twinkled. "All the same, I was hoping that, after the first meeting, the children themselves might not want to continue. But they love it!"

They not only loved Malgosia's club, they were soon to change through it and the outcome was so pronounced that I was to hear about it in the staff room at school. Three of

Malgosia's little charges were from difficult homes and had behavioural problems so great that the teacher had suggested relocating them to a special school. One term later, though, she said that, "by some miracle", they had been transformed. I could say nothing, of course, but I knew the other side of this story. Malgosia had told me that these children had now found Pan Jezus and He had wrought the miracle.

I was pleased to see the number of gardeners increase but, oddly enough, I found within myself a strange new reluctance to stand up in public and call for more. This was a personal thing. Now that I understood how the rejection syndrome had caused me to step too often on stage in the past, I wanted to step well out of the limelight in the present.

Friends noticed. "Jasia, you are the one who always talked about multiplying yourself. What's happened? Why are you now leaving that to others?"

Brave enough, by now, to speak of the rejection battle, I explained my reticence. They confronted me.

"But you can't sit in the shadows! Besides, it's not yourself to whom you're drawing attention now. It's the Lord Jesus and His call to children. People won't catch the bug if you don't tell them about it!

"Get out where you can be seen, Jasia. Preach the vision. Teach the vision and, if necessary, write the vision!"

Those words gave me the shake-up I needed. I had wanted to shed every vestige of the rejection syndrome, but in this case I was going about it the wrong way. The vision had indeed to be spoken and, with the depth of need increasing in our country, none of us could afford to be silent.

"Shoot or emigrate!" had become a popular expression in Poland during the late eighties, so desperate was the mood of the people. Every month, rather than shoot the government, thousands took tourist trips abroad and simply never returned.

It was easy to understand why. By 1988, the average wait for an apartment had increased from fifteen years to twenty-five. Food had increased a further 40 per cent. Rent was up 50 per cent. Electricity was up 100 per cent. A 36 inch colour television cost a man one year's wages. A simple wedding-ring cost him a month's salary. Some were helped by packages from the West. Others floundered.

The government blamed the nation's ills on Solidarity and began a new programme of austerity. If they continued to put more money in circulation, they said, people would be walking around with suitcases full of worthless notes.

So the queues lengthened and tempers shortened. The jokes allowed no one to forget that there was a better way to live.

"A capitalist, a socialist and a communist have an appointment," said one. "The socialist arrives late, out of breath, carrying a shopping bag. He apologises, explaining he had to queue to buy meat. The communist turns to the socialist and asks: 'What's meat?' The capitalist turns to the socialist and asks: 'What's a queue?'"

Even as the depth of need brought increasing pain in the country, I gave thanks to see that the Master Gardener was ensuring the Rainbow Garden spread.

"People are catching the bug, Jasia," the Institute students announced triumphantly. "It *is* contagious!" Many had begun holding home meetings specifically to spread this contagious condition. They were multiplying themselves, just as Aunty Alice had recommended.

The Master Gardener allowed the numbers to grow. The next year, a second group of about fifty enrolled in the Training Institute. The following year, there was a third group. Some of the new gardeners were those I had known in the past. Falkonetti and the Angel joined us from the Foil House. So did a student named Renatka, who was none other than the sister of the tiny boy whom I had found, at my very first school, being beaten by the headmistress. The new students also included some who had been led to the Lord by the other Institute students, and they now, in turn, wanted to learn how to reach children themselves.

All had taken to heart the Lord's words in Matthew 9:37, "The harvest is plentiful but the workers are few." Each one soon became active in working with the children.

I longed to do the same. In the midst of organising the broader aspects of the Rainbow Garden I was missing the delight of having a little group of children with whom I could myself meet regularly.

To my surprise, this did not seem to have the sanction of the Master Gardener. I had no peace as I prayed about it.

"Why, Lord?" I asked, bewildered.

I was studying the life of Paul at the time and, as I read of the way he discipled Timothy and others, I thought I found my answer. The Timothys in my care needed support too. It was not enough to train children's workers and then leave them to it. They needed care and prayer. They needed love and encouragement. They needed, above all, I believed, to be as family to one another, to provide mutual support in the challenges their gardening would bring.

While I grieved that I could not give regular care to a pocket of the Garden myself, I realised that if I gave the same time to the gardeners they would plant many more pockets and see the work spread far more widely.

It was as though the Lord was teaching me one more secret needed for the Garden's growth: "If you want the Garden to grow, take care of the gardeners." That principle is one I have lived by ever since.

Decision made, Mamuska and I turned our tiny flat into a kind of Open House to which they could come whenever they needed. It became a very busy home. Sometimes, groups gathered for meetings. At other times, individuals came.

The authorities, however, continued to keep an eye on the growth of the work, and one visitor was less welcome than most.

Tobiah began by visiting on a regular basis and asking his usual questions.

He tried to justify himself. "Oh Jasia, I just love kids' work. That's why I like coming here. I need the fellowship." He certainly knew the right words to say, but continued to pull his hair in his nervous fashion, and Mamuska's eyes, which missed nothing, shot a dark warning in my direction.

Since our apartment is only small, I always had to receive

guests in my bed-sitting room where it was, unfortunately, all too easy for them to look at any Rainbow Garden material on my desk.

Tobiah liked to flick nonchalantly through my papers, asking questions about this and that, and as he did so I realised something had to be done. I needed to have greater privacy with visitors like Tobiah or, indeed, even Big Ears, who dropped in for neighbourly visits from time to time. Like his parents before him, Big Ears was quite often seen talking to the Moskal.

Remembering all the drafting skills that Tatusiek had taught me, I drew up plans to divide my room. The major part of it remained a bed-sitting room. One end, however, became a secret office with a bulging bookcase serving as a false wall.

The next time Tobiah came to visit, he sat on my lounge and looked around in surprise.

"You've renovated?" he said.

"Yes, do you like it?"

"Of course, but," he looked vaguely about him, "I thought this was a bigger room?"

At that moment, of all things, the telephone rang in my office. The entrance to it was via a cupboard door.

"Lord, I'm such an idiot!" I cried, silently. I had no choice but to reach through the door and answer it.

Somehow, in His graciousness, God seemed to prevent Tobiah from concluding the truth.

"You keep your phone in a cupboard, Jasia?" he asked, looking, to my astonishment, impressed with the idea. "How creative! It keeps it out of the way!"

He never commented again on the phone, nor on the change in my room. Neither did Big Ears. At last I had a secret office in which I could work freely.

That tiny office, only ten feet by five, served a second purpose as well. It became the place where I could meet with the Master Gardener and listen to His plans for the growth of the Garden.

I loved this place and the sense of the Lord's presence I found in it. He still had university lessons to teach me, however, and although I wanted to be open to His leading, there were times when I was a difficult student. Being too sure of my own ideas, I was on occasion closed to His. As He pulled me towards the next step for the Garden's growth, I resisted with all my might.

In summer, a knock at the door brought the lady who had organised the help given by the Christian Mission to the Communist World. Her name was Chris Fox and she was to become a regular visitor to the Rainbow Garden.

"It's a car you really need, Jasia," she told me, knowing that I was frequently clambering on and off trains carrying heavy materials for the children's work.

"Definitely not!" I had always been stubborn on this issue. Too often, I had seen Western money spoil people working sincerely for God behind the Iron Curtain. I did not want to be another casualty.

"It needn't be extravagant. Just a simple car would do," Chris persisted. "Everyone in our mission is behind the idea and so are others who know you in the West."

"But I don't need those fancy foreign things!" I complained, as she suggested purchasing a Western make.

"What do you plan to drive here?" she asked, while driving me one day in her car. A stream of locally-made vehicles was coming the other way and, as I looked at them, I took her point. The options were certainly not great. There was the tiny Polish Fiat, which some described as a sewing machine on wheels. There was the Syrena, a toy-like vehicle made of plastic and wood. There was the Skoda, a poorly-made Czech car which tickled the Poles' sense of humour since, in our language, the name means "a pity". There was the heavy, infamous Russian option, popularly known as "Stalin's Revenge". There was the Eastern German Trabant, looking and smelling rather like a frog, as it hopped its way along the road. People called it "Honecker's joke".

"Which of those would you choose, Jasia?" said Chris, "if you wanted one reliable enough to take you to children all over Poland?"

She made good sense, but I was still nervous.

"I don't even know how to drive!" I protested. I could not afford to learn, either, though I did not tell her this. Chris must have picked up the problem, however, for just after she left I found an envelope containing money under a vase in the house. In it was a note that this was for driving lessons. The sum was just what I needed.

In the end I realised that to refuse the car would be to refuse God Himself. I got my licence and the mission started to gather funds.

I had no sooner adjusted to this new step in the Garden than, back in my secret office, the Lord seemed to point me in another direction for the Garden's growth: literature.

There were millions of children scattered around the country whom, as yet, we did not have gardeners enough to reach. The printed page, however, could go much further than the individual and CEF suggested I write a magazine for Polish boys and girls, explaining how they could find new life in Christ. Any interested kids could write to an address for follow-up through correspondence lessons.

The idea of writing something specifically for Polish children seemed right to me. Although foreign material was available for us to translate, there were issues unique to the Eastern European child who, after a diet of Communism, had been taught to see Christianity in quite a different way than his counterpart in the West. Moreover, although some Polish churches included a children's section in their general publications, no broader Christian magazine specifically for kids existed in Poland.

Again, though, I had trouble obeying the Master Gardener. "Lord, I'm sorry," I told Him in my secret office one evening, "but I just can't find time to get the job done!"

That same night, before bed, I read a chapter in the life story of Amy Carmichael, the English missionary who worked among Indian children. She, too, had longed to write but, like me, always seemed to be too busy. In the end, she broke her leg and on her sickbed found all the writing time she needed.

"Perhaps that's what I need? A broken leg?" I joked, as Mamuska hugged me good-night.

The next day, a truck came to our home to deliver a load of concrete slabs. Ewa and I were planning to construct a driveway to the garage that would later house my car.

As I helped with the unloading, however, I nearly lost my balance on the back of the truck and, getting my footing wrong, came down heavily on one leg.

"Are you all right?" the man said, concerned. "That looked as though it hurt!"

"Oh, it's nothing! I'm not made of sugar!" I replied. The phrase is typically Polish. Our people have never been encouraged to bother much about pain or sickness.

It wasn't quite truthful, however. That afternoon, as Ewa lent her wonderful strength to positioning the heavy slabs, I fetched and carried as much as I could, but my leg complained with each passing hour.

During the evening, Mamuska offered me another folk remedy, "sour water", in which to soak it and bring down the swelling. Next day, it had quadrupled in size and I could not walk on it. The pain had become excruciating.

"We'll have to put your leg in plaster," said the doctor we consulted. "And you'll be six weeks off work, Pani!"

"For a bruise and a bit of swelling?" I protested.

He held the X-ray against the light. "That's no bruise, Pani. That's what we call a hairline fracture," he said. "To put it simply, you've broken your leg!"

It was Amy Carmichael's principle all over again. I didn't know whether to laugh or cry.

Commenting yet again on the Lord's sense of humour, Mamuska set to work in caring for me. She was dependent on a crutch after her stroke, but she spent much of the next six weeks shuffling to and from my bed, faithfully bringing food and medicine for my health and art materials for my work.

I called the magazine *Tik, Tok, Tak*, the Polish expression for the sound of a clock. I wanted children to understand that, spiritually speaking, it could be five minutes to midnight for any one of us. They needed to turn to Pan Jezus for salvation while they still had time.

I finished the magazine at the end of my sick leave and collected the car with my leg in plaster.

Despite my former misgivings, the gift of a car made an enormous difference to the Rainbow Garden. With it, no corner of Poland was now beyond reach. As I travelled, moreover, I could see for myself the new pockets of children's work starting up, here and there, throughout the country.

The Training Institutes had been like stones thrown into a pond, and as I travelled I saw the ripples flowing in ever-widening circles. The students were now teaching their Sunday Schools with a new approach, confident they could offer children new life in Christ instead of trying to feed dead bodies. Knowing that many children never came to church, however, the trainees had also looked for other ways to reach them. They had prepared special programmes for festival times like Christmas and Easter. Inspired by Malgosia's example, a number now took the plunge, too, in opening Good News Clubs. Ela, the student whose mother had taken me to Mazury so long ago, opened one. Dasia and Lidzia did the same. Zbyszek and Nela did too, bringing the love of God into tall, soulless apartment blocks in our area. Camps and half-camps were flourishing as well. With the car, I could easily visit and "water" these and other areas of growth in the Garden.

As well as the car, moreover, Christian Mission to the Communist World had made it possible to get another tool for the Garden, a video player. To our people, in these years, video-watching was so rare a treat that, whenever I brought this to a town, I felt like the Pied Piper. Word spread and children came running, with their fascinated parents and grandparents in tow. It was an ideal opportunity to share God's love with them all.

I showed them videos of stories by the English children's writer, Patricia St John. No Christian writer for children is known and loved in Eastern Europe as much as she. I took her classics, *Treasures of the Snow* and *The Tanglewoods' Secret*.

After the videos, I spoke to the children, explaining how they could find new life in Pan Jezus. It was a source of constant joy to see Him draw many to Himself on each occasion.

One little boy proved unforgettable. He was skinny with a pale, freckled face and as he talked to me, his hands were tensed in anxiety.

"I'm just like the children in the video. I hate two people and I don't want to forgive them," he began.

I waited, loving this little fellow's honesty.

"It's my parents. They are alcoholics and, when they are drunk, they often hurt me and they forget to feed me." By the time his story was done, his little hands had twisted themselves into a great knot. That day, however, he found the peace he craved by beginning new life with Pan Jezus.

So did many others. Wherever I took the video player, I left a new pocket of the Rainbow Garden.

Back in the quiet of my secret office, however, the Lord never let me forget that, if we wanted to see the Garden's growth continue, it was crucial to look after the gardeners. "Be sure you know the condition of your flocks," I read one morning. "Give careful attention to your herds" (Proverbs 27:23). The imagery was different, but the point was the same. I increased the number of meetings for the children's workers.

We knew that the authorities continued to be interested in our activities and, strictly speaking, our meetings were illegal. Since we managed to keep Tobiah away most of the time, though, I did not expect much trouble. In that I was wrong.

One night, when a Western CEF worker was visiting our group, somebody reported a foreign car outside our house.

The police came to the door.

"You must show us everybody's documents," they announced. "You are holding an unauthorised meeting."

I continued to thank the Lord for Aunty Alice's advice. "Can you show me a search warrant?" I asked. To my relief, they could not.

"Then I'm not letting you in!"

"Now, just a minute, Pani! We know you have a foreigner in here and we want to see his passport."

"You have no right to enter!" I repeated.

"You . . ." the leader began and then stopped with a great cry. I had not realised it but, just as I had been closing the door, he had placed his brawny hand over the lock and I had jammed his fingers.

"Pani!" he shouted in pain, and I suddenly saw what had happened. I quickly released his hand and apologised.

"I'll get you for this," he shouted viciously, banging on the outside of the closed door.

Inside the house, we were not sure what to do. "Let's meet for as long as possible and hope they will not wait outside for us!" I said. "Then we'll have to leave the meeting in twos and threes, with intervals between. You'll have to arrive next meeting the same way."

After that, I was observed and my phone was bugged; their technology was so unsophisticated that I could hear the interference whenever I lifted the receiver.

Since it would now be more difficult to hold meetings, we decided to hold "birthday parties" or other festive activities as these occasions were permitted without special authorisation. The celebrants turned up at our house bearing cakes, jellies and ice creams in large glass bowls for any observing parties to see. We all gained weight, but the Open House continued.

Those watching us had far subtler tactics than they had used in the days of the smoker. Sometimes an electrician would work on the street light outside our house for three to four hours while we held our "party". At other times, a street cleaner would sweep outside for so long that we expected to find a hole worn in the road's surface. We were sure that, before long, the streets around my home would be the cleanest in our town.

For their own sakes and that of the Rainbow Garden, however, it was crucial that the meetings continued. Many of these young people struggled with personal problems even as they tried to garden.

The more time we spent together, the more I came to thank God again for the rejection battle that had marred my earlier years. It was, without doubt, a pattern that troubled many of them too as they battled different aspects of what I called the "A" syndrome; alcoholism, adoption, abuse, assault, authoritarian parents, absent parents or ambitious parents.

No wonder Bruce Thompson had said that, when counselling people, he found the great majority had experienced rejection at some point in their lives. He had, moreover, written an article about his teaching and I had translated this into Polish. I shared his insights with the gardeners and they took hold of them with the same eagerness as I.

There was one area, however, in which all of them felt a common sense of rejection that far out-weighed the others: singleness.

"Jasia, how do you cope with being single?" they asked one evening. Most of these young people were in their twenties or thirties, and I knew it cost them to open up on a topic of such sensitivity. It cost me, too, but their honesty demanded an honest response from me.

Since David's death, I had wrestled with this issue in prayer. At last, however, I had concluded that the "singles" picture did not have to be one of gloom and doom.

"I have come to see God as a kind of Master Musician," I told them. "He writes the perfect melody for our lives and He plays it. If we demand that God provides us with a spouse, it seems to me as foolish as the keys of a piano trying to make their own music rather than allowing the Musician to perform His piece. Let Him be the One to play. His are the nail-pierced hands, not ours!"

They agreed, but brought up the issues that had caused them pain.

"Some married people make rude jokes and comments. Don't they hurt you?"

"They used to." As I spoke, I realised that, since the all-important prayer time with Bruce Thompson, much of the sting had gone out of these situations. "Perhaps some married people won't accept you, but don't go and marry just to earn people's acceptance or you could end up with your life a disaster!"

"But often their comments make me feel second-rate!" said another.

"Yes, I know some think that people are like shoes and should be found only in pairs," I said. "But the Bible doesn't teach that. Tell your married friends that some of God's choicest people were single. Nehemiah was. So was Paul. So was the Lord Jesus Himself! Was anything second-rate about them? No! God simply needed them to be unmarried for His purposes to be fulfilled!"

A timid girl spoke up. "My parents always say I won't be a whole person or a real woman if I'm not married."

"I have heard people say that too, but does the Bible say it? No! The Lord Jesus promised that fullness of joy could be found through commitment to Him, not through commitment to a spouse! Look at John, chapter 15, verses 10 and 11."

"But other people try to be matchmakers!" said a young man. "It drives me crazy!"

I had to smile at this. Not long before I had been invited to friends who just happened to have a bachelor drop in at the same time. "What on earth did you think I would see in him?" I asked them later. "Well," they replied, "he had seven pigs and three cows, and during these hard times what more could you want in a man?"

The gardeners laughed ruefully at my story, but their pain continued to come out in the questions that followed.

"How do you handle the loneliness?" asked someone else.

"I believe there's a difference between living alone and being lonely," I said. "It can be very hard coming home, alone, to an empty house. But that, in itself, is no reason to marry. Why? Because it is much more alone to come home to a person you should never have married. The loneliness of a wrong relationship is the worst of all."

The night was getting late but, before it ended, they came up with a more delicate question.

"I feel awkward when married people show lots of physical affection right in front of me," said a young girl. "It's so insensitive."

"I used to hate it," I admitted, "until I realised it was not deliberate. Those who do so don't mean to hurt us!"

"But, Jasia, doesn't it bother you, anyway, not to have a physical relationship with someone?"

"Yes!" I wanted to be truthful. "I struggle with it. But I'll tell you something I have discovered. There was a time in my life when I was looking for a relationship with three dimensions: physical, intellectual and spiritual, in that order.

"In recent years, though, God has reversed the situation. Now, first of all, I long for people of spiritual unity. Secondly, it's a bonus if they are intellectually compatible. Thirdly, if God should bring these qualities in a man I find physically attractive too, that would be marvellous. But, since that is third priority, not first, I can still enjoy wonderful friendships that prevent my life from becoming lonely."

The group could probably have talked till dawn on this subject.

"Please, don't live your life waiting for a husband or wife!" I begged them, after what seemed hours. "Don't wait for a spouse, wait on God! Rest in His will. Marriage is a gift, but singleness is a gift too. So thank Him for the singleness you currently enjoy and let Him determine whether it will be temporary or permanent. If you go searching for a spouse, you'll become emotionally bankrupt and you'll be ineffective for ministry.

"Above all, promise me," I concluded, "that you won't go marrying someone just because he or she has seven pigs and three cows!"

Despite street sweepers and electricians, we continued to meet whenever possible and God, in His graciousness, kept us covered from any further trouble. Larger gatherings, however, required a bigger venue and preferably one situated in a location of greater privacy.

I heard of such a home in the mountains and, one glorious autumn day, set out to see it. I drove up a winding forest road surrounded by the burnished tones of the season. The sun winked at me through red and orange leaves and the forest floor was like a golden carpet. Suddenly, though, a red light on my dashboard flashed its warning.

I had been taught that, once this light came on, I must not use the engine. I was still a new driver, though, and had no idea how I was to get back down the mountain.

I stopped the car and looked over the precipice at the hairpin bends of the road and my head reeled.

There was only one thing for it, I decided. I would have to turn the engine off and coast back down. I began the descent and, at the first bend in this serpentine road, pushed the brake pedal. Nothing happened. Nobody had ever told me that when the engine of my car was not running the power-assisted brakes would not work. At the next corner, I had the pedal on the floor, but I simply gained speed and momentum. Every bend became more frightening than the one before as I hurtled around each, at absurd speeds, hanging on to the steering wheel and praying through every metre. What if I met a tourist bus on the road? What if I came upon a horse-drawn cart laden with hay? "Lord, I'm in Your hands! You know this car is committed to the Rainbow Garden and so, for that matter, am I! Please save us both!"

Again, He proved Himself the God of the impossible. I met no traffic at all on this usually busy road.

When I arrived, shaken, at the base of the mountain, I suddenly recalled that a friend's home was not far away and coasted on until, with one last terrifying manoeuvre, I swung up on to the slope of his driveway. The steep angle brought the car to a stop and I stepped out, stammering my story.

My friend looked inside and then asked in astonishment: "Jasia, what are your keys doing on the dashboard?"

"Well, I was told to turn off the engine if a red light flashed and, without the engine, who needs keys?"

"But that's impossible!" he said, staring at them. "When you remove the keys, your steering wheel should lock. Try it!"

I did. The steering wheel locked immediately and my stomach turned over. Now I understood what should have happened on the very first corner of that dangerous twisting descent.

"Jasia," my friend shook his head, "God obviously has work for you in this world before He lets you leave it! You've witnessed a miracle."

The mechanic at our garage fixed the car, but over the months that followed I found it necessary to go back to him repeatedly as one thing after another broke down.

Finally, he drew me aside. "Pani, the problems I'm finding in your car are not merely routine. Someone is tampering with it."

"Oh you're imagining things," I protested, laughing.

He did not return my smile. "The jobs are too neat, Pani. I'm sorry, but you seem to have yourself an enemy!"

17

THE EAGLE REGAINS ITS CROWN

"Papers, Pani?"

The Rainbow Garden was growing in another new direction. It was expanding across the border.

The Czech students attending our Institute had invited me to visit their country. I could not come empty-handed, though, and since for the moment my car seemed to be in working order, I had loaded it with hidden material to help their work.

Earlier, Chris Fox had delivered Polish and Czech literature to Poland and, in the shelter of the mountain forests, transferred it to my vehicle.

To cross this border, I had hidden the videos of Patricia St John's stories under the seat covers and stashed Czech literature under the floor mats and inside my deflated spare tyre. I was praying I would not have a puncture before I reached Czechoslovakia.

"I am sorry about your sad loss, Pani!" said the immigration officer, kindly.

"Thank you!" I tried to look solemn. I was dressed in black mourning dress and on the back seat there was a huge bouquet of lilies tied with heavy black ribbon.

As a rule, we were allowed only a limited number of visits to Czechoslovakia per year. Beyond that, we could not cross at short notice unless it was for a family wedding or funeral. Near the time of their children's outreach, therefore, my Czech friends had carefully observed the death notices and sent me an invitation by telegram to attend "Aunt Agnusia's sad parting from us".

The officer waved me through and I breathed a silent prayer of thanks.

"Anything to declare?" Customs was next. The officer looked at the lilies and I held my breath. Would he notice the raised level of the floor or the lumps in the seats where the videos were hidden?

"Open the boot, Pani." So far, so good. I lifted the boot for him and he checked its nooks and crannies.

"I'll need to take a look underneath your spare wheel," he said, and my stomach turned over. Its weight would give me away if I allowed him even to move it.

"Let me do it for you!" I offered hastily. "It has a tricky catch and I'm used to it."

Not for the first time, I could have bitten my tongue. Whatever was I thinking of, suggesting this? I could not carry that wheel even when it was filled only with air. My back had been seriously damaged while lifting Mamuska in her invalid condition and I was due for hospitalisation in order to repair displaced vertebrae.

Matthew 10:19 was one of Uncle Jozef's favourite verses for moments like this: "Do not worry about what to say or how to say it. At that time you will be given what to say." I tried to hang on to that verse and to keep "both hands full".

"Lord, I believe You can inspire the right words at the right moment," I prayed under my breath. "But can You help me lift the tyre?"

He must have. I grabbed it and held on for dear life. The second hand seemed to take for ever to work its way around the dial of the customs' wall clock. The veins in my forehead were pulsating and my palms sweating. He did not let me drop it, though. Satisfied at last, the officer allowed me to return it and declared me free to go.

I drove from the border until I could find a quiet spot in which to sit and allow God to still my beating heart. How gracious His care had always proved. This was the very crossing where Mamuska had so often passed with butter on her head. It was here, too, that I had been interrogated on my return from England.

Faced with the example of the Czech Christians, however, I felt quite ashamed about the fears I had entertained at the border. These believers paid a much higher price for their faith than we Poles. The building in which I was to address the Czech children, for example, had been specially designed to serve a double purpose. Much of the time, it was simply a regular home, but when needed it could open into a three-storeyed meeting place. Only believers of deep faith and courage would take on such a risk.

When I arrived at this amazing 'church', my Czech friends rejoiced to hear about the safe delivery of the literature. I went to the boot to pull out the wheel for them, quite confident that, after lifting it at the border, I could do so now as well. I couldn't. No matter how hard I tried, I could not get it to budge.

"I'll help, Jasia!" A young man lifted it for me, but even he puffed and panted.

"How on earth did you manage this?" he asked and only then did I see the size of the miracle God had wrought at the border. Clearly, He wanted to see the Rainbow Garden grow in Czechoslovakia and this material would be needed for it.

My visits to Czechoslovakia became a regular thing. It continued to be necessary for someone to die every time, but, dressed in black and armed with telegrams and lilies, I was able to come and go quite frequently.

I never really knew quite why the Czechs kept on inviting me, however, since they had now begun an excellent work among their children. Despite the restrictions of their government, they were holding secret camps, high in their magnificent mountains, as well as meeting in homes for Good News Clubs. The Czech gardeners were multiplying themselves too.

I was moved by their courage. Far from my being of help to them, I felt their example was an inspiration for us in Poland to keep on with the work, no matter what.

As the decade drew to a close, the tired, failing Polish System sensed it was losing its faltering grip on the country. Our people were starting to believe that Mikhail Gorbachev's policies of glasnost and perestroika could allow greater changes in Poland than even he imagined.

Without doubt, people had lost faith in the government and, despite the promised perks, very few could be tempted to join the Party. Membership, for those under thirty years old, had been 25 per cent in 1970. It was a mere 7 per cent in 1988.

Some said we needed a new set of leaders, but most Poles now believed that we did not need a change of drivers so much as a change of vehicle. The System itself did not work. Solidarity began to push for pluralism.

A political cartoon captured it best. It depicted a group of Party members sitting in conference and a giant hand writing on the wall behind them: *"Mene, mene, tekel . . ."*

A wounded animal, it is said, fights hardest and our government battled with all its might in the late eighties. It called for a resurgence of Communist dogma in the classroom, hoping that it might, even now, save the day by insisting upon ideological adherence among the young.

At prayer in my secret office, I believed the Lord was using this to push the Garden in yet another new direction. It was time for us to plant it in schools. I had not forgotten the emptiness of my own childhood diet of Communism and I was sure we needed to meet the grey, System teaching with the colours of the Rainbow Garden.

"This time, Jasia, your enthusiasm has really got the better of you. Schools are untouchable!" the gardeners protested at one of the meetings. "You know what's happening in the education world right now!"

Things were, indeed, tough in the schools at this time. It was not only students who were under pressure, but staff as well. Teachers, as guardians of the young, were being re-evaluated to determine their political correctness.

Those who proved acceptable at the first assessment were not bothered further by the authorities. Questionable teachers were interviewed and observed a second time. Severe cases were subject to a third round. A number of the gardeners were in the third category. So was I.

Lidzia had a story that inspired us all. A little boy in

her classroom had, despite the increased heat from the authorities, been unmoved in his bold stand.

"Filip is just four years old, but his parents have bred such a fearless faith in this child that he just stands for the Lord, no matter what. He prays before meals. He says 'Allelujia' all the time. If boys around him fight, he explains boldly that Pan Jezus wants us to love one another. When we give him blocks, he builds a cross and talks about salvation," she recounted.

"Recently, he brought the story of Noah's Ark and explained it to the class. 'The people of Noah's time were very naughty and they made God sad,' he said, adding, 'We can still make God sad today, if we don't follow Him.'"

"And a little child will lead them . . ." says God's Word in Isaiah 11:6. When I heard about Filip's example, I promised the Lord that, no matter what, I would begin planting the seeds of the Rainbow Garden in schools.

Word of this new step in the Garden may have spread, however, for soon after Tobiah turned up again, asking about growth in the work and new directions it would be taking in the future. His questions were so blatant that their purpose was unmistakable.

"Tobiah, who has put you up to all these questions? An ordinary friend does not need all this information!" I said, my patience exhausted.

"I don't know what you mean! I'm interested in the work, that's all!" he protested.

"It's not all and you're not leaving until you tell the truth!" I said, with Mamuska nodding approvingly in the background.

It took hours, but eventually he confessed that, like the Amazon in the Foil House, he had been permitted several trips abroad as long as he co-operated with the System. After that night of confrontation, however, Tobiah stopped his visits to our home.

To begin the planting at school, I decided to use one of Patricia St John's videos, *The Tanglewoods' Secret*, as the story is set in England's countryside and, arguably, is a legitimate tool for English teaching. I showed it to the first of my classes and they were abuzz afterwards. The word quickly spread and a friend on the staff warned me that, after school, I might be summoned to the headmaster's office. At that, I rescheduled my other English classes so that they too would see the film before the headmaster could stop me. Sure enough, when school was done, I was in trouble.

"Pani Jasia, I heard this film has religious elements!" the principal began.

"Well, it touches on the deep things of life," I said.

"Pani, Pani!" he sighed, frustrated with me. "Don't you realise you are already in trouble for your beliefs?" A long lecture followed until, at last, he reached his main point. "If you are to show anything else at all, you must be sure I see it first."

The idea sounded excellent. I would have loved this man to see *The Tanglewoods' Secret*.

"When would you like to view it?" I asked, trying to hide my enthusiasm.

He faltered. "Oh, I don't have time now. But perhaps the vice-principal can check it."

She did. I translated for her as she watched and, like the students, she was evidently touched by its message. At a subsequent Dziegielow crusade, this woman was to give her life to Jesus Christ, but "my change in direction really began when I saw that film," she told me, afterwards. Several students from the school later confessed the same thing.

Without doubt, the Rainbow Garden was needed in schools. Too many children were sitting in our soulless classrooms with unanswered questions and no one to ask about them. They desperately needed God's love and we would, I believed, be crazy to miss the opportunity to give it.

The government's nervousness increased as Solidarity became more sure-footed in its steps towards change. In March 1989, a history-making agreement was signed concerning our next election. Poland was now to have a freely elected upper house and a lower house in which two-thirds of the seats would be reserved for Communists. It was not a completely democratic arrangement, but it was a huge step forward and nothing like it existed in the Eastern bloc.

The people responded with good-natured humour. "Did you know that our electrician, Walesa, has set up a new firm with Jaruzelski, the General?" they joked. "It will be called 'General Electric!'"

The air was indeed electric with the possibility of change. What would it all mean for our country? We were not sure. For the moment, prices were as high as ever, queues just as long and the products in the stores very limited.

This resulted in another threat to the work in the Rainbow Garden. Travel restrictions had recently been relaxed and there was now a new pull on the gardeners for the use of their summer vacations. Often, they were invited to spend their holidays outside the country picking fruit and earning Western wages. Two months' wages could equate to one year's salary in Poland. The temptation was great.

I was specially grateful that year, therefore, to see the gardeners give their holiday time to the children's work. More than one hundred and twenty made themselves available for our major outreach at Dziegielow. The Children's Tent had continued to go up beside the Adults' Tent, year by year, with ever increasing numbers. Anything between six and eight hundred children now came, each day of the crusade. We needed our dedicated gardeners in force.

I never got used to the wonder of seeing children ushered into the Kingdom of God. Nor did I get used to the miracles that followed.

Two young boys, fairly new in their knowledge of the Lord, happened to be wandering outside the main tent when they met a man sitting alone.

"He looked unhappy, Aunty, so we explained our Wordless Books and then he gave his life to Pan Jezus too. But we're not sure we counselled him properly. Could a grown-up check?" Further adult conversation followed with the man, but, as so often happened, it proved almost unnecessary. Through the crystal-clear explanation of these little ones, he had realised that he could leave behind his old life and start all over again with Jesus Christ.

Other children who had been counselled in previous years

also showed the contagious nature of their commitment. One smiling girl had lived her new-found faith so fully that her parents, both alcoholics, had come to the Lord and overcome their addiction. Now she, though young, was also to enrol in the Training Institute.

Incidents like these were by no means isolated cases. Similar things were happening repeatedly wherever the work was being developed. To use the Polish term, they were "postcards" of the Rainbow Garden in general. We could only bow before God in gratitude.

The more the Garden grew, the more gardeners the Lord provided. That summer, in mid '89, a larger number than ever enrolled in our Training Institute. There was just one problem. Because of the shortages in the shops, and in our pockets, I could not see how we would be able to feed them all.

"Lord, we really need a raven this time!" I prayed.

I had to leave the answer with Him as there was little time to think more about it. The Institute was to start in just a few days and in the interim I needed, briefly, to leave the country. It happened that Malgosia, the student who had led Shirley Temple to the Lord, was to do further study at Kilchzimmer and I was to drive her there.

Before I could take such a long journey, of course, I needed to be sure of the car's dependability. After my garage attendant's warning, I had spoken at length on this subject with the Master Gardener in my secret office. Looking out its window, one dusk, I thought I saw the answer. For convenience I usually parked my car in the street and, that night, I saw Big Ears and the Moskal moving around it in a suspicious manner. I ran outside, but as soon as they saw me they disappeared. After that, I made it a point to park the car in the safety of our back yard. The long trip to Switzerland brought me reassurance that it was now running trouble-free.

The trip brought something else as well. It gave us the raven we needed for the coming Training Institute. The Kilchzimmer staff and students, aware of the shortages in our country, would not let me return to Poland without filling every inch of my car with goods for the Institute. They also handed me a covering letter stating this food was a gift for Poland. With it, I should have had no trouble at customs.

Ignoring the document, however, the Czech border guard demanded that I unload everything in my car. I knew what this meant. He and his friends would find some pretext on which to confiscate the Swiss food and keep it for themselves.

I was not completely surprised at this. Enmity between Poland and Czechoslovakia had, for four decades, been carefully fostered by the System, in order to prevent solidarity within the Eastern bloc. Polish people were often, therefore, victimised by Czech border guards.

"Empty your car, Pani. Every can! Every box!" the Czech guard repeated, his burly six-foot frame towering over me.

I stood to my full five foot nothing and tried to keep "both hands full".

"Very well, you may search the car, but Someone who holds a very senior position will hear about it!" I said.

He hesitated. "Very senior?"

"Yes, and He already knows about my document of authorisation!" I was speaking of Pan Jezus, of course, but the guard did not ask for names.

The guard searched my face for a moment.

"Well, Pani . . ." he began. "Perhaps if I look at your papers again . . ."

In a few minutes I was through the border. My heart was pounding and my stomach turning but the students at the Institute would be fed.

"At that time you will be given what to say . . ." That verse seemed to be becoming my daily creed. I had not planned, in advance, to offer the guard this answer but it definitely seemed to have been given and the Rainbow Garden, yet again, protected.

Once the Institute began, we could see the more clearly why God had wanted to keep it safeguarded. For the first time, we now had students enrolled at four different levels and they were, in themselves, a picture of the variety within the Rainbow Garden.

There were gardeners from all over Poland, as well as the closest regions of Czechoslovakia. There were people from every major denomination within the Protestant and Catholic ranks. There were both males and females; a healthy sign, I believed, because children's ministry is too often written off as mere "women's work". There were university and school students, as well as graduates already engaged in professional work, all of them retaining the high level of excellence in study that had marked the Institute from the beginning.

They had one thing in common, though. All were irrepressible concerning the news they brought from their different parts of the Garden.

"We've been to Bieszczady and met daily with a street gang, and most of its members came to the Lord . . ." said Olgierd. "They're so keen to attend the next Dziegielow crusade that they told us they'd rob a bank to get there if necessary. But," he grinned, "don't worry. They were only joking. They know now that is not the Lord's way of doing things."

"I definitely feel pulled towards orphanages," said Bartosz, who had established a Good News Club in the one near his home. Orphanages, under Communism, were places where the State knew it had an unchallenged hand in children's lives and, as such, were marked by atheistic, Socialist ideology. "Most have no concept of the love of Pan Jezus!" finished Bartosz. He told us he planned to make orphanage work his life's direction.

"We held a half-camp," said Falkonetti and the Angel. "We travelled to a town a hundred kilometres from home and kicked a football around until children came to play with us. Before the week was done, seven of them had given their lives to Pan Jezus and now we're looking for a way to get them into a Good News Club."

"I didn't plan to hold a camp. It just happened!" said Ela, Marysia's daughter. "My parents took me to the seaside and, on the beach, many kids seemed bored. They wanted to get together every day. I shared the Wordless Book with them, one colour for each day's meeting, and several came to the

Lord. Next time, I want to go back with something better organised!"

"We met opposition!" said Zbyszek, our biologist. At the half-camp he had held in the mountains, they had been chased by a drunken man, brandishing an axe. The community as a whole, however, had supported their work and the local children were growing in faith.

More reports came from holiday venues: the beaches on the Baltic coast, the lakes district of Mazury, the mountains of Beskidy and Tatry. Children everywhere were disappointed by the emptiness of life without God and were finding life abundant in Pan Jezus: "the Way, the Truth and the Life".

As well as regional work, some were focusing on groups drawn together by need. "I'm working with deaf children," reported one. "I spent my holiday time with gypsy kids," said a second. "I'm working with children of alcoholics," added a third. "And I am starting work for children in hospital," said Renatka, the girl from my first kindergarten post.

"Wait, wait!" I told them, as one report tumbled out after another. "I can't keep up with you all! You're just like borscht in one of my Mamuska's ancient saucepans, bubbling all over the stove."

"Do we need a bigger saucepan then?" one of them asked. He was half-serious. "We have put the theory into practice, and we all agree it works! So what happens next?"

I did not know the answer to that question. There were practical issues to consider. As the numbers involved in this work increased, the supply of resources would need to keep up. At present, though, all the material needed for the children's work was squashed into my ten by five foot office. It was hopelessly inadequate.

"I believe God will allow us to establish a formal organisation to co-ordinate the work," I said at last.

"But Christian organisations are impossible in Poland. Have you forgotten that?"

"I know, but one day," I said, not sure quite why I felt so absolutely certain, "God will permit it. I am convinced of it! We must look for windows or chimneys if necessary!"

Whatever our futures held, individually or collectively, Uncle Sam encouraged us to keep going. "You can expect four Vs in this work!" he said. It is his practice to begin each point with the same letter, whenever possible.

"First comes vision, when you come to see the need of children and respond to it. Second comes your venture, as you set out to see that vision fulfilled. Third comes the valley. You'll very often end up battling difficulty or disappointment. As you allow God to go ahead of you, however, you'll find He gives you the fourth V: the victory! Remember the four Vs! Vision, venture, valley, victory!"

At the close of the Training Institute, we held our first longed-for graduation ceremony. Four years' study had been completed and all of our seniors had passed their final exams.

"The Holy Spirit is doing a special work in Poland," Uncle Sam told me as he watched them.

"Do you think it might, in part, be in answer to Uncle Jozef's faithful years of prayer?" I mused.

"Aye, you could be right!" he said, in his Irish brogue. "I'll never forget a night Jozef asked me to pray with him for Poland's children. We knelt on the floor and Jozef said, 'Lord, let Your love be made known to the boys and girls of Poland . . .' and then he stopped and gave way to tears. It was, without doubt, the most unusual prayer meeting I have ever attended. I don't know how long we knelt there. It could have been minutes or it could have been hours. All I know is that, when we rose to our feet, Jozef told me, 'Sam, I am ready to serve Poland's children. Use me!'"

Uncle Sam and I watched as the graduates smiled their way among family members. Only Tobiah's presence brought a sour note to the occasion, but we were too happy to care.

"It's been a long journey since those early days in Warsaw, hasn't it, Jasia? It's been a long journey for you personally, too," he said quietly. "Are you glad, today, that you did not stay in England after all?"

I nodded, retracing the steps since the time in Switzerland when the decision had been made. I thought of the Foil House, the children's crusades and the Training Institutes. I thought, too, of the broadening work of the gardeners as they were at work in places scattered all over the country. How gracious the Lord had been to stop me from wandering down the wrong side of the mountain.

In August 1989, the nation's election took place. As promised, it was held under the terms of the "General Electric" agreement.

The world held its breath and so did Poland. When Solidarity took the Upper House with a resounding victory, we shook our heads in shock and disbelief. The first non-Communist government in the Eastern bloc was set in place. I was excited. Could this mean a whole new direction for the Rainbow Garden? Freedom would surely bring unlimited possibilities.

One weary, crumbling Communist regime toppled after another. The Berlin Wall came down. The statues of Lenin and Marx came down. The impossible had happened. Eastern Europe had broken free.

The face of Poland began to look different. The nation's eagle was given back his crown and the people felt, in many ways, that their lives were offered a new dignity as well.

Every week that followed brought change, in ways great and small. The *milicja* was replaced by *policja* and people raised their heads just a little higher at the knowledge that we were no longer under military rule.

The zloty was allowed to find its true value on the world market, and although prices quickly increased, so did the range of goods available. Our shops sprang into life. An influx of colourful, well-designed goods filled their shelves. Window-dressing, an almost unknown art before, began to make an appearance too. Queues disappeared, by and large, and meat was now readily available. Bazaars and flea-markets materialised, as "back seat" importers brought goods across the border and sold them from the boots of their cars or from blankets on the ground. Suddenly oranges, the fruit I had only ever seen at Christmas, were available all the time. So were bananas. Ham was too. Instead of one or two kinds of bread, we quickly had a dozen varieties. It was certainly not yet comparable to the red and white checked baker's shop I had frequented in England, but it was much better than we had ever seen before.

New restaurants began to open, offering foreign fare and fast foods instead of the usual cabbage, borscht and potatoes. Chinese restaurants, hamburger joints and popcorn machines appeared. One pizza house included on its menu "Communist" pizza: the cheapest and most tasteless option available, made entirely of red ingredients.

Architecture reflected the same changes. Style and grace appeared in the new homes that went up beside the dreary blocks built by the System. Western cars came on to the streets, making the Eastern bloc vehicles look more toy-like than ever.

Change of quite another type took place as well. For the first time, the truth about historical facts could be aired as the government filled in what it called the "blank spots" of history. With each revelation, I found myself remembering the words Tatusiek had so often repeated to me as a child. "One day, my girl, you'll understand. One day, the whole world will know . . ."

An important spot was, of course, the Warsaw Uprising, the tragic event of the Second World War when the Soviets had failed to cross the Vistula river to help Poles against the Nazis.

Another spot was Katyn, the forest which saw the slaughter of Polish officers. Russia officially apologised for this atrocity and Katyn was now documented in print and film and featured even on stamps. Memorials were placed in different parts of the country for its victims.

A third spot dealt with the true story of the resistance fighters during the war, men like those I had met in England. Many of them came home for the first time in almost fifty years.

A fourth spot was of personal concern to me. My beloved Wujek Morcinek, long discredited among Polish people for renaming the industrial city of Katowice after Stalin, was cleared of blame. Morcinek, journalists revealed, had been set up.

There was one further spot which had previously been taboo as well. Pollution, the issue over which Tatusiek had often taken his employers to task, was now discussed openly. Yes, it was confirmed, the proximity of the Nowa Huta ironworks was definitely damaging parts of beautiful, historic Krakow. It was also revealed that the Vistula, our national river, was so badly polluted that its waters could not even be used for industry.

General Jaruzelski remained president after our country's change of government, but the post of prime minister was filled by a Solidarity man, Tadeusz Mazowiecki. When confirmation of his nomination was handed down, journalists said he looked like a prisoner awaiting his death sentence.

He saw what many of us, at first, did not see. Impossible as it seemed, we were soon to discover that toppling Communism was going to prove the easy bit. The hard part was finding a way to rebuild the country.

Lech Walesa was quoted as saying that while it is easy to take live fish from a tank, chop them up and cook fish soup, it was quite another story to take the fish pieces from the soup, put them back together and turn them again into live fish. Essentially, that was the problem that lay before Poland.

There was no "How-to-do-it" book on converting Communist economies to Capitalist ones. The new finance minister, Leszek Balcerowicz, chose a radical solution so severe that many called it "shock therapy". As the zloty was exchanged at its true rate on the world market, Poland's inflation ran at 100 per cent a month to begin with. Ailing business firms that had long been supported by the government were to be privatised, if viable, or otherwise permitted to go bankrupt.

Prices continued to rise with the new economic plan, and so did unemployment. The people, now anxious, began telling jokes again.

"What is a lizard?" went one. "A crocodile after one year of Balcerowicz's reform package."

"What is Balcerowicz's favourite sport?" said a second. "Lifting prices."

"Do elephants have hernias?" "It would be possible," came the answer, "if one tried to lift our economy."

We all knew things had to get worse before they got better, but Poles were shocked to see the standard of living drop 40 per cent. Some tried to brave it out. Some left the country, for either short periods or long, to earn dollars in stronger economies. Some turned to corruption, whether on small scale or through well-organised syndicates. Some blamed each other and factions began to appear within Solidarity.

When I think of the Polish character, I think of three Rs. Poles are rebellious; excellent in bonding together to fight oppressors but less good at living together in unity. They are religious; good at going to church regularly, though the outward adherence does not always reflect inner reality. They are romantics; often keen to idealise their situation and I, at this point in our history, was as romantic as anybody.

Our future would be marvellous now, I believed. The possibilities would surely be unlimited for the ministry. I rejoiced when Henry Wieja registered a new organisation which would permit the long-standing prayers of the Wednesday group to become reality. Called "Christian Foundation: Life and Mission", it provided an umbrella for the women's work organised by Henry Wieja's wife Alina, youth work, couples' ministry, prison work, apologetics, literature outreach and, of course, evangelism among children.

We called the children's ministry "Child Evangelism Mission" and ten of the seniors agreed to work full-time, while the rest would actively continue at the volunteer level. At last we could have the resource and administration centre we had longed for.

I was euphoric. With our new freedom permitting limitless opportunities, I believed there could now be no stopping the children's work.

It was my wise, far-seeing Mamuska who tried to bring me down to earth. Now that she was a little stronger, Ewa and I had taken her to one of her favourite spots in the Beskidy mountains, the Secret Church.

She gazed about her, drinking in the scene she loved so well
as the sun's rays, always diffused in this place, lit her gentle
face. Ewa's face glowed too as the pair reminisced about the
generations of Polish Christians who had suffered in one way
or another.

"Don't think your troubles are over yet, Jasia! Life has
always been tough on God's people," she said, gesturing to
the rough-hewn beech trunks and stone altar which bore silent
testimony to the struggle of earlier generations.

"I thank God for keeping us safe when times were hard,"
she said, "but, these days, I pray He will protect us now times
are easy."

"Oh Mamuska, life in Poland is going to be so much better
now, you'll see!" I said. I was always more of an optimist than
a realist.

She shook her head. "If we go off guard, kochana, we will be
the more vulnerable to Satan's attacks! You know what Josef
Prower always told you!"

Of course I did. I had quoted his words often enough
to others. "You're facing the spiritual battle, Jasia, and as
long as you want to bring children to the Lord Jesus, Satan
will oppose you." It had been easy to see their application
under the pressure of Communism. Now, though, I was not
so sure.

"Tell me the poem Uncle Josef used to love about the
Secret Church," she said. "That's the kind of faith we need
today."

Like most Poles, Mamuska loved poetry and often asked
me to recite for her. That day, knowing her weakened limbs
would probably not permit her to visit the Secret Church again,
the words were of special meaning to her. She patted my hand
and, with eyes closed, nodded as I spoke the words she loved
so well.

The Beskidy forest was quietly rustling,
The moon, through a cloud, gently reached,
A handful of God's faithful servants ascended
To Hear His Word faithfully preached.

The trees' silent presence absorbed the hushed singing
About their Commander, so strong.
The One the saints worshipped as their "mighty fortress",
God, heard though they whispered their song.

"Begone, earth's delusions!" the group prayed in silence,
"For we have the altar of stone;
And it represents God's own Son, our true Saviour,
Whose blood flowed, our sins to atone."

With tears streaming softly, but hearts bravely pounding:
"No foe against God can prevail,
So keep your fine houses, we'd rather these trees! For
Our Gospel you cannot assail!"

It is a new time, now, yet these trees still rustle
And that timeworn altar remains,
As if, like our fathers, it too has lived by faith
Enduring life's winds and its rains.

"Enduring life's winds and its rains . . ." Mamuska repeated,
as she walked to the stone altar. "Don't think your storms are
over yet, kochana.

"Satan will fight you just as much in a democratic Poland as
a Communist one. Doesn't he fight for children just as hard in
England and America as he does here?"

"Yes, yes." I said, but I hardly heard her.

A bright new day had dawned in Poland and I was caught
up in the sheer joy of it. Never would I have believed that I
was about to face a foe far more deadly than any I had met
before.

18

LIVING IN THE LIGHT OF ETERNITY

"Are you saying I have cancer?"

"Oh, I could not say anything definite yet," my doctor told me. "All I can tell you is that we have found several lumps and we need to operate. Are you ready for that?"

I wasn't. With the Rainbow Garden stretching before me, I had never been less ready.

"My work is just at a critical point. Couldn't I wait a few months?"

The doctor's grey eyes dropped for a moment. "Pani, I'm not sure it can wait even one month. I would like you in hospital within the week."

I stood up to leave in a daze. On the one hand, despite Mamuska's warnings, I had not now expected the Rainbow Garden to come under any serious threat. On the other hand, I could not deny the pain that had plagued me for months.

In the days that followed, the doctor removed what she described as "more polyps than I could count".

The tests showed that they were benign, "although I have to warn you they may grow back," the doctor said. "Take it easy. Don't overdo things!"

I no more heeded her caution than I had Mamuska's. Life in our new Poland was brimming with possibilities and I did not want to miss a single one of them.

There was one other warning sign which I also ignored in my euphoria. Even after the operation, I had felt stabs of pain from a second source, together with strange feelings of sudden weakness. It was as though an uninvited guest had come to live inside me and I did not know quite what or where it was. I was quite convinced, however, that nothing, now, should be allowed to threaten the Garden and again sternly told myself I was not made of sugar. Ignoring persistent symptoms, I jumped headlong into the ministry.

Our new office was opened and the work began rapidly to expand. Good News Clubs sprang up like mushrooms after rain, their numbers growing so quickly that every month brought reports of more. Half-camps increased at the same pace. With so many gardeners at work, now, it was hard to keep track of all the growth.

From the office, we gathered seed for planting. Our workers prepared teaching materials and colourful visual aids. They wrote a curriculum for the Good News Clubs. They developed a training programme for would-be gardeners. In addition, as *Tik Tok Tak* found its way across the country, a correspondence course had to be started and followed up regularly. Each full-time worker's load was enormous. Nothing like this had existed in our country before and everything had to be prepared from scratch.

If, during the long hours at the office, my mysterious guest continued to plague me, I told myself I had no time to think about it. There was too much to do. As the weeks passed, I rejoiced to see the Rainbow Garden flourish and, in time, move into the community in an unexpected way.

At Christmas, the gardeners took a drama presentation to community clubs, theatres, culture houses and schools, as well as churches and Good News Clubs. It was so well received that they were asked to come back with a second one at Easter. After a lifetime of Communism, we had to pinch ourselves to be sure we were not dreaming. For the Christian message to be permitted, even welcomed, in the secular world seemed almost unbelievable.

Perhaps the community's openness stemmed from a sense of need. Our new Poland had already brought disillusionment for many.

In recent months, the nation had ached to see Lech Walesa competing against his former ally, Tadeusz Mazowiecki, for the presidency. In December 1990, Walesa had won and Mazowiecki had resigned from his post of prime minister.

The country grieved to see Solidarity fragmented and squabbling. We were seeing the sad truth of God's word in Matthew 12:25. "Every kingdom divided against itself will be ruined, and every city or household divided against itself will not stand."

A new prime minister may have replaced Mazowiecki in January 1991, but the government appeared to be doing little. It had promised to consider ninety new pieces of legislation that were urgently needed for our economy to recover. So far, however, few had been discussed and none passed.

Inflation, though somewhat reduced, continued to plague the economy. So did debate. Some advocated the Big Bang, radical approach to economic recovery. Others argued for Gradualism: slower, gentler reform. The problem with the easier path, experts said, was that, in the long run, it would not work. Too few inefficient, state-run firms had been closed, they claimed, and these were draining our economy. Yet, on the other hand, every factory that went bankrupt meant people lost jobs and families could not pay for food and rent.

Discouragement began to set in. "What is the half-way stage between Communism and Capitalism?" asked a joke. The bitter answer: "Alcoholism".

There were winners and losers in the "New System" as we called life these days. Many people were angry that members of the powerful Nomenklatura from the Old System were among the greatest winners. Most had substantial sums of capital to invest now and were making money on a grand scale. The Moskal and Iwonka were typical. They had bought a series of nightclubs, and with the profit were investing heavily in real estate.

"How did the Communists account for their past adherence to Marx and his book *Das Kapital*?" asked the cynics. "They rejected Marx, but kept the *Kapital*!"

Those who did not have capital strove to find it. The country saw a mass exodus of Poles to the West, seeking the right to German citizenship as "every Pole went looking for a

German grandmother", according to the popular saying. Big Ears was among them. He emigrated to Germany and turned up from time to time, driving a magnificent Mercedes, wearing a stylish leather coat and observing, with nose in the air, "how cheap everything is here!"

On a Polish salary, however, the smart new items in our boutiques were not cheap at all. A pair of jeans cost a week's wages. An elegant blouse cost two. A leather jacket cost four months' salary.

I realised that our gardeners, many of them young professionals, could have emigrated and found excellent jobs in the West, just as rats leave a sinking ship. Mamuska was right. Although we no longer had to deal with the restrictions placed upon us under Communism, Satan could yet attack the Garden through a new "ism": materialism. With the West so close and the borders open, the chance to get rich abroad had never been easier.

Thankfully, the gardeners remained unmoved in their dedication.

"I want to give my future to boys and girls," the Angel told me on my next visit to the Foil House. Her attitude was typical of them all.

She, together with Falkonetti and the Doll, had worked for some years now nurturing the younger generation in God's love. During this visit, I had brought a team of gardeners with me and, as they quizzed the young children who had gathered, the depth of understanding in the little Foil House kids was indisputable.

"Are you sure you're going to Heaven?" a visiting gardener asked.

"Yes!" the young voices shouted with confidence.

"Is that because you are never naughty?" Our team were testing the depth of their understanding.

"No!" they chimed.

"So how do you know you're going to Heaven?"

A sparkling-eyed poppet stood up, hair gathered in bunches tied with big bows either side of her round face. Her front teeth were missing and she spoke with a lisp.

"'Coth of the Bible!'"

"Do you know where it says this in the Bible?"

"John Three Thickteen!"

The whole group recited the verse. "For God so loved the world that He gave His one and only Son that whoever believes in Him shall not perish but have eternal life."

A flaxen-haired lad with glasses, looking and sounding like a little professor, added: "It's not because of what we have done that we are going to Heaven. It is because of what Jesus has done. We do bad things, but He died in our place!" he said, adding, "'He who has the Son has life. He who does not have the Son of God does not have life', 1 John, chapter 5, verse 12."

There was a murmur of surprise in the congregation. Many parents told us later that they had never realised the depth of spiritual knowledge in their children until this little test was given.

"You see?" the Lord seemed to be saying to me. "One generation of children is now reaching the next! Take a good look!" I did. I knew He did not want me to see this simply as a picture of the Foil House. This too, in a way, was a "postcard" of the broader work. We now had three hundred gardeners either fully or partially trained, together with many more who had caught the bug although they were not formally enrolled in our Training Institute.

After the service, the Lord had a surprise in store. One of the older ladies who had been a friend of the Chameleon's approached me with a smile and took my hand.

"Jasia, I am sorry that you suffered so greatly in the past," she said, to my astonishment, with tears in her eyes. "Can you forgive those difficult years? Today I understand why this work is so important. Children are our future! *Z Bogiem*, Jasia!"

When possible, we took more trips of this kind to different parts of Poland, but they could not happen often enough to meet the nation's need. The more I saw of the country, the more thoughtful I became. Our population was now placed at thirty-six million and, statisticians told us, twelve million were young people. All of them needed God's love.

But how, I asked myself, was it going to prove possible to get further work developed? Since starting this new ministry, I had allowed paperwork to fill my days and nights. The weight of administration had taken me by surprise, if I was honest. I had to ask myself whether, before long, the time would be ripe for this to be left in the hands of others so that I could get back to tilling the soil; which was, I knew, my true calling. So many children were waiting in those regions further afield, the "Furtherlands", as I dubbed them.

Of course, we were not the only people taking the love of God to the nation's children. In our country there has always been a multitude of churches from which many ordained men were reaching out to the community. Without doubt, however, an army of lay people needed to stand behind these men if every child in Poland was to be reached. When we looked at the alcoholism, depression and relationship breakdown in Poland's adult world, it was obvious that there were still far too many children growing up damaged by the same kinds of weeds as those which had marred my life as a child.

I agreed with the old lady at the Foil House. Children are a nation's future and that, I believe, is why Satan works so hard to get a grip on their young lives. If he can sow the seeds of destruction early enough, weeds can take root and later choke much of a person's life.

"And that, Jasia, is why I believe you are personally under attack!" said a friend, while driving with me to visit my local doctor. I had spent several days, bedridden, writhing in pain. My friends had insisted I seek medical help.

The doctor came straight to the point. I needed a hysterectomy but, she insisted, "your case is too difficult for us to treat here. Can you find a way to go to the West?"

In England, Chris, P and P, and Christian Mission to the Communist World organised support. So did the Shrewsbury church. So, too, did friends in other countries.

The British doctor spoke to me after the operation.

"Quite honestly, I don't know how you've managed all

these years," he said. "Did you not suspect something was wrong?"

It was no good reiterating that, in Poland, we were not supposed to be made of sugar. He shook his head and told me: "Another few months and the growth we found would probably have turned malignant." I sank into my pillow, weak with relief. Now I could work, unhindered, in the Rainbow Garden, I thought, sure that my mystery guest had been dealt its final blow.

"Oh and one other thing," he added before leaving. "It's a good thing you never tried to have children, my dear. With the other complexities we found, you might not have come through a pregnancy."

His words unlocked a mystery for me. When he left, I looked up a verse which had always spoken to me on the question of motherhood. "'Sing, O barren woman, you who never bore a child . . . because more are the children of the desolate woman than of her who has a husband' says the Lord" (Isaiah 54:1). The Rainbow Garden had proved that verse true. Many more spiritual children now called me Mamuska than I could ever have given birth to.

When I returned to Poland, I felt all the more like a mother, and a proud one at that. The gardeners had done a superb job. The Good News Clubs were increasing in number all the time, the half-camps were thriving, camps had been set up, the correspondence course was handling hundreds of letters and the Children's Tent at Dziegielow, the heaviest responsibility of all, was wonderfully organised. The gardeners still called me Mamuska, but mothers have to know when children are ready for independence and, in that moment, I knew the time was coming when these faithful workers could manage without having me around on a constant basis. Of course, I would always want to be available to them, my "first-born", if needed, but the focus of my work would, I believed, soon change.

It was a great moment. My own Mamuska, in her indomitable faith, had constantly reminded me of the verse God had given when I left the Foil House. "You intended to harm me, but God intended it for good to accomplish what is now being done, the saving of many lives" (Genesis 50:20). If Satan had, indeed, hoped to hurt the work through the illness, he had not succeeded. For, with the Furtherlands now in view, I realised the illness had not harmed the Rainbow Garden. It had made the way for it to expand.

The gardeners were not yet convinced they could manage, however. "We still need you," I was told when I broached the subject. "You are the one who began the work with children. It wouldn't be the same without you."

For the moment, I continued in the same role. In the next Training Institute, I allowed enthusiasm to get the better of me and immersed myself in the work. The gardeners begged me to slow down, but I had always been a workaholic and their words fell on deaf ears. I ignored obvious warning signs when each day's work was done and if, at times, I burst into tears for little reason or felt too weak to lift my head, I simply pushed myself harder.

Perhaps there was a deeper factor at work too. I wanted to prove to myself that now, at last, my battle with the guest was over. Of late, I had again experienced that tell-tale pain and weakness and I did not like to think about its implications.

"Lord, I hope this is not serious. I want to live!" I whispered, secretly, when the symptoms came. "The Rainbow Garden has still so far to go and I want to be on this earth long enough to see it in full blossom!" I tried to convince myself that the pain was merely my imagination. After all, a growth had been removed in England. Surely my problems were over now? Surely nothing else could be wrong?

In a way, that was the question the country was also asking itself during this time. Weren't Poland's difficulties over now that we had a new "ism" in place? The population was disillusioned to discover they were not. An immensely popular television satire, *Polish Zoo*, depicted every major politician as an animal and, each Saturday night, mirrored the events of the week. Its name was a little too close to home for many Poles. They did feel the antics of the politicians uncomfortably similar to those of animals in a zoo.

"Do you think Polish humour is becoming more political?" asked the comics. "No, I think Polish politics is becoming more humorous," was the disillusioned reply.

Late in 1991, we had our first full election following the end of Communism. Almost thirty parties participated, however, and it was hard for many Poles to take any of them seriously. Less than half the population voted and no party got more than 13 per cent of the ballot box.

We were given yet another new prime minister, one who believed in the gradualist approach and slowed down reforms again in order to quieten the discontent of the people. The country's leadership was, however, so utterly fragmented that the new government lasted only six months.

The life expectancy of a Polish government, it was said, grows ever shorter. By June 1992, when our first woman prime minister, Hanna Suchocka, forged a coalition of seven parties, Poland had already seen four prime ministers take office in as many years. The words "Polish Zoo" were on everybody's lips.

Nonetheless, from the perspective of the Rainbow Garden, our new freedom continued to offer wonderful opportunities for growth. I wanted to seize them all with my usual eagerness, but, try as I might, I could no longer deny the fact that my energy was lessening, and the pain increasing, with each passing week.

Mamuska was now staying at Ewa's picturesque mountain home as I did not have the strength to care for her invalid condition. Doctors prescribed further sick leave for me but, although rest helped, the symptoms still persisted.

Two more lumps were found on my back, and removed during yet another operation. Still, though, the guest seemed to increase its hold and my condition deteriorated.

I began to have slight but frequent heart attacks at unpredictable moments, finding myself out cold on the kitchen floor, slumped in a corner of the living room, or flat on my face in the hall.

Life became frightening. Sometimes, I was afraid to get out of bed lest I have an attack in some spot where I might hurt myself. At other times, I was afraid to get into bed lest I have an attack and never wake up again.

What was the matter with me? After three bouts of surgery in three years, I was exhausted, weakened and scared.

One doctor took hold of my case with tenacity. "You can't go on like this. You have to be able to live normally again," he said.

After months of testing, he found the guest. A tumour had been growing quietly for several years, he said, and it was disturbing the body's functioning. That was the reason for my heart attacks, high blood pressure and strange feelings of weakness. Every bout of surgery had irritated this guest the more.

"And the solution?" I asked.

He hesitated. "It will have to be removed, but the operation is considered a delicate one."

"Delicate?"

He took a deep breath and my heart knotted. "I'll be honest with you. This operation is classified as life-threatening."

At my blanched expression, he quickly went on. "But, Pani, if it is successful, you will have a brand new life. I promise you it is worth trying!"

"And if it is not successful?"

His eyes were compassionate. "That's a risk we have to take."

The professor to whom he referred me was the country's leader in the field and I knew, humanly speaking, I could get no better care. It was up to the Lord, now, whether I came out of this alive or not.

"But what of the Garden?" I repeated, before the Lord in prayer. "What of Poland's twelve million young people? So many are waiting to hear of Your love. Is this really the right time for me to die?"

Fear, grief and pain all played their part in the months leading up to the operation. Each special event took on a heightened quality as I knew it might be my last. I took particular care over preparations for Easter and Mamuska's birthday.

Every minute, every hour, suddenly became precious. I began to see life in a new light: that of eternity. When my daily Bible reading brought me to Ecclesiastes, I was struck by the words that God has "set eternity in the hearts of men" (Ecclesiastes 3:11). Eternity was certainly uppermost in my mind during those uncertain days.

Not surprisingly, that became the theme when I met with the gardeners at the end of their Training Institute. The group members had again come from regions all over Poland, together with Czech workers who had now begun their own mission as well. Not knowing if I would see the group again in this life, I could not help but speak to them in the light of the next.

"What does it mean to live in the light of eternity?" I asked, quoting again from Ecclesiastes. "It means we must not confuse the eternal with the temporal. Very often we prize the wrong thing. We do a little of this or that and call it ministry. But we frequently dig ourselves into activity which has no value in the light of eternity. Time is short. When eternity comes, our opportunity will be over.

"While we dally, lost children are starving for spiritual Bread. They are waiting for you. As the apostle Paul says, 'Be very careful then how you live – not as unwise but as wise, making the most of every opportunity.'" (Ephesians 5:15).

As my condition worsened, it became impossible for me to speak in public any more. Ongoing heart trouble, blood pressure problems and pain kept me quiet and, at times, bedridden.

Friends at home and abroad supported me with cards, letters and gifts. They sent ravens, too, which I badly needed since our under-equipped hospitals required patients to purchase their own syringes, drips, bandages and antibiotics. It was as if a wider Rainbow Garden family, in different parts of the world, was gently bearing me before the Lord. I often thought of the sick man who was lowered through the roof by four friends and brought to the Lord Jesus for healing. The support and care of international friends felt much the same to me.

One tiny gift that came was of such great coincidence that I knew it bore the Masterful touch of the Lord. It was a book by Patricia St John that I had not seen before. It told the story of a young English girl, Elaine, whose mother had initially little interest in her and who therefore felt she did not belong anywhere. The child thus developed a life full of weeds; she became a selfish, lonely, cranky little thing who "was so unhappy and so longed to be admired". She reminded me of myself during my childhood Communist days.

It was the title, however, which came closest to home. The book happened to be called, of all things, *The Rainbow Garden*. I thought it very appropriate. There were many little Elaines in Poland; many unhappy children who could not cope with the weeds in their lives and who needed to meet the Master Gardener.

"And if you do permit me to come through this operation, Lord, how would You have me care for these children?" I prayed, during the months of waiting before my operation was scheduled.

I spent a few days of quiet prayer at Zakopane, in the majestic Tatry mountain range that lies south-west of our gentler Beskidy slopes. I have always found Zakopane to be a feast for the eyes. Its glorious slopes are clad with conifers and the architecture seems built to match, with every home resembling a Christmas tree in shape.

As I sat on this "roof" of Poland, it was easy to imagine I was looking far across the country and seeing the needs, as yet unmet, in the Furtherlands. Months of pain and rest had given me ample time for prayer and now my head was brimming with ideas.

The weather in the mountains is always unpredictable, and that morning I found myself ducking for cover when a massive downpour began. From the shelter of a shepherd's wooden hut, I watched as the cloudburst created raging torrents down the mighty slopes.

As abruptly as it had started, the storm came to a sudden halt and, through the mist, a glorious rainbow appeared, its seven colours clearly defined.

Rainbows speak of only one thing in my life, of course: the Garden. I found a dry spot and watched it.

"Perhaps the red, white and blue colours of the Garden are no longer enough?" I said to the Master Gardener. "Poland has changed and the Rainbow Garden has surely now grown beyond all three."

As I sat, warmed by the golden sun, I saw a way in which the children's work could be expressed through those seven colours.

Red: training Red stood for the very heart of the ministry and that, to me, is training. Many were crying out for training now, both teachers and parents. It was proving impossible to keep up with the requests that were coming from all over the country.

Orange: prayer With my life now full of pills, I connected orange with vitamins and my favourite vitamin for spiritual life is vitamin P: prayer. For a long time, I had wanted to establish prayer bands in Poland, groups in which children could come together for the specific purpose of intercession. As well, I wanted to set up a prayer telephone ministry, with a hot line which children in need could call. A line had already been offered to us. We needed only for gardeners to be trained.

Yellow: media Media, like the yellow rays of the sun, could penetrate the country far more thoroughly than people. Magazines were needed; at home I had twelve new issues of *Tik Tok Tak* already on the drawing board. Cassettes were needed too. Christian artists had already offered me their services for music and teaching. An excellent Christian studio was available. Television and radio work were also possibilities.

Green: outdoor work Camps and half-camps were being held in abundance each vacation, but still far too many children were bored during their holidays and therefore vulnerable to all kinds of trouble. We needed to multiply the outdoor work many times over if all of Poland's children were to be reached.

Blue: minority groups Blue has always been associated with minority groups for me, because it is the colour of Israel. Now, in the nineties, Poland is starting to see more Jewish children once again. Sadly, post-Communist Europe has also brought a return of neo-Nazism. Full-time workers were needed for Jewish children.

There was a second minority group in need as well. Gypsy children had long been seen as beggars or thieves and treated as outcasts by our community. They needed gardeners with special understanding to take them God's love.

Indigo: itinerant evangelism This, the colour of kings, I connected with the most royal task in the Rainbow Garden: the fulfilment of the Great Commission. We needed to send gardeners, skilled in itinerant evangelism, throughout the length and breadth of Poland.

Christian Mission to the Communist World had recently provided a huge tent for the Garden. It could be taken, by a full time team, to towns and villages all over the country.

Violet: special need groups This dark, sombre colour reminded me of children with special need in hospital wards, orphanages and children's homes, centres for handicapped children and corrective homes. Work had been pioneered in all of these areas but much more was needed.

The colours of the Zakopane landscape were all the brighter after the rain shower. The Christmas-tree houses glinted as the sun painted their roofs a golden hue. The trees were a vibrant green, standing like sentinels on the slopes. The alpine flowers at my feet were a riot of colour, yellow, purple and blue. Marvelling at the power of the Creator, I asked Him to paint the colours of the Rainbow Garden just as surely, in the Furtherlands of Poland.

"So, Mamuska, whatever Satan's attack, God can bring good out of it." It was my final visit before the operation and I had described the seven colours to Mamuska in an attempt to put a smile on her sad face.

She nodded, but I could see tears threatening. "I just can't bear to think of your suffering any more. You have struggled for so many months already," she said.

"But good things have come out of those months, Mamuska! In a way I can be grateful for them!" I replied.

"Grateful?"

"Yes. For one thing, with my workaholic tendencies, probably nothing less than illness would have stopped me long enough to have seen the full need of the Furtherlands. So, in a way, this illness has not been a hindrance. It's been a window."

She nodded, but she sniffed.

"There's another blessing in it as well, Mamuska. I've been sick for so long now that the full-time workers have seen how good a job they can do on their own. If the Lord keeps me alive, I will be able to work fully in the Furtherlands now."

"But you're just one person. How are you going to get the rest of the children's work done, Jasia?" she asked.

"Multiplication! We'll need at least a thousand children's workers," I began. "The CEM team is already fully stretched with its current responsibilities. We must keep mobilising more gardeners . . ."

"A thousand?" Ewa asked, incredulous.

"Well, that's not unrealistic. A few hundred are already trained. Many more are requesting training and the Lord will make sure they multiply themselves as well. They always do once they catch the bug."

"And how will you pay them?" Ewa was always practical.

"They don't need to be full-time. We can use volunteers like Bartosz, Olgierd, Ela, Falkonetti and the Angel!"

Loving as always, Ewa served me borscht and meat carefully cooked according to my doctor's strict instructions. She was going to do everything in her power to see I came out of this illness alive.

"Besides," I told them as I ate, "there are the other groups that are now working with Polish children!" CEF had begun another new ministry under the direction of a young pastor, Czeslaw Bassara, who was one more of Uncle Jozef's disciples. An American group, New Hope, had started one as well and I was on their board. "We will all need each other if we are to get the job done. Twelve million young people is a big number."

"But what if the political situation in the country changes?" asked Mamuska. There was so much discontent in the country now that the unthinkable was being discussed. A kind of nostalgia for Communism was creeping into people's thinking, fuelled by Communist promises of easier times if only they were re-elected.

"Well, you were right in the warning you gave me, Mamuska. Satan will battle the Garden just as hard no matter what 'ism' we have, Communism or Capitalism. He'll use anything he can to stop children finding Christ. So whatever the future holds, we have to go on with the Rainbow Garden."

After the meal, Mamuska brought me her Bible and turned to the Old Testament. "Kochana, I have asked the Lord again and again why you have suffered with these years of illness," she said, "and I've reached a conclusion. Whenever I read about a leader whom God calls for a special purpose, that person always comes under an unusual kind of attack."

She had placed bookmarks in several places which she wanted me to read. "Satan knows that if he can stop the leader, he can hurt the work God is trying to do. When I listen to your vision for the future, I know it's true.

"But, kochana," Mamuska continued, "I still believe what I have always said, that God will bring good out of evil. And I'm praying you will live . . ." The tears that had been threatening all day now welled up in those chocolate eyes that had watched over me for so many years.

"Have you made a will, kochana?" she asked, sniffing bravely. She had asked me to do so the day she heard my diagnosis. As a nurse, she knew the odds.

"Yes, Mamuska. It's all settled. If the Lord takes me, you'll find I have left everything in order." I bit my lip, afraid that I too would give way to tears.

"That's wise . . ." she could say no more. Trying to be brave, she pulled herself out of her chair and hobbled on her stick to the next room.

There, Mamuska has an electronic keyboard that is easy for her arthritic fingers to manage. All at once, she began to play the hymn which, for her, was an anthem for life: "A mighty fortress is our God". It was her practice to play on this keyboard morning and afternoon, so that the people of these mountains could hear the notes of their best-loved hymns cascading down into the valley.

I looked out of the window as she played, watching workers in the fields. One man took his hat off and placed it over his heart. A couple of women, planting seeds in the soft earth, turned towards the music with a grateful smile. An old lady raised her hand to wave. She had told Mamuska earlier that, whenever she heard "our music", she found added strength to work.

These God-fearing people, like Mamuska herself, had proved their Fortress time and again through decades of suffering.

I raised my eyes to look at the pine-clad ridges standing black against the brightness of the sun. Their jagged lines reminded me a little of an ancient stronghold and I thought of my favourite castle in Krakow as Mamuska fingered the notes.

"Lord, be my mighty fortress in this next trial!" I whispered. "Whether I live or die, I am in Your hands."

The surgery was performed at last, and what followed for me were days in which morning and evening seemed to merge into one. I heard the voices of doctors and nurses discussing me, but I was not always sure what was happening.

One afternoon, there seemed to be a dilemma, although it was only when others described it to me later that I could reconstruct the events in full.

Apparently, my heartbeat and blood pressure had plummeted to crisis point. I heard distant voices shouting, "We're losing her! Quick!"

For me, at that point, something else was happening. A deep sleepiness had overtaken me, one greater than I had ever known before. It felt very peaceful and rather cosy too, as though a golden light was enveloping me.

In a way, I was comfortable with the situation. Heaven had never felt so close. The Lord was near, His presence so real it was almost tangible. I half-fancied that I glimpsed Him and, with Him, my David as well. In that moment, I almost welcomed the prospect of death. I was not sure I wanted to return to Earth with its pain and struggles.

"She's going! Jasia, you have to fight!" I heard a voice saying at my side.

"Jezus . . . Jezus!" I could not formulate a whole sentence. I could speak only that one word. My mind, though, was asking Him a question. Did I really have to fight for my life? Couldn't I come to Him now? I was so tired after the long months of pain and weakness.

"Fight, Jasia! You can't go yet!" I later learned this was the professor's voice.

It reached me. Suddenly, I remembered why I had to fight. The face of a little girl with missing front teeth floated into my thinking. Another, who looked like Shirley Temple, followed. A boy who would one day be a professor came after that. Then came a laughing procession of little Bujoks from the mountain school. At last I was looking at a sea of faces, just like those I had gazed upon so often under our Children's Tent at Dziegielow.

"Let the little children come to Me!" Those words of the Lord Jesus, so often a part of our work, floated into my consciousness too.

"How many have you brought to Me?"

I didn't know exactly. I had never counted.

"Aren't more waiting?"

"Yes Lord." I realised I had to live. I had to see many more children adopted by God.

"Jasia, are you going to help us? Are you going to fight?" It was the professor's voice. I heard it more clearly now. What I did not hear was a similar cry from prayer partners in other countries who wrote that, at this precise moment, God had pulled them to their knees. One lady awoke at midnight in her time zone, certain she had to stay awake to pray for me. Another friend stayed up for several hours because "I felt you were fighting and, in prayer, I wanted to help you." A third called for a circle of praying friends to go into fasting for me during this time.

I gave the doctors my all. With trained precision, they leaned over to jolt my heart into action again. The blood pressure slowly rose and, at last, normal sleep enveloped me.

"Good girl, you're going to make it!" the professor told me later. "Your tumour was benign and the surgery successful. Your new life stretches before you!"

"Thank you!" I said, gratefully.

"No. Don't thank me. Thank yourself," he replied.

"Why myself?"

"We thought we were losing you. But," he looked at me for a moment, "there is some kind of inner power in you which brought you back to life. So don't thank me!"

That power, of course, was not of my own making at all. What the professor saw was God at work, pulling me back to the most beautiful job on earth.

I was returning to the children.

In the months that followed, I rediscovered a life free from pain. I found my old strength returning. I could think more clearly and move more freely. Best of all, I saw the colours of the Rainbow Garden springing into life.

Red, for training, was one of the most strategic colours. "Jasia, how do you lead kids to Christ?" asked a serious student during a spring training conference at Dziegielow. "I met Pan Jezus as a child, but I don't know how to bring others to Him!"

I smiled at her. She could have been me, twenty-four years earlier, when Jozef Prower had invited me to hear Uncle Sam answer the same question. Now Uncle Sam and I were teaching students who had been drawn from the third generation of gardeners.

"A lot's happened since the early years," Uncle Sam said to me. "Look!" In the Dziegielow sisters' guest book he had found the entry for our very first training course. "The current students are younger, but seem really serious and committed," he observed. I thought the same. Almost all of them had told me they wanted to multiply themselves and bring others to the next course.

"The bug", it seemed, was as contagious as ever. With this kind of enthusiasm, the Garden could not help but grow, and indeed, despite a new Communist victory in Poland's elections, I had already seen the Rainbow's other colours brightening in recent months.

Orange, for prayer, had definitely been strengthened. New prayer groups had begun for the work, not just among young people, but also among some old enough to be my grandparents.

Yellow, for media, was coming more clearly into the picture too. "I'm available to work with you on the next issues of *Tik Tok Tak*," a talented young writer had promised. The magazine was of high priority with me.

Green, for outdoor work, was being given new application. Summer programmes in the recently donated tent would provide opportunities for large numbers of children to be offered new life in Christ.

Blue, for minority groups, had surprised me by appearing so early. "I'm very interested in Jewish children. Can you train me to work with them?" one earnest gardener had volunteered.

Indigo, for itinerant evangelism, had been discussed by older gardeners. "We want to take salvation to the kids in the 'Furtherlands'," these more experienced workers told me. They had seen too many unsaved children to ignore the depth of need.

Violet, for special need groups, had its adherents as well. One student group wanted to help retarded children, others had persevered with hospital needs and one person continued to pioneer orphanage work.

"It's like an explosion of colour!" I said to a visiting foreigner, as I began drawing a newsletter for friends in the West. "I can hardly keep up!"

"If the work multiplies at this rate, how ever will you supervise it all?" she asked.

"Supervise?" I laughed. "This work will be a family of individuals and ministries, caring for different parts of the Garden. So they won't need a boss as much as they will need a Mamuska. If I can keep my administrative role to a minimum, that's what I want to be." I knew now, without a doubt, that the Master Gardener had used my illness to free me from an office role so that I could move more freely in the Garden.

"But which colour will you major on?" my visitor persisted.

"Oh, I don't believe the Lord wants me to work with just one part of the Garden," I replied. "I think He wants me to water all of it; to take His encouragement to the gardeners at work and to help them pioneer new patches wherever possible."

My guest watched as I started to draw at the top of the newsletter. "And what will you call this ministry?" she asked.

"That's the problem." I chewed on my pen. "The needs of Poland's children are so diverse that I can't find any name broad enough to encompass them all."

My guest smiled. "As far as I can see, this ministry already has a name."

"Already? What do you mean?"

"Didn't the Lord give it one years ago?"

I stared at her for a moment and then, as realisation dawned, my smile matched hers. "Of course!" I said, grabbing my pens to redesign my letterhead. I laughed out loud as flowers and children began to appear on the paper in front of me. Only one name gave sufficient scope for the depth of need.

It had to be called the "Rainbow Garden".

If you would like to write to Jasia, she can be contacted at the following addresses:

RAINBOW GARDEN MINISTRIES
P. O. BOX 26568
COLORADO SPRINGS
80936-6568
USA

RAINBOW GARDEN MINISTRIES
C/O RELEASE INTERNATIONAL
P. O. BOX 19
BROMLEY
KENT BR2 9TZ
UK

RAINBOW GARDEN MINISTRIES
P. O. BOX 602
PENNANT HILLS
NSW 2120
AUSTRALIA